Future Tourism

This book investigates and considers the urgent political, social and economic challenges that confront society and tourism. It attempts to look at what is threatening society, and makes suggestions on what the impact will be and how tourism will be changed to integrate with the new socioeconomics of a newly emerging society with its novel peculiar challenges and opportunities in a post-energy era.

The book draws on the views of leading thinkers in tourism and considers a broad range of issues from multidisciplinary perspectives facing the tourism industry for the first time in one volume: dwindling energy, new technology, security (like war and terrorism), political economy, sustainability and human resources. By critically reviewing these social and economic challenges in a global scale, the book helps to create a comprehensive view of future tourism in the unfolding and challenging society of the third millennium.

This innovative and significant volume will be valuable reading for all current and future tourism professionals.

James Leigh is Associate Professor of Tourism at the University of Nicosia, Cyprus.

Craig Webster is Associate Professor of Political Science in the Department of European Studies and International Relations at the University of Nicosia in Cyprus.

Stanislav Ivanov is Associate Professor and Academic Director of International University College in Dobrich, Bulgaria.

Routledge Advances in Tourism
Edited by Stephen Page
School for Tourism, Bournemouth University

Future Tourism

Political, social and economic challenges

Edited by
James Leigh, Craig Webster and Stanislav Ivanov

Routledge
Taylor & Francis Group

LONDON AND NEW YORK

First published 2013
by Routledge
2 Park Square, Milton Park, Abingdon, Oxon OX14 4RN

Simultaneously published in the USA and Canada
by Routledge
711 Third Avenue, New York, NY 10017

Routledge is an imprint of the Taylor & Francis Group, an informa business

British Library Cataloguing in Publication Data
A catalogue record for this book is available from the British Library

Library of Congress Cataloging in Publication Data
Webster, Craig
  Future tourism: political, social and economic challenges / Craig Webster,
  James Leigh and Stanislav Ivanov.
    p.cm.
  Includes bibliographical references and index.
  1. Tourism – Forecasting. I. Leigh, James. II. Ivanov, Stanislav. III. Title.
  G155.A1.W366 2012
  338.4'791 – dc233

                                                        2012003295

ISBN: 978-0-415-50902-2 (hbk)
ISBN: 978-0-203-12503-8 (ebk)

Typeset in Times New Roman
by RefineCatch Limited, Bungay, Suffolk

Printed and bound by CPI Group (UK) Ltd, Croydon, CR0 4YY

To our wives and children

Contents

Illustrations

Figures

Tables

Contributors

Susanne Becken: Griffith University, Gold Coast Campus, Queensland, Australia
Dr. Susanne Becken is also the Director of the Land, Environment and People Research Centre (Lincoln University, New Zealand). Susanne has undertaken extensive research on tourism, energy, oil prices, climate change and related policies and she is interested in how these affect the future of tourism. She is on the editorial boards of the *Journal of Sustainable Tourism, Journal of Policy Research in Tourism, Leisure and Events* and the *International Tourism Review*; she is also a Resource Editor for *Annals of Tourism Research*. Susanne acted as a contributing author to the Fourth IPCC (International Panel on Climate Change) Assessment Report and represented the United Nations World Tourism Organisation at the UNFCCC (United Nations Framework Convention on Climate Change) conference in Bali in 2007.

Michael Clancy: University of Hartford, USA
Michael Clancy is Professor and Chair of the Department of Politics and Government at the University of Hartford, where he also serves as coordinator for the interdisciplinary International Studies program. He is the author of two books, including most recently *Brand New Ireland: Tourism, Development and National Identity in the Irish Republic* (Ashgate 2009). His work on the political economy of tourism and development has also appeared in the *Review of International Political Economy, Latin American Research Review, Studies in Comparative International Development, Annals of Tourism Research, Globalizations*, and forthcoming in the *Journal of International Relations and Development*.

Ulrike Gretzel: University of Wollongong, Australia
Dr. Ulrike Gretzel is an Associate Professor for Marketing at the Institute for Innovation in Business and Social Research, University of Wollongong, and Director of the Laboratory for Intelligent Systems in Tourism (LIST). She received her Ph.D. in Communications from the University of Illinois at Urbana-Champaign and holds a master's degree in International Business from the Vienna University of Economics and Business. Her research focuses on persuasion in human–technology interaction, experience design, use of technology for interpretation, adoption and use of social media, interorganizational information systems

and other issues related to the development and use of intelligent systems in tourism. She uses qualitative and quantitative research methods and has a particular interest in network analysis and text mining.

Werner Gronau: University of Applied Sciences, Stralsund, Germany
Professor Dr. Werner Gronau is Director of the Tourism and Transport Research Center of the University of Nicosia, Cyprus and at the same time holds the position of Professor for Tourism, Travel and Transport at the University of Stralsund, Germany. He holds a German degree in Human Geography from the Technical University of Munich and a Ph.D. in Tourism Studies (Leisure mobility and leisure style) from the University of Paderborn. He is a member of several research groups in the field of Tourism and Mobility, such as the British Leisure Studies Association, the German Society of Tourism Research and the EuroMed Research Business Institute. Furthermore he is editor of the transport journal *Studies on Mobility and Transport Research* and works as Reviewer for several journals, such as *EuroMed Journal of Business*, *Tourism Management* and *Leisure Studies*. His research interests focus on sustainable tourism planning and destination management, with a specific focus on transport-related issues. He has worked in several research projects granted by different institutions, for example, the German Ministry of Research and the European Commission, and presented the results in international conferences, various journals and books.

C. Michael Hall: University of Canterbury, New Zealand
Michael Hall is Professor in the Department of Management, University of Canterbury, New Zealand; Docent, Department of Geography, Oulu University, Finland; and Visiting Professor, Linneaus University, Kalmar, Sweden and co-editor of *Current Issues in Tourism*. He has wide-ranging interests in tourism and mobility, environmental history and gastronomy.

Stanislav Ivanov: International University College, Bulgaria
Stanislav Ivanov is Associate Professor and Vice Rector for Academic Affairs at International University College in Dobrich, Bulgaria. He holds a Ph.D. in tourism economics from the University of Economics – Varna, is the Editor-in-chief of the *European Journal of Tourism Research* and serves on the editorial boards of 17 other journals. His research interests include destination marketing, tourism and economic growth, political issues in tourism and special interest tourism. Dr. Ivanov's publications have appeared in different academic journals – *Tourism Economics*, *Tourism Management*, *Tourism Today*, *Tourism*, *Journal of Economic Studies*, *Journal of Southern Europe and the Balkans* and the *South-Eastern Europe Journal of Economics*.

Kostas Karadakis: University of Florida, USA
Kostas Karadakis has published two manuscripts; he is second author of the article 'Understanding the legacy components of a host Olympic city: The case of the 2010 Vancouver Olympic Games', published in *Sport Marketing Quarterly*. He is first author of his second manuscript published in the *International Journal of Event and Festival Management* entitled 'Event leveraging of mega sport events:

A SWOT analysis approach'. Kostas has ten peer-reviewed conference proceedings and presentations, in five of which he is the first author. He has presented his research at the North American Society for Sport Management Conference (NASSM); the North American Society for the Sociology of Sport (NASSS) conference; the European Association for Sport Management conference and the Fourth International Conference on Tourism in Athens, Greece. Kostas has also been involved in a number of international research projects dealing with the Vancouver Olympic Games, the 2010 World Cup where he assisted with the preparation and writing of a technical report and the examination of legacy aspects among the residents of the four latest Olympic Summer cities: Atlanta, Sydney, Athens and Beijing.

George Karlis: University of Ottawa, Canada
Dr. George Karlis is a Full Professor in the School of Human Kinetics at the University of Ottawa, Canada. He completed his Ph.D. at Michigan State University (USA), his Masters degree at Acadia University (Canada), and his Bachelors degree at the University of Ottawa (Canada). His area of specialization is leisure and society. He has written over 50 articles and his research has been published extensively throughout the world. Most notably, he is the author of *Leisure and Recreation in Canadian Society: An Introduction* (Thompson Educational Publishers), a textbook that is used as a required reading in universities and colleges. He has researched tourism from a leisure studies perspective in Canada, as well as sport volunteer tourism in mega sport events.

Nicos Kartakoullis: University of Nicosia, Cyprus
Nicos Kartakoullis is a Professor of Organizational Behaviour and Sports Management and Head of the Department of Hospitality, Tourism and Sports Management of the School of Business at the University of Nicosia in Cyprus. He is the Chairman of the Board of Directors of the Cyprus Sport Organization (Ministry of Sport of the Republic of Cyprus). His work has been published in many scientific journals and texts and he has presented his work in conferences around the world.

James Leigh: University of Nicosia, Cyprus
Dr. James Leigh has international experience and a lifelong interest in applied geopolitics and civilization clash, and more recently in crude oil geopolitics. These culminate in his third and fourth books, *Death of Nation in Civilization Clash* (Afi Touch Editions), and *Beyond Oil Bust: Investigating Oil Economics, Society and Geopolitics* (Atlantic Books). He has researched and published as a futurist, considering, through macrohistorical precedents and political geography, what current events and trends portend for our future world. As a geopolitician his work often makes dramatic geopolitical predictions which are gaining some considerable attention. James is an Assistant Professor of Cultural Geography at the University of Nicosia, Cyprus. He is a visiting professor at several universities and a reviewer for several journals, and has published and worked in five continents. James is a Chartered Geographer (C.Geog.) and a Fellow of the Royal Geographical Society (FRGS). Visit his personal professional webpage www.freewebs.com/jas4.

Scott Richardson: Central Queensland University, Noosa, Australia
Scott Richardson is a Senior Lecturer in Tourism and Marketing at Central Queensland University, Australia. He obtained his doctorate degree in Tourism and Hospitality Management from Griffith University, also in Australia. His thesis focused on the experience of students working in the tourism and hospitality industry while studying for their undergraduate degree. He has published a number of papers on Generation Y and the impact this generation will have on tourism and hospitality organizations in the new millennium. His research interests are human resource management, sport tourism, event tourism and special interest tourism.

Amanda Sharaf: University of Ottawa, Canada
Amanda Sharaf is currently a Ph.D. candidate completing her doctoral degree with the University of Ottawa, Faculty of Health Sciences, in Ottawa, Canada. Ms. Sharaf's educational credentials include a Bachelors Degree in Social Sciences, with a concentration in Leisure Studies, and a Master of Arts Degree in Human Kinetics, both from the University of Ottawa. Her doctoral areas of research include understanding the relationship that exists between leisure and the sociology of work, leisure and quality of life, work–life balance in the workplace, as well as contemporary understandings of leisure, tourism and recreation. Ms. Sharaf's professional work experience includes teaching and research assistantships at the University of Ottawa within the School of Human Kinetics, as well as policy and research advisory and analysis within the Canadian public service.

Chris Stone: Manchester Metropolitan University, UK
Dr. Chris Stone is an academic tourism expert and qualified university educator, and teaches on undergraduate and postgraduate Tourism Management programs at Hollings Faculty at Manchester Metropolitan University. He was appointed as an EU TEMPUS Academic Expert in 2003, and re-appointed in 2007. Chris acts as External Examiner for tourism degree programmes at the University of Bedfordshire (Masters) and at Bournemouth University (Bachelors), and has served on programme validation and revalidation panels at several universities. He reviews manuscripts for international academic journals including *Tourism Management* and also on behalf of major book publishers, and is a member of the Editorial Review Board of the *European Journal of Tourism and Hospitality Research*. Chris formerly held the position of Managing Consultant, managing consultancy contracts commissioned by private, public and not for profit clients in the tourism and leisure industry. While in academia, he completed further consultancy contracts including work for British National Parks, local authorities, European governments and private organizations and, in addition, he successfully bid for and managed Knowledge Transfer Partnership projects with UK tourism industry partners. As an experienced Ph.D. supervisor, Chris's academic interests lie in discourses around tourism and sustainability; the responsible tourist; tourism policy, planning, management and performance; social tourism; tourism and events, including cross-cultural festivals; destination image, marketing and management; and tourism futures.

Craig Webster: University of Nicosia, Cyprus

Dr. Craig Webster is an Associate Professor of International Relations at the University of Nicosia in Cyprus whose research focuses on the major social, economic and political issues faced by people worldwide. In recent years, he has focused on the state's regulation of tourism. He has published widely on topics related to the political economy of tourism, public opinion analysis and comparative foreign policy. His research interests include human rights, the political economy of tourism, public opinion analysis and comparative foreign policy. He is the Editor in Chief of *Tourism Today*, a co-editor of the *Cyprus Review* and has published in many peer-reviewed journals. He studied Government and German Literature at St. Lawrence University in New York State, where he was inducted into Phi Beta Kappa. He later received his MA and Ph.D. in Political Science from Binghamton University in New York State and an MBA from Intercollege in Cyprus.

Ian Yeoman: Victoria University, New Zealand

Dr. Ian Yeoman is the world's only professional crystal ball-gazer or futurologist specializing in travel and tourism. Ian learned his trade as the scenario planner for Visit Scotland, where he established the process of futures thinking within the organization using a variety of techniques including economic modeling, trends analysis and scenario construction. In July 2008, Ian was appointed an Associate Professor of Tourism Management at Victoria University of Wellington, New Zealand. Ian has published extensively within the field of tourism futures, with articles published in leading academic journals such as *Tourism Management*, *Journal of Travel Research* and *Journal of Vacation Marketing* on a variety of topics from climate change to the future of energy and consumer trends – all within the context of travel and tourism. He is a popular speaker at conferences and was described by the UK *Sunday Times* as the country's leading contemporary futurologist. Ian is the holder of a number of honorary positions, including Visiting Professor at Stenden University, Netherlands and Visiting Research Fellow at Sheffield Hallam University, England. He has undertaken consultancy projects for the UN World Tourism Organisation and is sought out by many organizations for advice about the future. Ian is presently undertaking research for the Ministry of Tourism examining the future of tourism in New Zealand in 2050 (see www.tourism2050.com) and a European regional project for the Dutch government. His most recent book, *Tomorrow's Tourists: Scenarios and Trends* (www.tomorrowstourist.com) looks at where the tourist will go on holiday in 2030 and what they will do. Forthcoming books include *Tourism and Demography* (Goodfellows 2010), *Revenue Management* (Palgrave 2010) and *2050: Tomorrow's Tourism* (Channel view 2011).

Acknowledgments

Many people have contributed in one way or another to the production of this book. First and foremost, we are grateful to the contributors to the book whose minds and enthusiasm made the book far greater than we expected it to be. Their hard work enabled us to produce a book that will have value to many in and out of academic circles. In addition, James and Craig would like to thank their employer, the University of Nicosia, our colleagues at the University, the staff of the university and our students. The University of Nicosia is a great place to work and the support in our enterprise from the university and from our fellow faculty members has been a tremendous help in the production of this book. Stanislav is grateful to the management team and colleagues at International University College, Bulgaria, for creating a wonderful working environment that stimulates research. He would like to thank the college students as well for constantly giving him new reasons to love his job.

There are other noteworthy people who should be thanked, since their assistance led directly to the creation of this book. Stephen Page is to be thanked, because he recognized the value of the book and supported it by encouraging us to publish with Routledge. Emma Travis of Routledge was also a major help in the creation of this book. She was supportive of the book and her assistance has strengthened the book in many ways. Carol Barber at Routledge was also a major asset to us, giving us advice and assistance in the editing of the text.

Finally, we are grateful to our wives, children and other family members and friends who have endured a period in which our attention was distracted by the book. Their love and support during the writing and editing of this text is appreciated and greatly enhances the quality of our lives daily.

1   Introduction

What future for tourism?

Craig Webster and James Leigh

The idea for this book began with James Leigh pondering how the major economic, political and social changes in the world would impact upon the tourism industry. It seems that most tourism studies concentrate upon short-term superficial concerns such as marketing, profitability and the creation of new products and services for tourists. Few academic journal articles deal with longer-term issues such as real sustainable tourism, the impact of climate change on tourism and other issues that are of a longer-term concern. We have sought to create a book to deal with the fundamental drivers of tourism and build a longer-term vision of the future and what tourism would look like 20 to 50 years from now. This is a book that evolved out of the concern to give a platform to those in tourism studies who want to speculate about the future and what the future may mean for tourism.

As a book of composed of submissions from multiple authors, we were able to include the perspectives of many leading academics worldwide who have contemplated the future of tourism. This is a major strength of this book – it enables tourism researchers from around the world to have their say regarding the future of tourism. The authors come from many countries and are also based in many countries, giving readers the benefit of the insights and opinions of researchers from 'the four corners of the Earth'. Another major benefit for the reader is that the authors come from many different academic backgrounds (such as geography, political science, management, economics and, of course, tourism). The variety of academic backgrounds adds diversity to the perspectives expressed in the book.

The contributors to this volume are some of the best academics in the field who have practiced and published widely and have excellent academic reputations. We are honored to have all these contributors and appreciate that they were willing to collaborate with us to produce this unique and ground-breaking book. We are especially grateful for having Ian Yeoman as a contributor, since he is largely recognized as the leading futurist in tourism studies. Having a book on this topic would have seemed inappropriate without his input.

It may be intriguing to those reading the book from beginning to end – chapter to chapter – that the 'experts' disagree about what the future is going to look like and what future tourism may be like. Also noteworthy is that some of the authors take a softer view towards the future, by not confronting some of the dramatic issues as seen by others. Such authors tend to see historical continuity, believing that the next hundred years will be more or less like the economic boom since World War Two. These authors see a future with prosperity and further economic development for much of the world's population. It may be that the majority of our readers will hope these optimistic views prove to be correct.

Astute readers will note strong clashes in the trajectories of tourism put forward by the different authors. For example, it would be harder to imagine more diametrically opposed views of the future of tourism than those given by James Leigh and Ian Yeoman. Such a dissonance would not appear in a single-author book and is one of the book's strengths, since it is a reflection of the free expression of ideas that a book of readings offers.

Although such dissonance between the authors may undermine the coherence of an argument about the future, it is a reflection of our intention to enable multiple voices a space to express themselves. This is beneficial, because it will urge readers to think critically about the future and the forces driving humanity to a variety of potential futures. However, in spite of the dissonance, it is apparent to most of the authors that there are serious challenges ahead for tourism to surmount.

When dealing with something that has not yet happened, there is the risk that the speculation may not fully play out. Some of what is speculated about in the book may prove to be laughable in hindsight, while much of it risks being astutely accurate, illustrating trends that the tourism industry now should take into account, because the implications of some of the trends could be substantial. Just because some speculation may not be vindicated by future events and trends, readers should not be put off. Instead, we urge readers to read through the chapters to determine for themselves which chapters have perspectives that should be of practical use for tourism planning. Indeed it would be a good exercise to consider the most serious potential threats and prepare for them, without neglecting some of the less serious ones or even opportune possibilities ahead.

Apart from this introduction and a concluding chapter, the book is composed of three major sections. Part I deals with global changes and their probable impact on tourism in the future and consists of two chapters. In Chapter 2, James Leigh looks at the issue of Peak Oil, the decline of petroleum supplies/production in the next few decades, and relates the decline in petroleum supplies to implications for society and tourism. In Chapter 3, Craig Webster and Stanislav Ivanov look into competing visions of the global political economy of the future, exploring various ways that states may organize themselves to react to the challenges of tourism and the likely responses of the state to crises in the tourism sector in the future.

Part II looks into the political and social trends and issues that will likely influence tourism in the future. Chapter 4, by Michael Clancy, considers the issue of security and the future of tourism. This includes political violence and terrorism, vital issues that are currently on the public's mind in many countries. Chapter 5, by Chris Stone, explores the under-researched phenomenon of social tourism, exploring how developed countries supply tourism opportunities to their least fortunate citizens and how states, civil society and the private sector are likely to deal with supplying the least fortunate people tourism opportunities in the future. In Chapter 6, Susanne Becken looks into forecasting tourism by considering some of the key drivers (Peak Oil, environmental decline, demographic change, terrorism, etc.) in an attempt to predict which ones will shape future tourism. In Chapter 7, Nicos Kartakoullis and his coauthors deal with future tourism and its role in the quality of life of citizens. Finally, this section ends with a reflection by C. Michael Hall in Chapter 8 on future tourism and academia's perceptions of the future of tourism.

The third part is dedicated more to the managerial issues that future tourism professionals will have to deal with. In Chapter 9, Ulrike Gretzel speculates about technological change and how tourism will be experienced differently in the future due to rapidly developing technologies. In Chapter 10, Scott Richardson deals with human resource issues and needs for the future, including a look into role of education and training of professionals in the field. In Chapter 11, Werner Gronau assesses the much-discussed topic of sustainability in tourism and the future trajectory of these efforts in tourism. Finally, in Chapter 12 Ian Yeoman focuses upon what he expects tourism will look like in the future, using New Zealand as a case study.

Chapter 13, our final chapter, is a conclusion, tying together what has been learned from the insights of the authors in the book. The conclusion highlights that there is a very real divergence in how the authors view the future, some with a sense of optimism about the economic, political and social future of humanity, and some with a more pessimistic outlook. We feel that the conclusion could be a powerful motivator as a call to action for some.

The intention of the book is largely to stimulate thinking about the future of tourism. Indeed, we feel that this will be useful for several reasons. Thinking of the future is necessary because there has been little or no discussion about the major drivers and their impact on the long-term future of tourism. Much of what has been produced in academic circles for some time has been superficial and short term.

Speculation about the future should also be an incentive to plan and prepare for future challenges. Indeed, predictions and forecasts about the future may be quite accurate or off the mark. However, without thinking about the future it is impossible to plan for it or proactively prepare to overcome more dramatic scenarios. Thus, this book should help readers to speculate about a different future that they may have to deal with, and thus begin pre-emptive planning for likely challenging and unexpected futures that they may have never contemplated before.

This book goes into largely uncharted territory without precedents in society and tourism. Going into such territory is a bold step. Many of the projections may be vindicated, while others may become invalidated by future history.

While this is an edited book of readings, we made no attempt to edit the intentions of the authors. The book has been left to reflect the bold concepts expressed by the authors. There was no attempt by the editors to 'tone down' the chapters to make it more digestible to readers. As such, the assertions, predictions and forecasts of some of the authors may seem bold or wide of the mark. Readers will have to use their own intuition and minds to evaluate the arguments and forecasts made by the authors.

The authors all appear to take the Western assumption that there is a past, present and future and that humans are experiencing all of this in a linear way. With this assumption, we see that there is the notion that humans are empowered and have the ability to change the future, whatever it may be. This means that humans can empower themselves to change the course of the future and it only requires them to take action to avert those events that are undesirable in the future. It may be, as in the Terminator film franchise mantra, that there is 'no fate but what we make'.

This is a very 'political' assumption, since different warnings about the future presume that political means must be taken to avert the unpleasant futures some of the authors assume will happen under the current trajectory. However, it is also a very political notion that the current trajectories of the global economy will ensure a bright future for all humans and have all the positive things that some of the authors assume will happen. Indeed, this book is at its core highly political and seems to embody the notion that political thought is a form of political action. Even if it does not appear to be an overtly political book, with a little reflection, readers will be able to see that this is a political book. The viewpoints of the authors suggest that humanity should do little or nothing to expect a bright future or that humanity must either take action to avert disaster or prepare for dark days ahead.

We expect that readers will find this volume interesting, challenging and even provocative and confrontational. It is an important time for us all to ponder the future seriously and take action. Even though readers may find some chapters more relevant to their interests than others, we will be pleased if this volume stimulates readers to think about the future, not only of tourism, but also of humanity.

Part I

Global changes and their impact on future tourism

2 'Peak Oil' confronts society and tourism

A futuristic view

James Leigh

Introduction: peak phenomena

The comprehensive concept of peak phenomena is not a new concept. In their seminal work *The Limits to Growth*,[1] the authors predicted almost 40 years ago that the world could not continue to support universal and unlimited economic growth because resources, including world conventional oil supplies, were finite (Meadows *et al.* 1974). Donella Meadows and her coauthors (1993) talk of 'overshoot'. This occurs when human consumption grows beyond the level which the Earth can supply. Paul Cherfuka (2007) defines this overshoot point as having occurred when human consumption exceeds the ability of the Earth and its environment to maintain the demanded supply. At this point, when the Earth cannot supply the level of humanity's desired consumption, people may increasingly experience various barriers that limit or slow civilization's ability to continue in its established ways of development to care for the world's growing population. At the same time, a high level of denial, manipulation and intentional misleading of society from the establishment may reach dangerous levels.

Within this context, it may be that we are on the blistering edge of a peak phenomena storm with looming dwindling resource supplies across the board for many necessities (Baland and Platteau 1996; UNEP 2007; Grubb 2010). Oil is at the heart of humanity's massive and voracious energy economy as well as the basis for a food supply (Cherfuka 2007). The abundant supply of cheap resources has fueled modern developed society with its unquenchable, escalating and huge appetite for goods and services and the progenitor, making the supply of all those resources possible through the various processes of extraction, production and transport of them, was cheap and abundant oil.

Within this context of a possible peak phenomena era, in this chapter I will investigate the Peak Oil model and consider its contemporary relevance to understand the implications of dwindling conventional oil supply on society and tourism.

'Peak Oil'

Well before Meadows and her coauthors presented *Limits to Growth* on the world stage, the 'Peak Oil' model originated in the 1950s from the work of geologist

Dr. Marion King Hubbert. Peak Oil suggests that the rate of world oil production typically goes through several phases that follow a bell-shaped curve. First, discovery, then the rate of exploitation, will rapidly rise to meet increasing demand and as production becomes more efficient, and so costs increasingly fall. Second, as oil is consumed at ever increasingly higher rates, the oil resource is set to become increasingly scarce: costs therefore will increase as production levels off to an all-time peak (Peak Oil level). Third and finally, increasing depletion or scarcity, from dwindling available oil in the ground, leads to a rapidly growing decline in the rate of oil extraction, faster than new supplies are discovered. Available oil is increasingly difficult to extract as the price to do so becomes prohibitive, and the limits of technology for continued extraction are reached – oil flow stops.

The term Peak Oil refers to the maximum production level point when typically half the available oil inventory in the ground has been extracted: from here the rate of extraction falls into increasingly higher rates of decline until the exhaustion point of the available oil. Figure 2.1 shows the production levels of the various phases of Peak Oil.

This final Peak Oil phase, at a global level, will also be a prompt for the development of conventional oil alternatives. One of these alternatives is nonconventional oils which are heavy or deep-ground oil, or oil from oil sands and shale. All of these nonconventional oils are difficult and costly to access or produce. There is also the possibility of synthetic oils and other non-oil-based technologies; however these are typically costly and need much more development. Oils from biomass (plants and crops) are another possibility, but this solution is problematic when we consider using significant amounts of arable land, and its crop produce for oil. Surely this has the potential to greatly exacerbate any food shortages.

Some critics argue that there may be much oil yet to be discovered, and so are sceptical against Peak Oil. They have a point. No one really knows how much unconventional oil may yet be discovered. However, it will likely fall under one of the following categories: impossible to extract; or due to difficult extraction circumstances, not worth it because of low or negative net energy gain (it takes more energy to extract than it offers); or not extractable with present technology at today's prices.

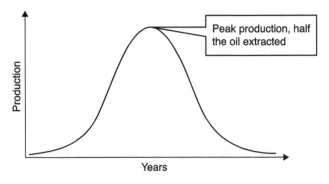

Figure 2.1 Hubbert's Peak Oil curve.

It is important to note that any future technology needed to extract this 'available' oil, is likely to be astronomical in cost by today's standards (The Hubbert Peak for World Oil 2003). Finally, while anticipating any such oil as a theoretical possibility for future use is not illogical, it is still indeed a long shot, and somewhat against the odds. At any rate, the ability to extract such oils would involve a long lead time, for field development (10 to 15 years or so), and eventually higher-cost fuel.

In considering that there may be much oil yet to be discovered, there is the point that developing any new oil field is a very capital-intensive project with long lead times of 10 to 15 years. Any new discoveries now could easily take a decade or more to make any significant difference to the available oil in the markets. And as we haven't new significant conventional oil fields to bring online now, or the extra refining capacity, or transport vehicles to carry the oil and its products (Hoyos 2008; Timmons 2004; Mouawad 2009), we are at least in a world of 'Virtual Peak Oil' for another 10 to 15 years, assuming we can even eventually find the extra supplies of extractable oil. Otherwise, we are in 'Real Peak Oil'. Either way will not make any difference for the next 15 years or so, and that is a long time for ailing energy-starved economies and societies to wait.

World energy sources

As shown in Table 2.1 (EIA 2008a), while oil is most important as the direct supplier of 34 percent of world energy, it is only one of the main world energy sources. For example, coal and natural gas combined offer the world 46 percent of its energy, and along with biomass combined, they give the world way over half its energy – 57 percent.

However, while these figures may be assumed to be correct, they belie the comprehensive importance of crude oil as the vital energy source – the progenitor of all other energies. To understand just how all important oil is, we need to ask one question, 'How would we have the other energy sources without oil?' The answer is probably that we would not have these other energies without oil.

These other energy resources need the supply of oil to fire up the both heavy extraction machinery and transport vehicles (trucks and ships) for their carriage to

Table 2.1 World energy sources

Resource	%
Petroleum	34.0
Coal	25.0
Natural gas	21.0
Biomass	11.0
Nuclear	6.5
Hydroelectricity	2.2
Renewables	0.4

(Figures are rounded up or down)

Source: EIA (2008a).

refineries or processing factories, and eventually to markets. Without oil we could not extract these other energies or process them. We would be largely without energy, and definitely not with the prodigious levels we have learned to take for granted in modern technological society. To put it succinctly and simply – without oil, we are without energy.

Oil supply

This means that the abundant supply of cheap oil is of paramount survival importance to our modern hi-tech society. Richard Duncan (2001) has shown that world oil production per capita peaked in 1979 and has since fallen off in a general decline to the year of 2000. Later figures, as shown in Figure 2.2 (EIA 2010), are interesting in extending the trends shown by Duncan, and they also concur with Heinberg (2005), who suggested 'The global production peak is expected to arrive between [2005] and 2010'. World oil production generally increased from 1999 to 2005 but fell into a general trend of decline from 2005 to 2009.

Figure 2.3 (EIA 2010) is even more disconcerting: it shows that world conventional oil production per capita has been rapidly and consistently declining from 2005 to 2009.

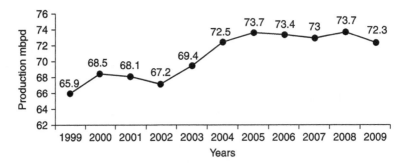

Figure 2.2 World conventional oil production.
Note: mbpd, million barrels per day.

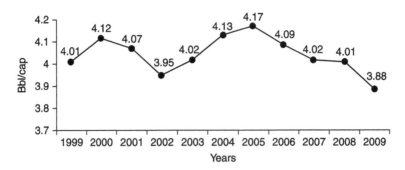

Figure 2.3 World conventional oil production per capita.
Note: Bbl/cap, barrels per capita.

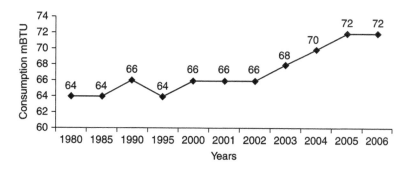

Figure 2.4 World primary energy consumption per capita.
Note: mBTU, thousand British Thermal Units.

From a more comprehensive point of view, Duncan (2001) has shown the world energy production per capita from 1979 was on a bumpy plateau up to the year 2000. Again if we consider later figures for this in Figure 2.4, we see that world primary energy consumption per capita was on a plateau until 2002, increased significantly to 2005 and again plateaued until 2006 (EIA 2008b).

Let us pause and take an overview of what the facts have shown us up to now.

- World conventional oil production per capita declined from 1979 to 2000.
- World conventional oil production has declined erratically since 2005.
- World conventional oil production per capita has been declining consistently since 2005.
- World energy production per capita declined from 1979 to 2000, increased from 2002 and peaked to a plateau in 2005.

To simplify further – conventional oil production (and per capita) may be in terminal decline, and world energy production may be in the early stages of a plateau leading to decline.

More specifics of energy and the future

According to Desmarest (2008: 13) world energy demand was 152 mboed (million barrels of oil equivalent per day) in 1980, grew to 244 mboed in 2005 and is predicted to be a whopping 328 mboed by 2030. That is a hefty 34 percent increase in demand for the 25 years to 2030. He has also shown that demand for oil by 2015 will be about 100 mbpd (million barrels per day), and considering conventional crude oil supply for 2009 was around 72 mbpd, we would need a formidable 39 percent increase in the next five years. No one knows where the extra supply will come from. Conversely he predicts a growing shortfall of crude oil supply of about 50 mbpd by 2015, about 50 percent of the predicted demand.

The fall off in world conventional crude oil supply is now being mirrored in the world production of energy. Energy consumption actually grew steadily from 9,260 mtoe (million tonnes oil equivalent) in 2000 to 11,315 mtoe in 2008, an increase of 22 percent over an eight year period, but fell 1.3 percent in 2009 over 2008 as shown in Figure 2.5 (BP 2010: 40–42). However, the increase in coal and natural gas overwhelmingly account for much of this increase up to 2008, and in 2009 coal's share of global energy was 29 percent, the highest since 1970. With conventional oil declining in supply, coal and gas have made up the shortfall so far (Desmarest 2008: 13; BP 2009: 41–42, BP 2010: 41–42).

With the increasing use of other energies to replace the conventional oil shortfall and the continuing expected rising cost of all energy (UN 2009: 1–4) we also see, in Figure 2.6, that world GDP per capita fell 4 percent in one year from 2008 to 2009, back to the 2006 level (Shane 2009). It must be conceded that this fall may be largely due to the global economic crisis. However, it is also reasonable to suggest that the rapidly rising oil price to US$147 a barrel in July 2008 could have been one of the foundational factors (in addition to gross financial mismanagement and overly high ubiquitous debt) that brought on the economic crisis.

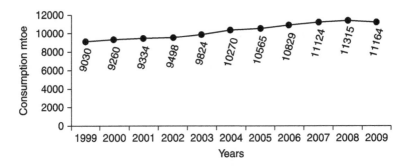

Figure 2.5 World primary energy consumption.

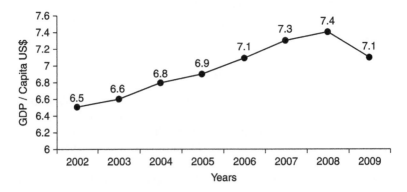

Figure 2.6 World GDP per capita.

Note: in thousands of US$.

We can now pause to make some summative observations:

1   Oil is important for 34 percent of world energy.
2   Oil is the quintessential progenitor of all energy.
3   Crude oil prices are erratic but probably generally on the rise.
4   World conventional oil production is declining.
5   World conventional oil production per capita is declining.
6   World conventional oil production may be beyond peak in permanent decline.
7   World conventional oil will probably be increasingly expensive to threatening levels.
8   World energy production per capita growth rate may be leveling off towards decline.
9   World shortfall in oil supply may be significant and probably increasing.
10   Other energies are probably only partly filling the gap and may be increasingly unable to meet the growing shortfall.
11   World energy production is in recent decline.
12   World energy may be increasingly expensive.
13   World GDP per capita is in recent decline.

In a more recent paper (2007: 148) Richard Duncan has predicted that we are in a transitional period for energy. He shows that even though world energy production and world populations have been increasing, there has generally been an energy per capita plateau for the past 30 years. Energy production rates have not kept up with the population growth rates – hence the plateau.

However, it is his prediction for energy production that is alarming. He suggests that the peak in world energy production in 2008, and world energy production per capita in 2005, heralded a permanent trend in the decline in energy supplies on the market. More specifically, he argues we are not now entering a slow die off of available energy, and that a 'cliff' was reached in 2008, with subsequent rapidly declining total energy supplies and energy per capita.

Fundamentally, Duncan argues that the declining supplies of the progenitor of all energy, conventional oil, will be responsible for falling energy supplies across the board. Within this context, some have struggled to understand the fluctuating prices of oil since July 2008, even though oil was not increasingly abundant. The unstable oil price is probably a result of three main factors. First, worldwide recession has eased the demand for oil to what it could have been, giving some relief to stresses on the supply side. Secondly, in an uncertain period of unstable oil prices, it may be that the opportunistic and manipulative actions of individual and corporate investors in the financial markets have had unpredictable effects on the price of oil. Thirdly, the 'queuing theory' suggests that when demand rises close to supply and even beyond, there may be an unstable period when prices of a commodity can be very erratic, and this has probably also exacerbated any other fluctuating tendencies in the price of oil (Deffeyes 2008). However, the overall trend of increasing decline in oil supply is anticipated with increasing prices.

Trends in tourism

At a time of threatening dwindling supply of conventional oil and its rebounding price levels, rising energy costs and potential shortages and an entrenched world economic crisis continuing to choke the world with falling GDP per capita, we may ask the question, 'How is tourism going and what may be its future?'

Tourist arrivals data, as shown in Figure 2.7, had a poor showing with monthly arrivals for the latter half of 2008 and most of 2009 with declines of up to about 13 percent. For the last two months of 2009 and the first four months of 2010 monthly arrivals were positive (UNWTO 2010). It may be that arrivals data will move into negative territory again towards 2010 summer, the high season for tourism, with the economic crisis continuing and oil prices in mid 2010 rising to significantly higher levels, at US$83 a barrel in early August.

We can see in Figure 2.8 that world tourism arrivals and receipts began to slow in 2008 and had absolute substantial declines in 2009 with −4 percent and

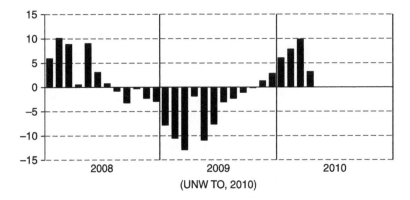

Figure 2.7 International tourist arrivals, monthly evolution (percentage change). *Source*: UNWTO (2010). Reprinted with permission.

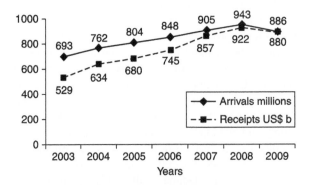

Figure 2.8 World tourism arrivals and receipts.

–6 percent (according to preliminary results) for arrivals and receipts respectively (Vogeler 2010: 3).

We can deduce that tourism worldwide is in a state of flux or anxious uncertainty with the following present and potential challenges (Vogeler 2010: 31):

- unemployment;
- worsening economic crisis as many positive signs are weak;
- pathological and increasing public and private debt levels;
- pandemic disease outbreaks;
- security and terrorism threats;
- intervening events such as floods, fires, earthquakes, volcanoes and hurricanes;
- other intervening events such as geopolitical and military conflicts;
- declining government stimulus packages;
- oil (and energy) scarcity and high prices.

In the wake of these interlinked and potentially dramatic challenges, we may see an extended period of economic slowing and entrenched downturn. In the remainder of this chapter one of these factors will be emphasized: that is potential oil scarcity and its implications for new society and new tourism.

New society

Various models of a post-oil and post-energy society have been suggested. However, to be viable, Heinberg (2005) says that any 'suggestion must describe a fundamental change of direction for industrial societies: from the larger, faster and more centralised, to the smaller, slower and more local; from competition to cooperation; and from boundless growth to self-limitation'. Agriculture will have to be integrated into the lives of many more citizens, to the point of being a typical even if a part-time pursuit, outside of the full-time job, in the lives of most (Heinberg 2005).

If the full effect of Peak Oil is beginning to play out, it may be about to forge a new society. That society will have to be compatible with (and integrate with) the new environmental circumstances – an end to the plentiful supply of cheap energy to fire up machine-based industrial civilization.

Put simply, humanity needs to drastically reduce its horrendous addiction to excessively high energy levels. The future society, to conserve energy, will likely be clustered into local communities, and as much as possible be self-contained and self-sufficient, with agriculturally based economies. This society does not however, exclude, for example, local industry, services and shops. This new decentralized society, with localized, largely self-sufficient communities, will automatically drastically reduce personal travel, packaging and transport for products – amounting to great savings on energy requirements.

We should not underestimate the need for a whole new mindset in such a close knit, locally organized, and largely self-sufficient community. However, this by itself would not be enough if we want to have a relatively high standard of living with comfort something like mankind now enjoys in the early twenty-first century. Various other changes in the daily behavior of citizens will be required in what we do and how we do it.

In this new society alternatives will have to be found for activities that once required large doses of energy. A quality of life is workable in a post-oil and even post-energy society, but the orientation and values of mankind will have to undergo a serious converting change, even to the extent of a metamorphosis. Eventually with the rise of a new truly sustainable lifestyle, in harmony with the physical laws surrounding us, many will be healthier and not in need of so much medical attention. Emphasis will have to be placed on sharing and cooperation, to replace the age-old excess baggage competition and strife. This will facilitate the new low-energy localized self-contained communities working well in a non-conflicted social environment.

It may not be a matter of whether we want to go this way or whether this is the lifestyle we want – there may be no choice. Actually the quality of human life and enrichment, it can be envisioned, could even be higher than we have now in both the rich and poorer countries of the world at present.

Looming oil depletion, and the concomitant lack of abundant energy from today's systems, trumpet the end of the industrial civilization and life as we know it. Classical economic development ideas and principles, largely dependent of cheap oil and energy supplies in permanent economic development, will soon be largely historic artifacts. A whole new approach and mindset is needed for a new society which will afford worldwide a quality and sustainable life. We will all need to embrace this new opportunity for a social community, living with harmonious behavior within sustainable circumstances (Leigh 2011, Leigh and Vukovic 2011: 67–95).

New tourism

Tourism is a human activity within the overall society and is subject to the general circumstances extant at any particular time. For example, economic development in the last 50 years, built upon cheap energy, has brought forth a consumerist society with machinery, technology, services, wealth, paid holidays and an inquisitive attitude for exotic adventure, fuelled by information technology and the entertainment industry. Many of these largely post-World War Two societal characteristics will be curtailed and re-channeled into new more frugal activities due to less wealth generally and higher prices.

Tourism will be modified, or more appropriately transformed, to fit within looming society's new context – the lifestyle and limits of that society. With the combined trends of increasingly scarce and more expensive oil, leading to greater scarcity and expense for energy in general, there will be significant knock-on effects for all human activities, with many goods and services also increasingly scarce and expensive.

Those activities with the greatest need for high levels of energy input will be the hardest hit. Our present living style, addicted to overly high doses of energy, may be about to change. Our present style of tourism uses prodigious amounts of energy, and so will also be hard hit in the post-energy era. Tourism will have to become much leaner in its use of energy generally and particularly oil. Suggestions of touristic behavior change in challenging circumstances are borne out by the findings of Steinnes (1988: 39) who found, in a regression model analysis, that both tourism expenditures and behavior are significantly related to gasoline prices.

We may then ask, what may be some of the specific changes we could anticipate for tourism of a new nature and scale? The following points are based on the assumptions that oil (and energy) will be scarce and expensive in the emerging world. Of course intervening challenges like dramatic geopolitical conflicts or natural catastrophes could greatly exacerbate the problems to be confronted by the tourist industry.

In this looming touristic context, within a new society we could expect to see the following factors emerge to make dramatic changes to the tourist industry:

1   Tourism with large energy doses will be very expensive and scarce. There may be esoteric luxurious facilities for the super rich who will be able to afford air travel, but for most people air travel and sumptuous holiday facilities will be out of reach.
2   Most people will use efficient popular transport modes of train, bus and ships (for intercontinental travel), although sea travel may be quite expensive too.
3   There will be a high demand for local tourism. For the great majority a typical holiday may be at a local beach or mountain resort (including forest or seaside camping).
4   Popular tourism will have to be simpler, less luxurious and more localized, to cut down on the total price and expensive consumption in a life that is more frugal overall.
5   This could mean that there will be a great opportunity for sustainable tourism to become more serious and real, beyond the lip service and window dressing of today's sustainable tourism.
6   Mass highly commercialized tourism will decline – smaller localized industry will (re)appear.
7   Generally people will travel less, and enjoy tourism with simpler cheaper requirements.
8   There may be a revival for the true soul of tourism, hospitality, to begin to overshadow and replace sumptuous amenities, which became the main focus in luxurious consumption-oriented tourism of the recent energy-hungry decades.

Peak Oil could set the context for a new society, which in turn will lay the foundations for new tourism. We can anticipate dramatic changes at all levels of society and its tourism (Leigh 2011, Leigh and Vukovic 2011: 67–95).

Conclusion

We are likely already in the outer edges of the Peak Oil storm beginning to play out. This heralds declining supplies of crude oil, and possibly even with increasing use of alternative oils, will lead to permanent (and yet erratic) price increases. Yet brief periods of cheap oil may lull the world into thinking the problems of oil and energy supply are over.

The present recession shows that levels of economic growth, or decline, can also affect demand for oil and its price, but surely the overall trend will be increasingly scarce crude oil and energy, and rising prices. This will erode established wealth and eventually forge a new society.

A brief blip on the historical record is about to disappear. Mass international tourism has come and will soon flee. This 'universal' mass tourism is a recent post-World War Two phenomenon, and blossomed upon technological development, and with the introduction of jet airliners, and cheap energy supplies, to grow at a spectacular rate since 1960. However, it looks like the reality of world Peak Oil is occurring now. Dwindling supplies of oil, and therefore of energy in general, are about to drag the world into a post-energy era, with increasing energy scarcity and more expensive goods and services.

Society may be on the edge of undergoing dramatic change, to be less dependent on abundant cheap supplies of energy and oil. It will be much more frugal in its energy use, and gravitate towards being localized in self-sufficient agricultural-based communities. Energy will be scarce and much more expensive. In this context, tourism will also change, metamorphosing to integrate with the new society and the constrictions placed upon it.

The new tourism will be largely 'back to the future'. Typically travel and tourism will be relatively local with much less travel (and mostly by road, rail, or possibly ship), in facilities that are more frugal. It is then that we may begin to see and experience the full measure of hospitality as it blossoms without the clutter of abundant supplies of sumptuous amenities. This may be a golden era for more frugal tourism of a new type, in which hospitality becomes central.

We can start planning now so that the transition to this new world society and tourism will be relatively easy and comfortable. Sage advice for the tourism industry may be encapsulated in the following dose of reality, 'those who harmonize with the trends today get on top of future history, before it gets on top of them' (Leigh 2009).

Note

1   This seminal work was also updated many decades later by most of the scholars in the original team (see Meadows *et al.* 2004).

References

Baland, J. and Platteau, J. (1996) *Halting Natural Degradation of Natural Resources*, Rome: FAO.

BP (British Petroleum) (2009) *BP Statistical Review of World Energy*, online. Available at   www.bp.com/liveassets/bp_internet/globalbp/globalbp_uk_english/reports_and_ publications/statistical_energy_review_2008/STAGING/local_assets/2009_downloads/ statistical_review_of_world_energy_full_report_2009.pdf (accessed 1 June 2010).

BP (British Petroleum) (2010) *BP Statistical Review of World Energy*, online. Available at www.bp.com/liveassets/bp_internet/globalbp/globalbp_uk_english/reports_and_publications/statistical_energy_review_2008/STAGING/local_assets/2010_downloads/statistical_review_of_world_energy_full_report_2010.pdf (accessed 5 June 2011).

Cherfuka, P. (2007) *Population: The Elephant in the Room*, online. Available at www.youtube.com/watch?v=e5wSHSvIMro&feature=player_embedded (accessed 5 September 2010).

Defeyyes, K. (2008) 'Oil Production, Oil Price, Beyond Oil', *Current Events*, 27 May, online. Available at www.princeton.edu/hubbert/current-events.html (accessed 5 September 2010).

Desmarest, T. (2008) *World Energy Prospects According to Total, Earth Resources: Threat or Treat?*, online. Available at www.yearofplanetearth.org/content/GLE/ThierryDesmarest.pdf (accessed 5 September 2010).

Duncan, R. (2001) 'World Energy Production, Population Growth, and the Road to the Olduvai Gorge', *Population and Environment*, 22(8): 503–522.

Duncan, R. (2007) 'The Olduvai Theory: Terminal Decline Imminent', *The Social Contract*, 17(3): 141–151.

EIA (Energy Information Administration) (2008a) *World Consumption of Primary Energy, 1980–2006*, online. Available at www.eia.doe.gov/pub/international/iealf/table18.xls (accessed 5 September 2010).

EIA (Energy Information Administration) (2008b) *World Per Capita Total Primary Energy Consumption, 1980–2006*, online. Available at www.eia.doe.gov/pub/international/iealf/tablee1c.xls (accessed 5 September 2010).

EIA (Energy Information Administration) (2010) *World Crude Oil Production, 1997 to Present*, online. Available at www.eia.doe.gov/emeu/ipsr/t11d.xls (accessed 1 September 2011).

Grubb, A. (2010) 'Peak Oil Primer', *Energy Bulletin*, online. Available at www.energybulletin.net/primer.php (accessed 1 June 2011).

Heinberg, R. (2005) 'Back to the Post-Oil Future', *Energy Bulletin*, online. Available at www.energybulletin.net/node/4943 (accessed 1 June 2011).

Hoyos, C. (2008) 'Saudis Warn of Oil Capacity', *Financial Times*, 22 April, online. Available at www.ft.com/cms/s/0/db03994e-109f-11dd-b8d6-0000779fd2ac,dwp_uuid=f2b40164-cfea-11dc-9309-0000779fd2ac.html?nclick_check=1 (accessed 1 June 2011).

Leigh, J. (2009) 'Tourism and Peak Oil Threat: Fact or Fiction?', paper presented at the Third Annual Student Conference What's Going on: Putting the Pieces Together into the World of Tourism, University of Nicosia, 31 March 2009.

Leigh, J. (2011) 'New Tourism in a New Society Arises from Peak Oil', *Tourismos*, 6(1): 165–191.

Leigh, J. and Vukovic, P. (2011) *Beyond Oil Bust: Investigating Oil Economics, Society and Geopolitics*, New Delhi: Atlantic Books.

Meadows, D., Meadows, D., Randers, J. and Behrens, W. (1974) *The Limits to Growth*, London: Universe Books.

Meadows, D. Randers, J. and Meadows, D. (1993) *Beyond the Limits*, White River Junction, VT: Chelsea Green.

Meadows, D. Randers, J. and Meadows, D. (2004) *Limits to Growth: The 30-Year Global Update*, White River Junction, VT: Chelsea Green.

Mouawad, J. (2009) 'Chilly Climate for Oil Refineries', *New York Times*, 23 December, online. Available at www.nytimes.com/2009/12/24/business/energy-environment/24refining.html (accessed 1 June 2011).

Shane, M. (2009) 'Real Historical GDP and Growth Rates of GDP per Capita for Baseline for Countries (in 2005 dollars) 1969–2009', *ERS*, 2 November, online. Available at www.ers.usda.gov/Data/macroeconomics/Data/HistoricalRealPerCapitaIncomeValues.xls (accessed 4 June 2010).

Steinnes, D. (1988) 'A Statistical Analysis of the Impact of Oil Price Shocks on Tourism', *Journal of Travel Research*, 7(2): 39–42.

The Hubbert Peak for World Oil, 2003, online. Available at www.oilcrisis.com/summary.htm (accessed 24 June 2010).

Timmons, H. (2004) 'Got Oil? Now Try to Find Tankers to Carry It', *New York Times*, 9 June, online. Available at www.nytimes.com/2004/06/09/business/got-oil-now-try-to-find-tankers-to-carry-it.html (accessed 4 June 2010).

UN (United Nations) (2009) *World Water Development Report 3, Water in a Changing World*, online. Available at www.unesco.org/water/wwap/wwdr/wwdr3/pdf/WWDR3_Facts_and_Figures.pdf (accessed 4 June 2010).

UNEP (United Nations Environment Programme) (2007) *Global Environmental Outlook 4: Environment for Development: Summary for Decision Makers*, online. Available at www.unep.org/geo/geo4/media/GEO4%20SDM_launch.pdf (accessed 4 June 2010).

UNWTO (United Nations World Tourism Organization) (2010) *Barometer*, 8(2), June, online. Available at www.unwto.org/facts/eng/barometer.htm (accessed 1 June 2010).

Vogeler, C. (2010) 'World Tourism: 2009 and Beyond', a presentation given at Tourism Outlook Seminar: Challenges, Changes and Opportunities in Tourism, Rising above the Current Global Economic Landscape, 23 February, Montego Bay.

3 The political economy of tourism in the future

Craig Webster and Stanislav Ivanov

Introduction

Tourism is big business, and there are various measures of how big it is. Indeed, there is a growing literature that is dedicated to measuring the size of it both from demand- and supply-side perspectives (e.g. Song *et al.* 2010; *Tourism Satellite Account: Recommended Methodological Framework* 2008). However, the question remains how large tourism will be in the future as an industry, how tourism and the experience of tourism will evolve and what role the state will have in terms of regulating and subsidizing tourism. This paper will explore these questions to look into how the state will interact with tourism in the next 20 to 50 years.

There are three separate issues that must be explored in order to make an analysis of what the role of the state in the future will be. The first of these is an analysis of what we can expect the future to look like in the next few decades. This is critical and can be viewed as a forecasting exercise, since the economic, social and political environment of the world in the next 20 to 50 years will indicate the sort of environment in which tourism and the state will operate. Indeed, this is the critical element to explore since there are various futures we can expect to experience, although some environments seem to be more likely than others as an outcome of the current global situation.

The second of these issues is a full description of tourism regulation regimes that are currently available to states. A full description of the archetypes of tourism regulation will be explored. These archetypes (or 'regimes') are linked with the various paradigms of political economy and with ideological views of what the role of the state is vis-à-vis the society and economy. These are critical to explore because the way in which the state will choose to interact with the economy and society are ideologically based, so a full understanding of the ideologies and the political choices such paradigms limit are critical to understanding the role of the state in the future in terms of its relationship with tourism.

The third of these issues is the importance of tourism and the question of whether, as an industry/sector, it is critical enough to warrant substantial governmental subsidies/supports. This issue is important to deal with because tourism, as a part of the non-financial service sector, is qualitatively different from banking, real estate and some manufacturing industries that governments often favor. The critical question is whether governments will find that tourism is worthy of governmental support, whether that be through subsidies, protection, or some other approach.

In this analysis, we will deal with each of these critical issues. First, we will discuss what the future of the world is likely to be and what role tourism will have in it. Next we will turn our attention to the question of how governments can deal with the regulation of tourism and subsidies given to the industry, given their ideological views on the role of the state vis-à-vis the market and society. Then we will address the likelihood that governments will view tourism as being an industry important enough to warrant governmental attention/subsidies/protection. Finally, we will make an analysis of the likely role of the state in the future and its relationship with the tourism industry/sector, given the analysis of the future of the world, the ideological approaches available and the importance of the industry.

World futures and tourism

There is a great deal of speculation in terms of what the possible futures are for the world. Such speculation has been going on for years and has been used all sorts of technologies and approaches. For example, apart from standard econometric analysis and more organic approaches to the future, there has been a great deal of scholarly work into the nature and logic of the future based upon computer simulations (see for example, Bremer and Hughes 1990; Meadows *et al.* 1993, 2004). This is a vast field and deserves some attention, although central for us are the two very different views of the future that emerge.

One view is optimistic, viewing the future as a positive place in which the liberal ideal has largely been realized, with a globalized economy and free markets. This view can be epitomized with the 'McWorld' vision outlined by Barber (1996), although Barber makes it clear that he is not entirely a fan of such an outcome. This world, in the most optimistic outcome, should be one with a minimal interference in international trade. Such a world is the logical outcome of a successful liberal agenda that has been pursued progressively since the end of World War Two, something often referred to as 'globalization'. Such a world relates to the intensified integration among countries and the creation of regional politico-economic blocs with common currencies. Those who champion such a world, for example Thomas Freidman (2005), project a future that is significantly better because technologies and liberal systems are bringing wealth and development around the world. However, such a world will bring challenges, because the more developed countries will be forced to compete against workforces that are less expensive and are highly skilled. This is a very optimistic view of the future, with development occurring because of the successes of the free market over the past few decades.

A less optimistic view of the future often focuses on resource depletion, a critical issue in the research forecasting of the world's economic, social and political future. For many, the center of the discussion is the depletion of oil, and a number of recent books have dealt with the question of peak of oil production and what happens after this occurs (see for example, Deffeyes 2006; Goodstein 2004; Heinberg 2003; Leggett 2006; Roberts 2004). Indeed, there has been concern about the dependence of modern industrial and post-industrial societies on the existence of vast quantities of petroleum at a low cost, while the supply is considered finite and diminishing. This discussion is not new (see Caldwell 1977), but with the increase of the global population and a rapid rate of economic development in China (among other countries), the issue becomes more commonplace and urgent. The crux of the argument is that petroleum is in finite supply and that our modern economy is entirely dependent upon it for fuel, transportation and as a raw material to enable humanity to feed itself via pesticides and fertilizers. When the fuel runs out, the argument is, humanity will have to substantially change the way it does things and many may die due to a dependence of food production upon petroleum.

There are others who write about other types of materials that will be increasingly scarce in the next few decades. Meadows *et al.* (1993, 2004) deal with materials other than petroleum (such as copper, zinc and platinum) and view a future scarcity in them. Kennedy (1994) views population growth as the chief challenge to humanity, because the increasing number of humans will create greater demands for resources, with critical issues arising in food production. Such an approach has a long history and there are many who have been influenced by the work of Malthus; indeed, there has been increased interest in the growth of the global population and its impact upon the sustainability of humanity since Paul Ehrlich published his best seller *The Population Bomb* in 1968 (Ehrlich 1968; Ehrlich and Ehrlich 2009). There are others who warn of general issues of ecological decline due to the way in which humans have treated the earth (see for example Catton 1982, 2009; Diamond 2005; Lovelock 2006). Thus, there is reason to believe that there could be 'overshoot' and 'collapse' (the computer simulation language to describe the phenomenon) due to a large population of humans, a diminishing supply of petroleum (as well as other resources) and extensive damage to the ecosystem caused by human activity.

In terms of thinking about the future, the question will remain to what extent the limitations on natural resources will exist in the future, and to what extent this will inhibit economic growth as humans have experienced it since the end of World War Two. In terms of reconciling the optimistic view of the future with the more pessimistic one, the optimists usually have the argument that humans are so ingenious that they will (or already have) found resources that will replace those that are depleted. There are occasional references to technologies that are superior to those presently known that are kept out of the public's knowledge. For example, Icke (2007: 393) mentions that he was informed of a technology that has been developed which harnesses the unseen energies in a house and can power and heat a house without cost. Of course, there would be significant interests who would want to keep information of such a technology suppressed. There is also the consideration that petroleum is not a seriously limited resource and may not actually come from fossils. An alternative theory, the 'abiogenic' petroleum approach, assumes that petroleum is not actually a result of fossils being changed chemically but is a naturally occurring substance excreted by the Earth. The implication from an abiogenic approach to petroleum is that it may not be nearly as limited in supply as supposed, since the substance may keep bubbling up through the Earth's crust in nearly infinite quantities.

One of the weaknesses in these arguments is that there is no currently known resource that can replace petroleum in terms of supplying energy to humanity (Leigh 2008) and can be used in such versatile ways in order to sustain the population via building materials/fabrics and (more importantly) creating a large food supply. So, even if energy were available from an alternative source, the other uses of petroleum remain so critical that humanity remains dependent upon it. Indeed, the massive production of food using efficient modern methods of agriculture (despite the costs) was made possible largely by the use of petroleum with petroleum-based fuels, pesticides and fertilizers. As Kennedy (1994) mentions, the era of agricultural overproduction that has occurred since the end of World War Two may be a mere historical anomaly, although recent developments with genetically modified organisms might expand food production over its current limits. Another concern is that the scarcity of petroleum can be manipulated via political means, as was done during the petroleum shortage of the 1970s.

In terms of visions of the future and how they relate to tourism research, the majority view the question of the future of tourism is generally optimistic. The most important work looking at this issue of future tourism is Yeoman (2008), who views the future of tourism as a continuation of post-World War Two economic expansion with greater leisure opportunities for all, including a growth in space travel. However, he is not alone, and the major textbook in the field (Goeldner and Ritchie 2006) views the future in a very similar way. Also typical of this approach is Henderson *et al.* (2001) who view the future of tourism as something in constant expansion, but one need not look into the literature very deeply to find that there is a general consensus that the growth of the middle class means greater opportunities for tourism and leisure for all. In other words, the consensus of those who study tourism and the future trajectory of tourism is that we can expect continued economic expansion and an expanding middle class. These authors generally perceive the future as a continuation of market-generated wealth, with people throughout the world increasingly exposed to the notion of leisure, recreation and tourism, since markets have produced wealth for societies to enjoy at a fairly constant rate since the end of World War Two.

Most of these authors' view is that the unfolding of liberal capitalism and its spread globally has led to an expansion of wealth and economic development. The natural outcome of such a process is the evolution of leisure, recreation and tourism. What less optimistic views of the future make a good point of is that such a process of development is not a one-way street historically but, perhaps, just a golden age of wealth that is made possible because of certain political and economic circumstances and the abundance of cheap petroleum. However, some have disagreed all along about whether the wealth that seems to have spread along with capitalism around the world was a benefit to all (see for example Wallerstein 1996). It may well be that the perceptions of those writing about the constant expansion of capitalism, higher living standards and greater leisure may not be writing their theses in countries in which poverty is widespread, so they are merely writing from a perspective of the wealthy developed countries, assuming that the less developed countries are merely going through the same process as did the West decades ago.

So the question of what the future looks like for tourism is tightly bound with the question of what the future looks like in general, as Table 3.1 summarizes. If a shortage of necessary materials is not problematic, because humans are ingenious enough to find alternatives and substitutes, then the expansion of leisure and tourism would seem to be a sure thing, as Yeoman (2008) and others seem to think. However, if one takes the view that (above all else) petroleum and other necessary inputs into economies (including water) are in finite supply and there are no suitable replacements for them, then it would seem that the future of tourism will be radically different. All humans should hope that the more optimistic view will prove correct, although reason would suggest that a more pessimistic outcome will be the case, given the current prevailing notions of the nature of petroleum and publicly available technologies. In the negative scenario, countries impose carbon taxes on any industries that have a negative carbon footprint on the environment, many of which are directly linked with tourism – e.g. transportation, food production, commercial hotel accommodation. These carbon taxes, that might be in the form of global taxes used to finance the UN-led environmental initiatives, will lead to increased costs of travel and tourism-related services, thus reducing their consumption.

Table 3.1 Possible futures, drivers and impact on the tourism industry

	Optimistic future	*Pessimistic future*
Driving to the future	• Globalization • Technological innovations • Liberal democracy	• Petroleum depletion • Mineral resource depletion • Overpopulation • Environmental collapse
Mitigating factors	• Protectionism • Petroleum depletion • Mineral resource depletion • Overpopulation • Environmental collapse	• 'Abiogenic' petroleum • Innovation in energy technologies • Innovation in agricultural technologies • Population growth slowing
Expected impact on tourism	• Continuation of low-cost air travel • Newly wealthy markets created • Space travel	• End of low-cost air travel • End of mass tourism from developed countries • Fewer people with resources to afford leisure/tourism

If the more pessimistic outcome is the case, there will still be tourism, but the mass tourism that is experienced in the Mediterranean, the Caribbean and Asia will largely be a thing of the past, since for many the transportation costs will be unaffordable for the dwindling middle class and less affluent. Indeed, there may be a return to a more localized approach to tourism, less dependent upon cheap fuels. Most probably, the tourists of the future will use trains and other forms of public transportation to get to the location of their holidays and engage in activities that are less dependent upon petroleum and less costly in terms of capital expenditures. They may search for leisure activities in the nearest natural surroundings of metropolitan areas in order to reduce travel costs and the carbon footprint of their holidays. In short, the future tourists may actually have camping types of vacations that are not far from home and do activities such as bicycling, canoeing, sailing and hiking. The future tourist may actually experience tourism in ways very similar to how it was experienced during the Great Depression or shortly after World War Two in Western countries, before the rebuilding of much of Europe and Japan and the rise of mass tourism via jumbo jets.

An additional issue to be looked at is the question of politics in the future and trends leading to political change. The movement of states into larger units is a general movement that will say a great deal about political structures in the future. The evolution of the European Union is the most advanced example, although other collections of states seem to be moving in a similar direction. Such evolving political unions (Europe, North America, Africa and others) will play an increasingly important role in the future, if current trends toward political and economic integration continue. This will have immense political, economic and social consequences and will influence tourism a great deal.

Tourism management paradigms

Little is written about the political economy of tourism, although almost anything in terms of policy or politics and its link with economics could be labeled 'political economy'. It seems that the literature on the political economy of tourism is experiencing a growth spurt (see for example Mosedale 2011). Although there are a large number of works that could be categorized as researching tourism from the standpoint of political economy (see for example, Britton 1982, 1991; Cornelissen 2005; Desforges 2000; Hall 2004; Jeffries 2001; King 2002; Ooi 2002; Page 2007; Pearce 1996; Palmer and Bejou 1995; Tang and Xi 2005; Vail and Heldt 2000; Williams 2004), this approach is generally underdeveloped in the literature.

Political scientists usually classify regimes in the world into three or four major typologies. The language and the theory comes largely from the leading texts in international political economy (see for example Balaam and Veseth 2007; Caporaso and Levine 1992; Frieden and Lake 1999; Gilpin 1987, 2001; Lairson and Skidmore 2002; Pearson and Payaslian 1999). A typical categorization of regimes of political economy conceptualizing four major types of economy is presented by O'Neil (2007), and this conceptualization is consistent with others in the field (see for example, Draper and Ramsay 2007). The four major approaches to political economy are outlined in Table 3.2 along with each approach's relationship with tourism regulation, because the issue of the regulation of tourism in the future is linked with current practice. The paradigms (or 'archetypes') are general guidelines, indicating a description of how the state views its role in the regulation of the state and economy. This has important implications for tourism management, most specifically for the national tourism organization (hereafter NTO), as the state's organized response to tourism. These paradigms and the implications for tourism regulation are mentioned elsewhere in depth (see Webster *et al.* 2011). One brief point that should be made is that states generally take approaches towards the regulation of their tourism industries consistent with how they envision the state should be involved in the economy (Webster *et al.* 2011).

The liberal approach to political economy (e.g. US, UK, Canada) puts faith in the efficiency and self-correcting ability of market forces. Liberal approaches to political economy stress the need to allow market forces to work independent of political forces to ensure that the markets function in the most efficient ways possible. For example, in the 'liberal' USA, there is no NTO. The closest

Table 3.2 Political economy systems and tourism regulation/management

	Liberalism	*Social democracy*	*Communism*	*Mercantilism*
Role of the state in the economy	• Modest • Minimal welfare state	• Some state ownership and regulation • Large welfare state	• Complete state ownership • Extensive welfare state	• Extensive state ownership or direction • Small welfare state
Role of the market in the society and economy	• Dominant	• Vital but not sacred	• Almost none	• Restricted and managed by state
Scope of NTO	• Limited powers granted, or they may not exist	• Limited to moderate powers granted to coordinate, market and regulate tourism	• Powerful state organs	• Powerful regulatory powers granted to them
Role of NTOs	• Data gathering, data analysis, possibly marketing	• Data gathering, coordination between private and public sectors, marketing, redistribution of wealth	• Command and control of entire tourism industry	• Regulation and coordination of private and public sectors in order to encourage efficiency, quality and competitiveness

Note: Based upon the four regimes presented by O'Neil (2007).

thing that the USA has to an NTO is an office within the Department of Commerce, the Office of Travel and Tourism Industries (OTTI), which is mostly responsible for the collection of tourism data. Canada, also classified as 'liberal', has the Canadian Tourism Commission (CTC), a public–private partnership that performs research and advertising for Canadian tourism. What is liberal about the Canadian approach is that the CTC is a public–private partnership, meaning that market forces and input are an integral part of how the organization is envisioned in its regulation of tourism in Canada.

The most statist political economies, the communist ones, are very different from the liberal ones. In the communist model (e.g. Cuba, North Korea, the Soviet Union) the market is almost completely marginalized, in order to prevent the inequalities that seem to emerge naturally from market forces. Thus, it should be no surprise that the state dominates, coordinates and controls the tourism industries in such political economies.

Mercantilist political economies (e.g. Japan, South Korea, India) are somewhat different from the communist ones, since they allow for the private ownership of the means of production and markets, although they allow a great deal of governmental regulation and interference in such markets, making them also quite statist. In mercantilist political economies, the state plays a leading role in terms of managing, regulating and controlling market forces. Unsurprisingly, Japan and South Korea have a very statist and mercantilist approach toward the regulation of tourism, in that they both have NTOs that are highly involved in the regulation, marketing and coordination of the tourism sector.

The social democratic model (e.g. Sweden, Finland, Denmark) is a blend of the liberal and mercantilist approaches, although commonalities with the communist approach are also apparent due to a common Marxist philosophical heritage. In social democratic economies, the state plays a leading role in regulating the economy and is sometimes an owner of industries. Social democratic economies permit market forces to function but entail significant political interference in markets to prevent wildly unequal outcomes from occurring. In terms of implications for tourism, we would expect such political economies to have institutions to regulate tourism (in contrast to a liberal approach) while at the same working in ways to alleviate inequalities within the country. What is interesting is that in recent years, Finland and Sweden (two clearly social democratic political economies) have to some extent abandoned their traditional statist and social democratic approaches to tourism regulation, in favor of a more liberal model.

The question relevant for the future is to what extent free markets are deemed to be desirable or workable as institutions to provide goods for societies absent massive support from governments. With the market failures of capitalism in the past few years, we may see that faith in markets will be so eroded that the entire foundation upon which liberalism rests (the efficiency and productivity of markets) will make liberal approaches either undesirable or impossible to pursue. This may steer political choices to deal with tourism issues towards social democratic and mercantilist approaches, with more managed economies and state involvement. However, in recent years we have witnessed several social democratic countries (like Sweden and Finland) adopting a more liberal market-oriented approach to destination marketing by cutting NTO's offices abroad (see further details in Webster *et al.* 2011). Additionally, due to the rise on regionalism we can expect that the role of the individual state governments in destination marketing will decrease at the expense of the regions within countries and the supranational bodies (such as the European Union, North American Union, African Union), because much responsibility for tourism may be taken away from states and given to the political unions.

How important is tourism?

The final thing to consider is the role of tourism and the importance of tourism in the economy in the future. This is a critical exercise, because it is really a matter of a political decision of the authorities in each country. To be sure, a country such as Malta or Cyprus with about two-and-a-half tourism arrivals per resident in a year will view the importance of tourism differently than a country like the USA, with only about 160 tourism arrivals per thousand inhabitants. The countries most dependent upon tourism as a basis for a strong economy will be more likely to use the state to organize and coordinate the tourism industries in their countries. However, for those countries which are not particularly dependent upon tourism, the state will be less likely to intervene and help to stabilize and expand the industry. Table 3.3 illustrates the attributes of industries correlated with state support, suggesting that there will likely be little or no sustained support for tourism in many countries.

There are two major variables that should be considered. The first point to note is that the importance of tourism for the economy will be a critical variable. Although many authors praise the economic importance of tourism (e.g. Ivanov and Webster 2007), it is wise to highlight some regional initiatives that undermine the ability of governments to measure the size of tourism in countries correctly. The introduction of the Shengen Agreement removed border checks among participating countries: this means that if a tourist travels from Germany to the Netherlands (for example) their trip will not be counted by the statistical authorities of both countries, unless they use commercial accommodation in the Netherlands. If the tourists visits friends and relatives or stays in their own property, the statistical authorities have no means of accounting their trip. The entry of many more countries into the Shengen agreement (with Bulgaria and Romania

Table 3.3 Correlates of state support for an industry

	State subsidizes/supports
Perceived as 'Too big to fail'?	Yes
Linked with an influential lobby?	Yes
Integral part of military–industrial complex?	Yes

expected to join in 2012–13) means that the international tourism arrivals among participating countries will look more similar to domestic trips within countries rather than international trips. If national statistics authorities experience difficulties with measuring such basic statistics as number of international tourism arrivals, what can one say about other tourism statistics?

However, the question of the size of tourism is highly integrated with the question of the future of tourism. In the more pessimistic view of the future, the beach holidays of Europeans in Thailand, Greece and Turkey will largely be limited to only the wealthiest of citizens. In such a scenario, it may be futile for states dependent upon mass tourism from far away to try to bolster the industry with state action over an extended period of time. In such a scenario, states such as Malta and Cyprus may, in the initial stages, experience large doses of governmental infusions of money and support to the tourism industry but it would seem that such support will eventually wither away, because the attempt to bolster tourism in the face of decreasingly wealthy source markets and increasing transportation costs will be largely futile, at least to boost mass tourism. In fact one could expect that future tourists will swap long distance trips for trips to nearby destinations, longer holidays for shorter holidays and expensive trips for less expensive trips. This may benefit continental countries with easy access by car/train to tourist resources (beaches, ski runs) but may disadvantage island destinations even within the Mediterranean whose accessibility is based predominantly on air transport sustained by low-cost petroleum.

The second major variable to be considered is the structure of the tourism industry itself, vis-à-vis other industries. While banks in the UK and USA and other developed countries have been bolstered by the state in this depression, tourism in the future may not face such massive subsidies and supports. The major argument in the UK and USA is that the banks are 'too big to fail'. The notion behind that is that if the banks fail the entire economy collapses, which translates for political officials into a desire to subsidize bank losses. There are other industries that are centralized and have the ability to secure political support because the ownership are organized and influential, have organized workers and are more visible to governments and the public. For example, if an auto company is in trouble government frequently intervenes, because the closure of a plant means a loss of jobs and this usually leads to legislators willing to do what it takes to bolster the industry: the workers are likely unionized, or if not, the spillover effects into the community are unacceptable for other businesses and politicians. The closure of a hotel or restaurant does not generally create the same level of problems for political and economic elites as do closures of manufacturing industries or financial service bankruptcies. The lack of centralization, unionization and the perception that it is not 'too big to fail' will definitely be a problem for tourism industries, because the industry is unlikely to get the types of governmental support that financial institutions and manufacturing industries will tend to enjoy. Another weakness that tourism industries will have to face is that they are linked with the military–industrial complex in only the most indirect ways, so that state support via that important channel will likely be minimal.

Conclusion: the unwritten future

If we accept the more optimistic perception of what the future will bring, we can expect more or less a continuation of what has happened since the rebuilding of economies following World War Two. That means there will be an expansion of mass tourism, with people flying around the world to experience different things and see different locations, and that more of the globe's population will be able to experience this. What will be noteworthy is that there will be an expansion of tourists from newly wealthy countries in Asia, as well as other parts of the world. What this means for the regulation of tourism in the future is increasing coopera-tion via intergovernmental institutions in order to enable the populations of the world who are increasingly affluent to get from place to place safely.

In this optimistic view, we expect that states will deal with regulating tourism within their countries in accordance with the prevailing philosophy of elites in power. However, since the European Union and North American Union (and perhaps some other political and economic unions) will be increasingly important in terms of regulations, it would seem that states within these unions will largely tend towards liberal types of regimes to deal with internal issues of tourism and its marketing, because much of the regulatory power will move upwards, to the polit-ical union level. To a large extent, the NTOs will tend to get smaller and will be increasingly dominated by market forces (as is the case in Finland in recent years). Even the gathering of tourism data within the nation-state may, in the future, be moved up to the political union level. The NTOs or organizations that resemble them that remain, under this scenario, will largely be administrative and may be mostly active in marketing the country's tourism product, doing surveys of the local market and industry and collecting data on tourism.

In the more pessimistic view of the future, a more interesting and turbulent political economy of tourism will appear. To begin with, the mass tourism of the post-World War Two years will largely be over. A dwindling middle class and expanding percentage of the population in economic trouble will have less cash available to afford vacations that involve air transport, a service that will increase in price in response to the scarcity of petroleum. Those governments deeming tourism to be critically important to their economy will likely look for ways to support the industry in the early stages and some enterprising ones may develop alternative opportunities for tourists. However, because in many of the countries that are tourism-dependent their ability to attract tourists is based upon inexpensive air fares, such interventions will in the longer term be largely doomed to failure. In non-tourism-dependent economies, if governments determine that tourism is not too big to fail, a liberal approach to permitting such industries to go under will likely be the outcome. In those states that choose more mercantilist or social democratic approaches, we will likely see more state intervention and planning to transform the industry into something that will be sustainable.

The major question, though, is how liberal approaches to the management of economies in general will persist, given the current economic circumstances and probable future ones. A new type of paradigm of economic management may arise and seems to have arisen as a field invention. This type of economic management is an odd mixture of liberalism and mercantilism that has sometimes been referred to as 'lemon socialism'. This way of doing things is not entirely new; it is merely the state infusing cash into industries that are troubled. If the industries succeed, the profits are privatized. If they fail, the losses become a public cost. This way of doing things is clearly not sustainable, especially when states have accrued massive debts that can never be paid back. However, such is the world we currently live in, with states that can never pay their debts and money that is printed that has nothing of value backing it up, apart from the statements of governments.

The future of tourism is interesting, and the very different paths that global tourism will take will be the outcome of major economic and political events in the next 20 to 50 years. The most likely outcome, unless you are optimistic about petroleum resources or a replacement for petroleum-based fuels, is that the type of long-distance travel that has been experienced by many and the mass tourism that was enabled by this is largely going to be over in the next few decades. For most of us, the leisure and tourism that we experience in the future will be more similar to what was experienced by Europeans in the 1930s and 1950s than the space tourism envisioned to be 'more mainstream by 2030' (Yeoman 2008). This change, an end of the 'golden age' with abundant fossil fuels, will have important meaning for everyone in a political sense, and tourism will not be immune from this. One thing that is certain, however, is that as long as there are humans there will be tourism, and the character of tourism in the future is really just a matter of the political, economic and social choices people will make, within the constraints of their circumstances.

References

Balaam, D. and M. Veseth (2007) *Introduction to International Political Economy*, 4th edn, Englewood Cliffs, NJ: Prentice Hall.

Barber, B. (1996) *Jihad vs. McWorld: How Globalism and Tribalism are Reshaping the World*, New York: Ballantine Books.

Bremer, S. and Hughes, B. (1990) *Disarmament and Development: A Design for the Future?*, Englewood Cliffs, NJ: Prentice-Hall.

Britton, S.G. (1982) 'The Political Economy of Tourism in the Third World', *Annals of Tourism Research*, 9(3): 331–358.

Britton, S.G. (1991) 'Tourism, Capital and Place: Towards a Critical Geography of Tourism', *Environment and Planning D*, 9(4): 451–478.

Caldwell, M. (1977) *The Wealth of Some Nations*, London: Zed Press.

Caporaso, J. and Levine, D. (1992) *Theories of Political Economy*, Cambridge: Cambridge University Press.

Catton, W. (1982) *Overshoot: The Ecological Basis of Revolutionary Change*, Urbana, IL: University of Illinois Press.

Catton, W. (2009) *Bottleneck: Humanity's Impending Impasse*, Bloomington, IN: Xlibris Corporation.

Cornelissen, S. (2005) *The Global Tourism System: Governance, Development and Lessons from South Africa*, Burlington, VT: Ashgate.

Deffeyes, K. (2006) *Beyond Oil: The View from Hubbert's Peak*, New York: Hill & Wang.

Desforges, L. (2000) 'State Tourism Institutions and Neo-liberal Development: A Case Study of Peru', *Tourism Geographies*, 2(2): 177–192.

Diamond, J. (2005) *Collapse: How Societies Choose to Fail or Survive*, London: Allen Lane.

Draper, A. and Ramsay, A. (2007) *The Good Society: An Introduction to Comparative Politics*, New York: Longman.

Ehrlich, P. (1968) *The Population Bomb*, New York: Ballantine Books.

Ehrlich, P. and Ehrlich, A.H. (2009) 'The Population Bomb Revisited', *The Electronic Journal of Sustainable Development*, 1(3): 63–71.

Frieden, J.A. and Lake, D.A. (1999) *International Political Economy: Perspectives on Global Power and Wealth*, London: Routledge.

Friedman, T. (2005) *The World is Flat: A Brief History of the Twenty-first Century*, New York: Farrar, Straus and Giroux.

Gilpin, R. (1987) *The Political Economy of International Relations*, Princeton, NJ: Princeton University Press.

Gilpin, R. (2001) *Global Political Economy: Understanding the International Economic Order*, Princeton, NJ: Princeton University Press.

Goeldner, C. and Ritchie, J.R. (2006) *Tourism: Principles, Practices, Philosophies*, Hoboken, NJ: Wiley.

Goodstein, D. (2004) *Out of Gas: The End of the Age of Oil*, New York: WW Norton & Co.

Hall, C.M. (2004) 'The Role of Government in the Management of Tourism: The Public Sector and Tourism Policies', in L. Pender and R. Sharpley (eds.) *The Management of Tourism*, Thousand Oaks, CA: Sage Publications, pp. 242–257.

Heinberg, R. (2003) *The Party's Over: Oil, War and the Fate of Industrial Societies*, Gabriola Island, British Columbia: New Society Publishers.

Henderson, K.A., Bialeschki, M.D., Hemingway, J.L., Hodges, J.S., Kivel, B.D. and Sessoms, H.D. (2001) *Introduction to Recreation and Leisure Services*, 8th edn, State College, PA: Venture Publishing.

Icke, D. (2007) *The David Icke Guide to the Global Conspiracy and How to End It*, Isle of Wight: David Icke Books.

Ivanov, S. and Webster, C. (2007) 'Measuring the Impact of Tourism on Economic Growth', *Tourism Economics*, 13(3): 379–388.

Jeffries, D. (2001) *Governments and Tourism*, Oxford: Butterworth-Heinemann.

Kennedy, P. (1994) *Preparing for the Twenty-first Century*, New York: Random House.

King, J. (2002) 'Destination Marketing Organisations – Connecting the Experience Rather than Promoting the Place', *Journal of Vacation Marketing*, 8(2): 105–108.

Lairson, T.D. and Skidmore, D. (2002) *International Political Economy: The Struggle for Power and Wealth*, 3rd edn, Fort Worth, TX: Harcourt, Brace & Co.

Leggett, J. (2006) *Half Gone: Oil, Gas, Hot Air and the Global Energy Crisis*, London: Portobello Books Ltd.

Leigh, J. (2008) 'Beyond Peak Oil in Post Globalization Civilization Clash', *The Open Geography Journal*, 1: 15–24.

Lovelock, J. (2006) *The Revenge of Gaia: Why the Earth is Fighting Back and How We Can Still Save Humanity*, London: Allen Lane.

Meadows, D.H., Meadows, D.L. and Randers, J. (1993) *Beyond the Limits: Confronting Global Collapse, Envisioning a Sustainable Future*, White River Junction, VT: Chelsea Green.

Meadows, D.H., Randers, J. and Meadows, D.L. (2004) *Limits to Growth: The 30-Year Update*, 3rd edn, White River Junction, VT: Chelsea Green.

Mosedale, J. (ed.) (2011) *Political Economy of Tourism. A Critical Perspective*, London: Routledge.

Office of Travel and Tourism Industries (OTTI), online. Available at tinet.ita.doc.gov/ (accessed 20 September 2011).

O'Neil, P. (2007) *Essentials of Comparative Politics*, 2nd edn, New York: Norton.

Ooi, C.-S. (2002) 'Contrasting Strategies: Tourism in Denmark and Singapore', *Annals of Tourism Research*, 29(3): 689–706.

Page, S.J. (2007) *Tourism Management. Managing for Change*, Oxford: Butterworth-Heinemann.

Palmer, A. and Bejou, D. (1995) 'Tourism Destination Marketing Alliances', *Annals of Tourism Research*, 22(3): 616–629.

Pearce, D.G. (1996) 'Tourist Organizations in Sweden', *Tourism Management*, 17(6): 413–424.

Pearson, F. and Payaslian, S. (1999) *International Political Economy*, Boston, MA: McGraw-Hill.

Roberts, P. (2004) *The End of Oil: On the Edge of a Perilous New World*, Boston, MA: Houghton Mifflin.

Song, H., Li, G., Witt, S. and Fei, B. (2010) 'Tourism Demand Modelling and Forecasting: How Should Demand be Measured?', *Tourism Economics*, 16(1): 63–81.

Tang, Fang-Fang and Xi, Y. (2005) 'Lessons from Hong Kong: The Role of Tourism Boards', *Cornell Hotel and Restaurant Administration Quarterly*, 46(4): 461–466.

Tourism Satellite Account: Recommended Methodological Framework (2008) Jointly presented by the United Nations Statistics Division (UNSD), the Statistical Office of the European Communities (EUROSTAT), the Organisation for Economic Co-operation and Development (OECD) and the World Tourism Organization (UNWTO).

Vail, D. and Heldt, T. (2000) 'Institutional Factors Influencing the Size and Structure of Tourism: Comparing Darlarna (Sweden) and Maine (USA)', *Current Issues in Tourism*, 3(4): 283–324.

Wallerstein, I. (1996) *Historical Capitalism with Capitalist Civilization*, 2nd edn, London: Verso.

Webster, C., Ivanov, S. and Illum, S. (2011) 'The Paradigms of Political Economy and Tourism Policy: NTOs and State Policy', in J. Mosedale (ed.) *Political Economy of Tourism. A Critical Perspective*, London: Routledge, pp. 55–73.

Williams, A.M. (2004) 'Toward a Political Economy of Tourism', in A.A. Lew, Hall, C.M. and Williams, A.M. (eds.) *A Companion to Tourism*, Oxford: Blackwell, pp. 61–73.

Yeoman, I. (2008) *Tomorrow's Tourist: Scenarios and Trends*, Oxford: Butterworth-Heinemann.

Part II

Political and social trends and future tourism

4 Security and the future of tourism

Michael Clancy

Introduction

On October 12, 2002 Islamist militants associated with Jemaah Islamiyah targeted the Kuta tourist district on the island of Bali in Indonesia with backpack, car and suicide bombs. When the carnage was over some 200 people were dead and an additional 240 injured. Higgins-Desbiolles (2007: 310) goes so far as to claim that combined with the September 11, 2001 attacks, the Bali bombings 'consolidated the war of terrorism as a war on tourism', by making clear the clash between affluent global tourists and the 'wretched of the earth'. Is this, in fact, the future faced by global tourists? This chapter will examine the future of tourism from the standpoint of security. It proceeds as follows: After discussing trends within traditional security concerns such as war, terrorism and political instability and their impact on tourist flows, the discussion moves to complicated notions of security. Finally, the chapter closes with speculation on how security concerns are likely to affect not so much the flows of global tourism, but more importantly their form.

Before starting, it should be noted that predicting the future, while fun, is always a bit hazardous as well. Following the fall of the Berlin Wall, many analysts predicted the obsolescence of armed conflict (Mueller 1989), but scarcely a decade later major terrorist attacks led others to note a 'new age' of global terror. This serves as a reminder that the world can change quickly. Moreover, the one thing that recent trends in tourism have underscored is the growing eclecticism of the activity. Today perhaps the greatest watchword in tourism is segmentation, and this is likely to continue. There are all kinds and a growing number of specialty forms of tourism, from ecotourism, to volunteer tourism, to adventure tourism and wine tourism, to dark tourism and medical tourism. The danger is that making broad predictions regarding *the* future of tourism ignores these specialties, which will most likely continue to flourish and run counter to broader trends. That said, many of these subspecialties will also be affected by changing developments in security.

International tourist flows depend upon, more than anything else, two things: affluence and security. As evidence of the former, in the midst of the current global recession the United Nations World Tourism Organization (UNWTO) reports global tourist flows falling 4 percent in 2009, this after a decline of 2 percent in the second half of 2008 (UNWTO 2010). Although the sector rebounded in 2010, that trend is tentative given renewed economic uncertainty in 2011. Others in this volume take up the issue of affluence, political economy and their impact on the future of global tourism in much more detail. With respect to security, upon first glance the relationship seems to be clear: Tourism requires security and insecurity harms tourism. Yet questions remain. What constitutes security and insecurity? How much of an impact does insecurity have and for how long? How much do perceptions matter and how do tourism stakeholders respond to these perceptions? Finally, and most speculative of all, what does the future hold in the realm of global security and what impact will these trends have on global tourism?

Trends in global tourism and security

Global tourism operates not only in the larger global economy but also within geopolitics. It should not be surprising therefore that the distribution of global tourists is not random but instead reflects existing global dynamics of power and wealth. As a result, when examining the world's top 10 international tourism spenders in 2009, one finds all five UN Security Council permanent seat holders, and nine of the top 10, are among the highest ranked countries in the United Nations Human Development Report. Wealthy and powerful nations are also disproportionately represented among the top tourism destinations and earners (UNWTO 2010). This suggests tourism flows in the future will continue to reflect the global distribution of power and wealth. To a certain degree, this is happening. Twenty years ago China was hardly a global destination for international tourists and had virtually no outbound market of its own. Today, however, the country ranks fourth in both global arrivals and departures. Other growing economic and political powers in the world such as Brazil, Russia and India (along with China, these are the so-called BRIC countries) are likely to see similar, if not such spectacular growth. The larger point is that tourists, as Phipps (2004: 82–3) points out, like to think of themselves as innocents abroad, but they are implicated in the global order. Or, as Jamaica Kincaid (1988: 17) puts it much more succinctly, who exactly gets to be a global tourist often depends on whose ancestors were 'clever'.

When Richter and Waugh (1986: 231) long ago wrote that 'political serenity, not scenic or cultural attractions, constitute the first and central requirement of tourism', they were raising the issue of security. Within the field of political science, security has traditionally referred to the absence of physical conflict between or within countries. The dominant theory of international relations, political realism, views the nation state as the ultimate protector of its citizens against real and imagined external threats. As neorealist Kenneth Waltz (1979: 126) writes, 'In anarchy, security is the highest end. Only if survival is assured can states safely seek such other goals as tranquility, profit, and power.' According to this understanding the main threat to security is external, coming from other nation states. And yet realists also point out that conflict is a normal, even natural feature of world politics.

The most common form of political conflict is war. By some estimates, in the last 3,500 years fewer than 300 of them experienced no war. Although estimates vary depending on how war is defined, today the incidence of war remains high. The Canadian ecumenical group Project Ploughshares identifies 28 armed conflicts involving 24 countries ongoing in 2009. The Uppsala Conflict Data Program in Sweden (UCDP/PRIO) estimates 36 wars in 2009, 29 of them intrastate and seven of them internationalized. Trends in the incidence of war remain unclear. On one hand, contrary to some liberal projections (Fukuyama 1993; Mueller 1989) the number of wars in the world actually *increased* rather than decreased following the end of the Cold War, peaking during the mid-1990s (Project Ploughshares 2010). On the other, since that point the number of global armed conflicts has been trending downward. Goldstein (2011) contends that not only is the incidence of war declining globally, but the overall destructiveness of war is also down considerably. Despite this, zones of conflict are not hard to find. The world has had at least 20 ongoing armed conflicts every year since before 1960 (Gleditsch 2002; UCDP 2010). Regionally, some three quarters of today's conflicts are centered in Africa and Asia, which accounted for 11 wars each in 2009 (UCDP 2010).

Although this time series data is useful, it tells us nothing of the intensity of war or about broader trends in armed conflict. Most analysts classify armed conflicts as wars when the conflict is political and results in at least 1,000 battlefield deaths. While some conflicts barely reach that floor, others have a much higher human cost: Russia's incursion into Georgia in 2008 was so fast and limited that for many this 'war' was not counted as a war. Meanwhile the conflict in the Democratic Republic of Congo has killed an estimated four million people. The war in Iraq has killed hundreds of thousands and created more than two million refugees. War has been a constant feature in Sudan, being present in all but 11 years since it gained independence and resulting in the deaths of more than one million. Despite these large-scale tragedies, the overall trend is that the size and scope of wars have been declining since the end of the Cold War.

This outcome may be related to the next factor: the predominant nature of war has also changed, from primarily interstate wars earlier in the twentieth century to intrastate or civil wars predominating today. According to the Uppsala Conflict Data Program, 95 percent of the armed conflicts taking place over the last decade have been intrastate in nature. Mary Kaldor (2007) distinguished between 'old wars' which are classic realist conflicts between nation states over power, and 'new wars' that are mainly internal but usually contain outside elements as well. These wars are characterized by identity-based (religious, ethnic) conflict, the breakdown of state authority, the use of irregular forces, a muddied distinction between war and organized crime and the high incidence of civilian casualties. This latter factor has been a profound development and appears to be the result of intentional targeting. At the outset of the twentieth century only one in eight war casualties was a civilian: by the close of the century that figure was seven out of eight (Kaldor 2007: 9). Others see a growing number of contemporary conflicts driven less by ideology or identity and more by scrambles over increasingly scarce natural resources (Homer-Dixon 2001; Klare 2001; Le Billon 2006). The rise of religious conflict, of course, has also been cited as a growing threat to global security.

Whether these trends will continue into the future is of course uncertain, yet if history is any guide we can expect the incidence and intensity of war to continue. Where and what form it takes remains to be seen. Those who emphasize resources may point to areas rich in petroleum and natural gas such as the Middle East and Caspian Sea regions. Others look to sub-Saharan Africa, where petroleum and rare earth minerals are concentrated, and where disputes over legitimate governance are commonly found. A third resource candidate is potable water. Among those who point to growing conflict over identity, some look at religious fault lines. Huntington's (1996) Clash of Civilization thesis envisions conflicts based on culture and religion. Similarly Griswald's (2010) *The Tenth Parallel* points to the fault line between Islam and Christianity over time, suggesting that much of past, current and future global conflict can be found there. Yet as her work and several others' demonstrate, making the distinction between religious wars and resource wars is often false. Global climate change or shrinking natural resources often reinforce and exacerbate ethnic and religious cleavages. The same is true of economic hardship. Thus, one reading of the Rwandan genocide is that of an ethnic conflict between Hutus and Tutsis. Another more nuanced account, however, would examine how economic crisis and structural adjustment policies, combined with population growth and increased pressure on scarce arable land, contributed to the conflict by increasing zero-sum politics.

Gleditsch (2002) surveys the more systematic studies of the causes of modern conflict, and his findings are instructive for thinking about the future. The overall probability that a country experiences war has, in fact, changed very little between 1946 and today, and while the number of identifiable armed conflicts has grown, so too has the number of countries in the state system (from 66 in 1946 to 192 in 2010). Kaplan's (2000) vision of a 'coming anarchy' may or may not come true, but his images of an overpopulated planet scrambling for increasingly scarce resources while the growth of identity politics coincides with the decline of public authority suggests that conflict and threats to security will remain a defining feature of the world. The question is less whether and more where. Gleditsch's (2002) answer is that among all the variables – power, politics, resources, ethnicity, religion – that analysts look to as causes of contemporary armed conflict, two stand out: poverty and prior violence. Wars mainly take place in poor countries and in those where wars have already taken place. No other variables are particularly predictive. With respect to poverty, a caveat is in order. It remains unclear as to whether it is absolute or relative poverty that contributes to the likelihood of armed conflict. Moreover, questions of the direction of causation remain: Does poverty cause war or is it the other way around? The other highly predictive factor, prior violence, is evidenced by the fact that of the 39 conflicts that have arisen over the past 10 years, 31 of them constituted what the CIDCM (2010: 2) calls 'conflict recurrences'. Together these two factors, poverty and prior violence, suggest that the war–poverty relationship is cyclical. Finally, while the *origin* and *location* of contemporary wars is largely predictable by income level and incidence of previous conflict, other countries often get involved. Data from the Human Security Centre in Canada (HSC 2010) suggests that over the longer term, 1946–2005, the countries most prone to war remain former colonial powers or Cold War superpowers.

What all this means for tourist flows is for the most part straightforward: Global tourists will, by and large, avoid war zones, and for the most part this is fairly easy and predictable. Zones of conflict such as southwestern Asia and various parts of sub-Saharan Africa caught in the cycle of violence and poverty already hold little appeal for most international tourists, and will continue to do so in the future. To be sure, the occasional popular tourist sites, such as Beirut and the Dalmatian coast, will also get caught up in armed conflict, but much as they do today, tourists will substitute alternative sites. New regional centers of tourism such as Dubai will take the place of sites scarred by war. Perhaps more ironic, many of the leading tourism-sending countries – the UK, France and the United States – are also the most war-prone countries over the past half century (HSC 2010), although again this underscores the geopolitical basis of international tourism.

Terrorism and political instability

Although war might be considered a 'stable' threat to security in that it is relatively constant and at least somewhat predictable, two other primary threats to security – terrorism and political instability – are much more unpredictable. The concept of terrorism is contentious and slippery. Terrorism expert Bruce Hoffman (2006) identifies 109 separate definitions of the term. What most academic experts agree upon is that terrorism contains several elements: violence (real or threatened), a political component, a psychological target and being extra-legal in nature. These definitional differences make tracking of terrorist incidents difficult, to say the least: What constitutes a terrorist attack? Where does terrorism end and war begin? What distinguishes crime from terrorism? These questions aside, efforts have been made to track incidents of terrorism. According to the most comprehensive databases, terrorist attacks and casualties have ebbed and flowed over the years, but both have increased significantly since 2001 (reported in Boulden 2009: 12–13). The MIPT (Memorial Institute for the Prevention of Terrorism) dataset, for instance, shows that the number of fatalities from terrorist attacks grew from 2,172 in 1998 to 12,070 in 2006 (reported in HSC 2007: 9).

Yet even shallow wading into the data reveals important caveats: Some 79 percent of the total fatalities recorded in 2006 took place in Iraq, where sectarian violence was peaking. Moreover, similar civilian casualties in many other civil wars were *not* classified as victims of terrorism. Authors of the 2007 Human Security Report, in fact, argue that outside of the Iraqi casualties, evidence suggests that terrorism in the world is actually *declining*. Boulden (2009), using HSC data, also argues that almost all of the increased reports of individual terrorist attacks can be accounted for by higher recorded numbers in just two regions: the Middle East and South Asia. Similarly, the Center for International Development and Conflict Management's 2010 report (CIDCM 2010) reports that global terrorist activity peaked in 1992, then fell until 2001. It grew between 2001 and 2006 but has fallen again since that point.

Much as the case with war, the effect of terrorism on tourism is expected to be predictable: Terrorism hurts tourism. Two factors, however, distinguish terrorism from war: first, terrorists may, and often do, target tourists. The 1997 attacks on tourists visiting Luxor in Egypt and the 2002 and 2005 bombings in Bali, Indonesia are prime examples. Most often tourists are targets either because of their particular identity (Americans, Israelis, Australians) or because of the economic dependence a country has on tourism. Egypt's economy, for instance, is heavily dependent on tourism and therefore constitutes an inviting target to those opposed to the Egyptian regime. As Wall (1996: 144) points out, targeting tourism often allows terrorists to reach their goals. Following the Mumbai attacks in 2008, one hotel marketing executive stated, 'Anyone who was thinking about a holiday in India will now think twice and many will cancel. Terrorists know the game' (Brancatelli 2008).

The second factor, however, runs counter to the first: While wars are clearly bound spatially, the same cannot be said for terrorism. Put differently, global tourists can view the world in terms of zones of conflict and zones of peace when it comes to war, but as residents of New York (2001), Washington (2001), London (2005), Tokyo (1995), Moscow (2002), Mumbai (2008) and Madrid (2004), to name a few, know all too well, terrorism is hardly spatially bound in the same way.

Oddly, this unbound geography of terror allows terrorism and tourism to operate side by side. Put differently, when terrorists strike sites whose main appeal is tourism and little else, the effect is immediate. Tourism is severely affected. Tourism arrivals in Bali fell by 25 percent immediately and only fully recovered in 2005, when new bombings adversely affected the area anew (Brancatelli 2008). Although some have argued that the effect of terrorist attacks on tourism arrivals is shorter than might be expected (Pizam and Fleischer 2002; Wall 1996), this is not always the case. Tourism arrivals in Egypt languished during much of the 1990s after terrorist attacks, and multiple attacks in Israel coinciding with the second Palestinian Intifada beginning in 2000 more than halved tourist arrivals, with numbers recovering to pre-Intifada levels only in 2007 (Brancatelli 2008).

The broader effects of terrorist attacks are even more complex. It remains unclear, for instance, whether terrorist attacks in more multidimensional destinations such as major cities have the same results in terms of declining tourism arrivals. Tourists may identify certain destinations as 'dangerous' due to a past attack combined with their overall lack of knowledge, but London and New York are known much differently. On the other hand, the indirect effects of attacks can be profound. After the September 11th attacks many Americans were afraid to board planes and many others saw travel abroad generally as now dangerous. *Overall* US outbound overseas travel fell 6 percent in 2001 and an additional 7 percent the following year (OTTI 2010). Among the markets most adversely affected were Mexico and Canada, two countries that had nothing to do with the attacks. Bonham *et al.* (2006) report that one side effect has been a boom in domestic travel to Hawaii.

The third main security issue for tourists is that of political instability. Global tourism relies upon a certain level of political calm. Note, however, that the requirement of stability is very different than a requirement of democracy. As Richter (2007) points out, some literature on tourism explicitly links itself with democracy and especially freedom. Yet any link between tourism and democracy remains unclear at best. During the Cold War tourism became a propaganda tool: the US and its allies explicitly linked the freedom to travel with broader freedoms associated with democracy and capitalism. Yet tourists have long flocked to tourism destinations under authoritarian or imperfect democracies. Whether democracy fosters tourism or vice versa remains unclear, but we might still consider the evolving nature of the world that makes up the landscape of tourism.

Among others, Huntington (1996) noted a 'third wave' of democratization emerging at the end of the twentieth century. As with previous waves, however, this third wave has been followed by a retrenchment (Diamond 2008). Freedom House (2010), which tracks democracy and freedom in the world with annual reports, lists 116 electoral democracies among 194 countries in 2010, a decline to the lowest level since 1995. Moreover, some 40 countries, 20 percent of the total, experienced absolute declines in freedom from the previous year. The Economist Intelligence Unit (2010) similarly produces a 'Democracy Index' and it, too, reports a decline in democracy in the world. It classifies countries in one of four categories: full democracies, flawed democracies, hybrid regimes and authoritarian regimes. In 2010 only 26 countries (15.6 percent) were listed as full democracies and an additional 53 (31.7 percent) as flawed democracies. Thirty-three (19.8 percent) were classified as hybrid regimes and 55 (32.9 percent) as authoritarian in nature. Perhaps most disturbing is that it classifies several stable and long thought of as open regimes such as Greece, Italy and France as 'flawed democracies'. Longer-term trends, however, are more encouraging. In 1979 roughly one-third of the countries in the world were classified under what Freedom House (2010) called 'free' regimes, another third under 'partly free' regimes and a final third under 'not free regimes'. In 2009, in contrast, 89 countries (46 percent) lived under free regimes, 58 countries (30 percent) were partially free and 47 (24 percent) were classified as not free.

While these trends are interesting in and of themselves, their impact on global tourism remains uncertain at best. It is not at all clear that democracy or freedom has any impact at all on tourist flows. In fact, tourists have in the past as well as today been quite happy to travel to countries with authoritarian political regimes (Hall 1994). As Richter (2007: 7) suggests, 'Nice beaches may be more relevant to tourists than human rights.' Instead, it seems that regime *change*, not regime *type*, is most important here because it tends to bring with it political instability. It is transition – whether from democracy to authoritarianism or the other way around – that may be most threatening to tourist flows. As a result, repeated coups in Fiji have had only a marginal affect on tourist flows, and the drop in numbers quickly recovered when order was restored. In contrast, pro-democracy demonstrations in Thailand during 2010 led to an immediate 15 percent drop in arrivals to Bangkok's international airport, and some officials projected the tourism industry to lose as much as $1 billion. Tunisia's experience with tourism mirrored the Thai case when protests led to the fall of the authoritarian Ben Ali regime in early 2011, as has Egypt's with the fall of Hosni Mubarak. Reports suggest that hundreds of thousands if not millions of trips were cancelled (*New York Times* 2011). This underscores the conclusion that it is political serenity, not specific regime type, that fosters and maintains tourist flows.

Before moving on to a deeper interrogation of security and its relationship to tourism it is important to note one additional aspect of tourism and its relationship to political violence. This is the time-bound nature of the violence and the issue of remembrance. Wars and terrorist attacks are profound human events. Not surprisingly, their significance becomes marketed through commemoration. This includes the creation of new holidays, historical markers and tourism sites. This practice fits under the larger heading of dark tourism or thanatourism, which Lennon and Foley (2000: 3) refer to as the growing tourist interest in death, atrocity and disaster. For Rojek (1993), this amounts to a modern form of pilgrimage. Others (Laderman 2009; Lisle 2004) have also noted that sites of war and atrocity – from Gettysburg to Pearl Harbor, the World War Two battlefields of France, Auschwitz and Birkenau in Poland, Vietcong tunnels of Vietnam to Ground Zero in Manhattan – have become tourist sites of remembrance. Moreover, they contain interpretations meant to convey a particular historical and social significance.

Securing tourist security

Several conclusions follow from the preceding section: First, it is not at all clear that the world is becoming a more dangerous place when it comes to political violence. Evidence shows that both the number and scope of wars and terrorist incidents have been declining. As Kaldor points out in the preface to the second edition of her 2007 book on war:

> there has actually been a decline in the number of wars in the world and a decline in the number of people killed in wars [. . .] Yet, paradoxically, the atmosphere of fear and our sense of insecurity has greatly increased.
>
> (2007: vii–viii)

This leads to the second conclusion, the importance of perception. Security and insecurity are ultimately perceptual in nature. As Hall and O'Sullivan argue, '*perceptions* of political stability and safety are a prerequisite for tourist visitation' (1996: 117, emphasis added). Third, and emerging from the first two, this requires much greater attention to the concept of security itself.

This renewed attention to security has been taken up in a couple of related ways in recent years. One effort has centered on broadening the concept of security by focusing on who or what is being secured as well as considering alternative threats to security (Hall *et al.* 2003; Levy 1995; Mathews 1989; Myers 1993). The human security paradigm, for example, argues that issues such access to food and water, poverty, resource scarcity, gender discrimination and violence, health, crime, human rights violations and environmental degradation all constitute threats to individual human security, and emphasis on the individual rather than the nation state leads to greater attention to these sources of insecurity. Focusing on human security is appropriate when considering global tourism because it is not the nation state that needs to be secured here but the individual tourist (see Hall *et al.* 2003 for an example). Threats to their real or perceived safety – or pleasure – are also broader than political violence and include several issues raised in other chapters in this volume including resource scarcity, climate change and sustainability. As they highlight, this insecurity through scarcity raises distributional justice issues, not least between hosts and guests.

In addition to broadening security to include additional actors and new potential threats, interrogating the very concept yields additional insight. The field of critical security studies does just that in asking not only who is being secured, but also what constitutes the condition of security as well as how ideas of security develop over time (Booth 2005; Krause and Williams 1997; Lipschutz 1995; Weldes *et al.* 1999). Common to many of these works is the idea that conditions of security and insecurity are socially produced, not just empirically through action but also discursively. As a result, although the actual incidences of war, terrorism and political instability appear to be *declining*, as evidenced above, ideas that the world is a more unstable and dangerous place proliferate. As Dalby (1997: 10) points out, in part this is because traditional security discourse contains a clear normative political element that favors order and the status quo over social change. In fact, change itself is often presented as a threat to security.

Tourism is not immune from traditional security discourse. As Goldstone (2001) makes clear, for instance, while much of security discourse during the Cold War revolved around realist concerns with the state's ability to provide physical security to its citizens within its territory, it also extended its protection to its citizens traveling the world by engaging in a discourse regarding 'the freedom to travel'. In addition, much of the emphasis of opening up markets in order to foster democracy contained a significant travel and tourism component. The end of the Cold War has done little to change this. Tourists themselves constitute the 'secure' portion of the ever-increasing flows of humanity across political borders. They are advised by governments through travel warnings and their passports are to serve as modern 'official' letters of transit.

Yet at the same time that global tourists are fostered and promoted by both sending and receiving governments, the modern discourse of security remain focused on danger. In part this is a holdover from the Cold War, where the security/insecurity dynamic at once promised protection from a foreign menace while simultaneously suggesting no protection was possible (duck and cover), the threat also came from within (McCarthyism) and finally that a threat anywhere in the world (Turkey, Vietnam, Mozambique) was of dire consequence to overall security. The message of terrorism today is consistent with these prior messages: The threat is both internal and global, and can strike anywhere without warning.

But this modern message of insecurity is much more comprehensive. Threats associated with war, terror, drugs, crime, urban violence and immigration dominate everything from cable news to popular movies and videogames. Often these 'threats' are tied to foreigners, the poor or people of different ethnic and religious backgrounds, leading to what Koskela (2009: 398) calls the 'new racism' that ties insecurity to race.

This new and intensified social production of fear (Koskela 2009) has profound consequences for the way in which the class that makes up the bulk of global tourists lives, both at home and abroad. Lockard (2005), writing about post 9/11, argues there is a political economy logic to this manufacture of fear, leading to everything from defense contractor Lockheed Martin's public relations campaign equating freedom with weapons production to increased domestic sales of duct tape. Individuals buy gold and hoard canned goods, not just in case of economic collapse, but also to prepare for other unspecified attacks. Similarly, David Campbell (2005) argues the boom in sales of sports utility vehicles in part results from changing cultures of insecurity following 9/11 that link external threats with internal behaviors and consumption patterns. We also witness the growth in global consumer classes living in gated communities or protected high rises as well as the now standardized surveillance of closed circuit television cameras in public spaces. Moreover, these practices have spread from the moneyed classes in the global north to become standard among the nouveau riche in emerging economies such as India, Brazil and South Africa. At home this global tourist class increasingly lives in spaces that are segregated and contain physical or technological barriers (home alarms) that insulate them not only from violence, but from perceived threats often associated with the poor and those from different races. In Europe these locales contrast with what some call 'dish cities', poor neighborhoods inhabited mainly by unassimilated immigrants from the Middle East, Africa and South Asia.

What does all this have to do with the future of global tourism? Quite a bit, I would argue. These messages of ever-present danger are likely to affect where people travel but perhaps more important *how* people travel. When it comes to where, it may be that people will travel more regionally, where the sensation of otherness is not so strong. Araña and León (2008), find that among US travelers going abroad, September 11th had a disproportionate and lingering effect on destinations with a high percentage of Muslim populations. As particular security threats become associated with peoples in the world, this trend is likely to continue.

These developments suggest that as the global tourist class lives in growing isolation and protection at home, so will they travel in the same manner. In other words, they are likely to travel behind real or perceptual barriers, where a major component of the tourist product itself will be safety and isolation. Tourism providers have already jumped in this direction. This will especially aid certain segments of the tourism market, most notably free-standing all-inclusive resorts as well as cruise tourism.

All-inclusive resorts have flourished for decades and they literally constitute the gated communities of the tourism sector. In recent years firms and even governments have worked hard to create new tourism facilities that segregate and protect tourists not only from the surrounding space but also from the spaces where tourism workers live. Many facilities include public and private security personnel. The planned Mexican tourism resort of Cancún exemplifies this trend. When it was created by tourism officials and city planners in the 1960s it demarcated tourist spaces from a zone where workers would reside. Over time, this segregation by zoning was not sufficient and subsequently walled and gated all-inclusive resorts cropped up throughout the Riviera Maya coast south of Cancún. Elsewhere governments have sponsored the construction of new tourist enclaves away from population centers in order to maximize foreign tourism revenues while avoiding unscripted social interaction with locals. These sorts of facilities have become ubiquitous in major tourism destinations throughout the world, especially in the global south, and there is every reason to believe they will continue to flourish in the future. Their emphasis on clear demarcation of zones of safety based on physical barriers, security personnel and surveillance allows tourists to maintain a sense of security similar to that they enjoy at home.

The cruise ship industry offers many of the same security promises to tourists and has become extremely effective in regulating tourist spaces and experiences. For that reason it is among the fastest-growing segments of the overall global tourism market. The number of berths in cruise ships effectively doubled between 1995 and 2005 (OSC 2005) and grew by another 50 percent by 2010 (Cruise Market Watch 2011). By 2009, in the midst of global recession, revenues were down but passengers were not and at least one analyst expects further growth in 2011 (Ibid.). Equally important, for years the two major cruise lines in the world, RCL and Carnival, were not able to acquire additional ships fast enough. Fifteen new ships were launched in 2009 with an additional dozen slated to launch in 2010. Many shipbuilders have been operating at full capacity in recent years, although there is some indication this is likely to slow in the future. While most global cruise ship passengers are concentrated in North America and Europe, this is beginning to broaden to other areas in the world, especially Asia.

Cruise ships are attractive because they amount to a traveling bubble. Much like all-inclusive resorts, they carefully regulate spaces, but unlike such resorts they are also mobile. Shore visits are also carefully orchestrated, with many cruise ship piers physically located miles from urban centers and where the built environment resembles shopping malls. Shore excursions most commonly take place through ship-approved local vendors. Finally, some cruise lines own their own private islands, making shore excursions to populated areas of ports of call completely unnecessary. Ultimately, what the modern cruise promises recalls the travel writings of Englishwoman Elizabeth Butler who, while on a Thomas Cook tour in Egypt in the late 1800s, remarked that travel by river boat was preferable:

> Travelling thus on the Nile you see the life of the people on the banks, you look into their villages, yet a few yards of water afford you complete immunity from that nearer contact which travel by road necessitates.
>
> Cited in Hazbun (2007: 19)

The final point about cruise ships is that, as Wood (2000) astutely points out, they are microcosms of power and wealth patterns in the world. Cruise ship tourism is labor-intensive, with ships typically employing more than 1,000 people from as many as 40 different countries, and he shows how labor is typically stratified ethnically. Ships officers and the upper echelon of positions on the hospitality side 'will be recruited from a specific nationality favored by the company; they in some sense form a separate caste' (Wood 2000: 353). Usually they come from North America or Europe. In contrast, many of the lower rung positions go to workers from the global south, with the least prestigious and poorest-paying typically going to those from the poorest countries. Ironically, when he wrote the piece in 2000, the lowest rung jobs typically went to Chinese labor. Who will be on that rung 20–50 years from now is uncertain but is likely to change.

Conclusions

Security remains of utmost concern to global tourists and will continue to do so in the future. This chapter makes two primary arguments: first, that as an activity rooted in politics and economics, global tourism in the future will reflect larger trends in these areas. As global power and wealth dynamics change, it will be citizens of those countries for whom the world awaits. Second, while global security trends remain uncertain both now and in the future, concerns over security have amplified and taken on new urgency. The global consumer classes – those that make up the bulk of global tourists – today are constantly reminded of their own insecurity, in their homes, in their workplaces, in public spaces, in their cars and of course when they travel. Any visit today to an airport, train station or border area provides a vivid example. These are simultaneously spaces of security and insecurity, where travelers are reminded that danger lurks. Passengers are profiled by ethnicity and surname, and tourists go through required processes so they themselves can be officially labeled as secure. This is but one more official reminder, this time just before embarking on global travel, that sources of insecurity and danger are everywhere. Is it any wonder that tourists will attempt to insulate themselves as global tourists?

References

Araña, J.E. and León, C.J. (2008) 'Terrorism and Tourism Demand: A Stated Preference Approach', *Annals of Tourism Research*, 35(2): 299–315.

Bonham, C., Edmunds, C. and Mak, J. (2006) 'The Impact of 9/11 and Other Terrible Global Events on Tourism in Hawaii and the United States', *Journal of Travel Research*, 45(1): 99–110.

Booth, K. (ed.) (2005) *Critical Security Studies and World Politics*, Boulder, CO: Lynne Rienner.

Boulden, J. (2009) 'Terrorism and Civil Wars', *Civil Wars*, 11(1): 5–21.

Brancatelli, J. (2008) Tourism and Terrorism. *Washington Post*, 9th December, online. Available at www.washingtonpost.com/wpdyn/content/story/2008/12/09/ ST2008120901240.html (accessed 29 December 2010).

Campbell, D. (2005) 'The Biopolitics of Security: Oil, Empire and the Sports Utility Vehicle', *American Quarterly*, 57(3): 343–372.

CIDCM (Center for International Development and Conflict Management) (2010) *Peace and Conflict 2010, Executive Summary*, College Park, MD: CIDCM, online. Available at www.cidcm.umd.edu/pc/executive_summary/exec_sum_2010.pdf (accessed 5 January 2011).

Cruise Market Watch (2011) 'Market Share', online. Available at www.cruisemarket watch.com/blog1/market-share-2/ (accessed 11 January 2011).

Dalby, S. (1997) 'Contesting an Essential Concept: Reading the Dilemmas in Contemporary Security Discourse', in K. Krause and M. Williams (eds.) *Critical Security Studies: Concepts and Cases*, Minneapolis, MN: University of Minnesota Press, pp. 3–32.

Diamond, L. (2008) 'The Democratic Rollback: The Resurgence of the Predatory State', *Foreign Affairs*, 87(2): 36–48.

Economist Intelligence Unit (2010) 'Democracy Index 2010: Democracy in Retreat', online. Available at www.eiu.com/public/topical_report.aspx?campaignid=demo 2010 (accessed 8 January 2011).

Freedom House (2010) *Freedom in the World*, Washington, DC: Freedom House.

Fukuyama, F. (1993) *The End of History and the Last Man*, New York: Avon Books.

Gleditsch, N.P. (2002) 'The Future of Armed Conflict', Madeleine Feher European Scholar Lecture, BESA Center for Strategic Studies, online. Available at www.biu.ac.il/Besa/feher6.pdf (accessed 5 January 2010).

Goldstein, J. (2011) *Winning the War on War: The Decline of Armed Conflict Worldwide*, New York: Dutton/Penguin.

Goldstone, P. (2001) *Making the World Safe for Tourism*, New Haven, CT: Yale University Press.

Griswald, E. (2010) *The Tenth Parallel: Dispatches from the Fault Line Between Christianity and Islam*, New York: Farrar, Straus and Giroux.

Hall, C.M. (1994) *Tourism and Politics: Policy, Power and Place*, Chichester: Wiley.

Hall, C.M. and O'Sullivan, V. (1996) 'Tourism, Political Stability, and Violence', in A. Pizam and Y. Mansfield (eds.) *Tourism, Crime and International Security Issues*, New York: Wiley, pp. 105–121.

Hall, C.M., Timothy, D. and Duvall, D.T. (2003) 'Security and Tourism: Towards a New Understanding', *Journal of Travel and Tourism Marketing*, 15(2/3): 1–18.

Hazbun, W. (2007) 'The East as Exhibit: Thomas Cook & Son and the Origin of the International Tourism Industry in Europe', in P. Scranton and J.F. Davidson (eds.) *The Business of Tourism: Place, Faith and History*, Philadelphia, PA: University of Pennsylvania Press, pp. 3–33.

Higgins-Desbiolles, F. (2007) 'Hostile Meeting Grounds: Encounters Between the Wretched of the Earth and the Tourist through Tourism and Terrorism in the 21st Century', in P.M. Burns and M. Novelli (eds.) *Tourism and Politics: Global Frameworks and Local Realities*, Amsterdam: Elsevier: 309–332.

Hoffman, B. (2006) *Inside Terrorism*, New York: Columbia University Press.

Homer-Dixon, T. (2001) *Environment, Scarcity and Violence*, Princeton, NJ: Princeton University Press.

HSC (Human Security Centre) (2007) *Human Security Report*, Vancouver: Human Security Centre/Simon Fraser University.

HSC (Human Security Centre) (2010) *The Mini Atlas of Human Security*, Vancouver: Human Security Centre/Simon Fraser University.

Huntington, S.P. (1996) *The Clash of Civilizations and the Remaking of World Order*, New York: Simon and Schuster.

Kaldor, M. (2007) *New and Old Wars*, 2nd edn, Stanford, CA: Stanford University Press.

Kaplan, R.D. (2000) *The Coming Anarchy: Shattering the Dreams of the Post Cold War*, New York: Random House.

Kincaid, J. (1988) *A Small Place*, New York: Farrar, Straus & Giroux.

Klare, M. (2001) *Resource Wars: The New Face of Global Conflict*, New York: Metropolitan Books.

Koskela, H. (2009) 'Fear and its Others', in S. Smith, S.J. Smith and R. Pain (eds.) *The Sage Handbook of Social Geographies*, Thousand Oaks, CA: Sage, pp. 389–407.

Krause, K. and Williams, M. (eds.) (1997) *Critical Security Studies and World Politics: Concepts and Cases*, Minneapolis, MN: University of Minnesota Press.

Laderman, S. (2009) *Tours of Vietnam: War, Travel Guides and Memory*, Durham, NC: Duke University Press.

Le Billon, P. (2006) *Fueling War: Natural Resources and Armed Conflict*, London: Routledge.

Lennon, J. and Foley, M. (2000) *Dark Tourism: The Attraction of Death and Disaster*, London: Continuum.

Levy, M.A. (1995) 'Is the Environment a National Security Issue?', *International Security*, 20(2): 35–62.

Lipschutz, R.D. (1995) 'On Security', in Lipschutz, (ed.) *On Security*, New York: Columbia University Press, pp. 1–23.

Lisle, D. (2004) 'Gazing at Ground Zero: Tourism, Voyeurism and Spectacle', *Journal for Cultural Research*, 8(1): 3–21.

Lockard, J. (2005) 'Social Fear and the Terrorism Survival Guide', in D. Heller (ed.) *The Selling of 9/11: How a National Tragedy Became a Commodity*, London: Palgrave Macmillan, pp. 221–232.

Mathews, J.T. (1989) 'Redefining Security', *Foreign Affairs*, 68(2): 162–177.

Mueller, J. (1989) *Retreat from Doomsday: the Obsolescence of Major War*, New York: Basic Books.

Myers, N. (1993) *Ultimate Security: The Environmental Basis for Political Security*, New York: Norton.

New York Times (2011) 'Tourism Industry in Southern Europe Benefits from Unrest', March 8. Available at: www.nytimes.com/2011/03/09/business/global/09tourism.html?scp=1&sq=north+africa+tourism&st=nyt.

OSC (Ocean Shipping Consultants, Limited) (2005) *World Cruise Shipping Industry to 2020 – A Detailed Appraisal of Prospects*, Chertsey: OSC Limited.

OTTI (Office of Travel and Tourism Industries) (2010) 'Historical U.S. Travel and Tourism Statistics and Analysis (U.S. Outbound)', online. Available at tinet.ita.doc.gov/outreachpages/outbound_historical_statistics_analyses.html (accessed 29 December 2010).

Phipps, G. (2004) 'Tourism and Terrorism: An Intimate Equivalence', in S.B. Gmelch, (ed.) *Tourists and Tourism: A Reader*, Longrove, IL: Waveland Press, pp. 71–90.

Pizam, A. and Fleischer, A. (2002) 'Severity Versus Frequency of Attacks of Terrorism: Which has a Larger Impact on Tourism Demand?', *Journal of Travel Research*, 40: 337–339.

Project Ploughshares (2010) *Armed Conflicts, 1987–2009*, online. Available at www.ploughshares.ca/imagesarticles/ACR10/98204_armed_conflict87-09.pdf (accessed 2 January 2010).

Richter, L.K. (2007) 'Democracy and Tourism: Exploring the Nature of an Inconsistent Relationship', in P.M. Burns and M. Novelli (eds.) *Tourism and Politics: Global Frameworks and Local Realities*, Amsterdam: Elsevier, pp. 5–16.

Richter, L.K. and Waugh, Jr., W.L. (1986) 'Terrorism and Tourism as Logical Companions', *Tourism Management*, 7(4): 230–238.

Rojek, C. (1993) *Ways of Escape*, Basingstoke: Macmillan.

UCDP (Uppsala Conflict Data Program) (2010) *Active Conflicts and Dyads 1946–2009*, online. Available at www.pcr.uu.se/digitalAssets/18/18072_conflicts_dyads_2009.pdf (accessed 3 January 2010).

UNWTO (2009) *UNWTO World Tourism Barometer: Interim Update, April 2009*, Madrid: UNWTO, online. Available at www.unwto.org/facts/eng/pdf/barometer/UNWTO_Barom09_update april_en_excerpt.pdf (accessed 29 December 2010).

UNWTO (2010) *Tourism Highlights*, Madrid: UNWTO.

Wall, G. (1996) 'Terrorism and Tourism: An Overview and an Irish Example', in A. Pizam and Y. Mansfeld (eds.) *Tourism, Crime and International Security Issues*, New York: Wiley, pp. 143–58.

Waltz, K. (1979) *Theory of International Politics*, New York: McGraw-Hill.

Weldes, J., Laffey, M., Gusterson, H. and Duval, R. (eds.) (1999) *Cultures of Insecurity: States, Communities, and the Production of Danger*, Minneapolis, MN: University of Minnesota Press.

Wood, R.E. (2000) 'Caribbean Cruise Tourism: Globalization at Sea', *Annals of Tourism Research*, 27(2): 345–370.

5 Wellbeing, equity, sustainable development and social tourism in twenty-first century Europe

Chris Stone

The term 'social tourism' describes the phenomenon of the provision of 'supported holidays' for those who would not normally otherwise be able to enjoy leisure tourism. Regular holidaymaking is regarded as a norm by many in the wealthier countries of Europe. Policy measures in the field of social tourism are intended to extend the benefits of vacations to disadvantaged individuals, households and social groups unable to participate in this activity. Despite the acknowledged benefits derived from participation in leisure tourism in personal, family and broader social welfare terms, about 40 percent of all EU citizens take no holidays. The reason most commonly suggested for this is a lack of available resources, most immediately monetary resources, but other factors including personal experience and abilities may also be relevant. The phenomenon of social tourism may be traced back for a century or more, and its very existence provides interesting perspectives upon the more familiar and glamorous commercial tourism industry and on holidaymaking as a social activity. However, social tourism has largely been overlooked in the academic literature and popular awareness of the concept also remains very limited.

It might be argued that many disadvantaged individuals and social groups would derive more benefit in relative terms from a holiday than those for whom an annual vacation is a norm, and some argue that the provision of supported holidays can yield improvements in aggregate social welfare. But while in the second decade of the third millennium little or no provision is made for supported holidays by many of the world's wealthiest countries, there are indications that the European Union may be moving towards a position under which the 500 million EU-27 citizens gain 'the right to tourism'. If this happens, it would represent a major development in terms of social equity, and could be interpreted as a logical and even appropriate development of social welfare policy trends in some of the more social democratically minded nations of the Union. Any such change in policy could be seen as the successful culmination of elements of several international agreements and conventions of the past 60 years, some specifically related to leisure and tourism but others only tangentially so, including such landmark global agreements as the Universal Declaration of Human Rights and the Convention on the Rights of the Child. A further and relatively novel perspective on social tourism of particular relevance to the twenty-first century may be derived from consideration of the phenomenon with reference to the social equity dimension inherent in the concept of sustainable development.

This chapter aims to examine the little-studied, low-profile and relatively unglamorous phenomenon termed 'social tourism' in the contexts of the UK and European Union. After a consideration of definitions and meanings of the term, the chapter will turn to a brief examination of the history and current status of social tourism provision in the UK and Europe, after which the issue of need or demand will be examined. An outline of international agreements and declarations of relevance to the theme of the chapter will be followed by an examination of social tourism with reference to the paradigm of sustainable development. Signed by over 170 countries, the Rio declaration of the 1992 Earth Summit will be interpreted in terms of its relevance for social tourism. The 2006 EU 'Barcelona declaration', perhaps a step towards a 'right to tourism' for European Union citizens, and subsequent initiatives will be introduced and some implications for the planned provision of supported holidays in Britain and the EU discussed. The chapter concludes on the issues associated with implementing any future European right to tourism, and proposals for further research are made.

Definition and description

The term 'social tourism' refers to enabling participation in leisure tourism (and day excursions) for individuals and social groups for whom such holidaymaking would otherwise be difficult or impossible because they lack the necessary resources or abilities. The European Union has employed a definition derived partially from the articles of association of the International Bureau of Social Tourism (BITS), which in turn referenced the principles adopted in the 1996 Montreal Declaration:

> All the concepts and phenomena resulting from the participation in tourism of low-income sectors of the population, made possible through well defined social measures.
>
> (European Economic and Social Committee 2006)

The range of individuals and social groups at which social tourism measures may be targeted may be extended more widely than simply those on low incomes to include a wide range of people suffering social disadvantage:

- those with disabilities;
- those suffering from physical and mental illnesses;
- children and families in need ('difficult circumstances');
- older people and the retired;
- those constrained by commitments as carers;
- those constrained by work commitments;
- youths;

- and even – in the most broadly drawn formulation – 'all population groups' (Jolin 2003).

The central objective of social tourism measures is the provision of supported holidays to beneficiaries termed supported holidaymakers (McCabe *et al.* 2010). The range of support necessary to enable the supported holidaymaker to take a vacation typically includes financial subsidy, but may also include assistance with trip and destination choice and booking, planning and packing, making travel arrangements, guidance on activities while away and other support during the journey and stay. In some countries, social tourism measures also include the provision of facilities specifically for the social tourist. Supported tourism initiatives may be provided by national governments, not-for-profit organizations, and the commercial tourism industry, and are in practice often provided by partnerships between these sectors. The UK has a limited tradition of supported holiday provision in comparison to that of several other European nations, and there seems to be little awareness amongst social welfare policymakers in the UK of the concept and practice of social tourism, despite its relevance to notions of social inclusion and perhaps also the more recent Big Society concept via social enterprise.

Purposes

Social tourism measures are regarded by some as a means to achieve certain social goals including equity (Minnaert 2008). Social equity implies fair opportunities in terms of livelihoods and resources, and full enjoyment of the social and cultural life of the community through meeting people's needs in a manner determined by each individual. The public sector is more involved in tourism than many other industries, and an argument can be made for national tourism policies to aim to spread the benefits of holidaymaking as widely as possible throughout society in an effort to address problems of poverty and deprivation (Swarbrooke 2003). Social tourism measures may also contribute to economic development and employment in less wealthy regions, and those suffering economic decline. The goal of many social tourism initiatives is to combine these various social and economic benefits in an efficient and effective way.

Vacations can be identified as merit goods. Merit goods:

- Can be described as goods or commodities whose true benefit may not be fully realized, and/or their production or consumption may be under-valued by the market.
- Tend to be underproduced and underconsumed in a free-market economy with reference to some socially optimal level – 'market failure'.
- Are judged to be sufficiently desirable for individuals and/or society for their provision to be assured by some means involving intervention, and on the basis of a concept of need rather than people's ability and willingness to

pay – so, perhaps involving subsidy or other support, or even provided free of charge.

- As having positive externalities or 'spillover effects', where the social benefits of their consumption exceed the private benefits: benefits are transferred to third parties, specifically wider society.

While the classification of goods as merit goods is based upon value judgments, meaning that there is a lack of agreement on the precise applicability of the term, health care services are often cited as examples of merit goods because they are generally considered to have considerable social merit and in turn a powerful claim on scarce government resources.

History

Until the mid-twentieth century, when seeking paid holiday time many employees were dependent on the goodwill of their employers, and in practice relatively few people in the UK and elsewhere could muster sufficient discretionary time and money to participate in holidaymaking. Working-class access to resorts varied across the UK according to household incomes and holiday traditions. While relatively well-paid Lancashire cotton workers saved together in 'going-off clubs' for an annual week at the coast in the late nineteenth century, provision – if any – for the poorest typically comprised an occasional one-day excursion paid for by charitable sources (Walton 2000). The notion of a paid annual holiday period for all employees, and even state sponsorship of holidaymaking, was coming to fruition in the 1930s. In industrialized countries in Europe and elsewhere, perceptions were developing that people needed a break from their working and everyday lives, often set in industrialized and urbanized surroundings, for health and social reasons. It was driven to a degree by political pressure from international labor unions and workers' associations, and one outcome was the International Labour Organization's 1936 Holidays with Pay Convention, which proposed an entitlement of a minimum of six days' annual holiday with pay after one year of continuous service. Several countries in Europe responded with legislation upon paid holidays. Although the convention was not ratified in the UK, the Holidays With Pay Act emerged there in 1938, though in practice this was more of a milestone than a landmark as it encouraged rather than required paid holiday entitlements (Walton 2000). The UK did not implement a general statutory right to paid leave until several decades later.

In the early 1950s only about half the British population took any kind of holiday (Bray 2000) and the very poor and unemployed were generally unable to travel at all. But other European countries were starting to make provision for tourism that was accessible to all citizens, partly at least as a result of 'the general democratising impact' of the Second World War in Europe (Davidson 1992). The two key agents in this process were the state (including local authorities) and the 'third sector' (not-for-profit organizations) sometimes referred to as the 'social tourism movement', which comprised a variety of cooperative and self-help groups (including the Workers' Travel Association in the UK), youth groups and faith-related organizations (including the Christian movement in France and Switzerland). The social tourism tradition has subsequently become embedded in the social systems of several European countries. In England, the Youth Hostels Association (YHA) had been established in 1930 as a charity with the specific purpose of providing low-cost holidaymaking accommodation to a primarily youth and young adult membership in order to promote travelling for the purposes of 'health, rest and education'. The YHA remains a provider of low-cost accommodation, with about 200 units in England and Wales, some located in major cities. Trades unions have a long history of making social tourism provision for members and families. For example, UNISON in the UK, with more than one million members in public sector employment, has owned and operated holiday accommodation for 70 years. A handful of private companies also make provision for holidaymaking, including high street retailer John Lewis, regarded by some as a relatively paternalistic employer, which owns five centers where employees may enjoy subsidized family holidays.

The overall effect of this combination of predominantly state and third sector-driven enterprise in the twentieth century has been credited as having had a major impact on the development of mass markets for leisure tourism travel and the development of destinations and associated travel facilities in Western countries. Social tourism measures accounted for much of the dramatic growth in tourism in post-1945 Europe (Davidson 1992), but despite the increase in holiday-taking propensity from the mid-twentieth century linked to growth in motor vehicle ownership and the growing availability of leisure air travel, the bulk of the tourism industry was still catering primarily for the tastes and budgets of wealthier social groups. The right to paid holiday time alone was frequently insufficient to enable many working families to go on holiday, because they were reliant upon their own limited means and abilities. Transport and accommodation for visitors were poorly developed and leisure time spent out of the home was still largely centered upon day excursions or short visits made to friends or relatives.

Supply

National governments

In the early twenty-first century, most of the tourism sector comprises private enterprises engaged in profit-seeking activities, most holiday trips are provided for on a commercial basis in response to market demand and social tourism measures account for a very low proportion of holidaymaking trips made in the EU. Provision for supported holidaymaking varies markedly across the member nations of the European Union: some European countries have national policies, legislation and policy instruments on social tourism to enable defined groups to take supported holidays, although many have few or none. Those that exist usually take forms that indicate a mixed economy pattern of supported holidaymaking provision across Europe, involving the state, the not-for-profit sector and frequently the private sector too. Several European states provide financial support in various forms to individuals and families judged to be in need, while others provide grants to organizations which develop holiday accommodation and facilities available at prices judged to be affordable.

In 1936, the Flanders region of Belgium determined to recognize tourism as a social right. As a result, it now has some of the most highly developed policies and programs for social tourism in Western Europe and a range of facilities for defined social groups. The publicly funded Holiday Participation Centre, linked to the Flanders tourism agency, establishes partnerships with tourism industry enterprises in order to provide affordable holidays. Holiday establishments seeking to register with and be promoted by the tourist office are required to provide free or discounted holiday nights for people in low income groups, and the Centre negotiates with about 500 tourism companies and accommodation providers to extend social rates to disadvantaged families. The offers are subsequently aggregated into a brochure distributed to disadvantaged families via a range of social organizations in Flanders. In 2009, the Office enabled more than 87,000 people to take budget holidays in the region, mostly in the form of low-cost trips to domestic social tourism centers, and 78,000 took day trips. Similar schemes are to be found elsewhere in Europe including France, Spain, Greece, Italy, Switzerland, Germany and Scandinavia. To date, the history of social tourism has been largely a European one, but there are indications of initiatives in Canada, Asia and Africa (Davolio 2003).

This mixed-economy pattern of state provision of holidaymaking opportunities in several western European countries stands in marked contrast to that of former centrally planned eastern European countries including Czechoslovakia and Poland, where tourism was often entirely controlled by the state. Working people there may have been granted the right to a holiday, typically taken at state-owned and state-run spa resorts and in the countryside, and while these centers are often no longer in use, the patterns of domestic tourism thus established frequently continue today.

In the UK, social tourism measures are not part of government policy and never have been in any significant sense. State provision for supported holidays is very limited and often of a local and ad hoc nature. This perhaps reflects a lack of national will on the subject and any consensus on holidays as a social right or being of social benefit. A limited range of enabling rather than direct legislation provides for minimal levels of provision for a very limited range of individuals and social groups with specific needs rather than disadvantaged groups in general. For instance, social care services in the UK may make funds available for family holidays to serve social welfare goals under:

- The 1946 National Health Service (NHS) Act (for convalescence).
- The 1948 National Assistance Act – providing recreational facilities for those with disabilities.
- The 1963 Children and Young Persons Act.
- The 1970 Chronically Sick and Disabled Persons Act.

- The 1989 Children Act — assisting families to stay together through the provision of holidaymaking (Hazel 2005).

Brief references to possible social tourism measures have been made in the UK government's occasional policy statements on tourism. An objective to widen access to tourism opportunities was mentioned in *Tomorrow's Tourism* (Department for Culture, Media and Sport 1999), which mentioned 'prejudice against some sectors of society' as a limiting factor to tourism. But no significant proposals were made. No further reference was made to the theme in the subsequent policy document, *Tomorrow's Tourism Today* (Department for Culture, Media and Sport 2004), despite a statement on the 'real [. . .] social benefits for the whole country' said to derive from the activity'. Subsequently VisitBritain, the UK tourism agency, identified 'making holidays available to all' as one of eight 'strategic challenges' in working towards 'sustainable tourism' (VisitBritain 2008). But the agency's proposed actions – including raising the industry's awareness of the size of the social tourism market, 'encouraging a broad price range in tourism facilities and experiences', and pursuing specific schemes to facilitate and encourage holiday-taking by people on low incomes – do not seem to have had any obvious outcomes. In a revised strategy of 2011, VisitBritain sought to encourage Britons to holiday domestically rather than abroad, but no further reference to social tourism measures was made (Department for Culture, Media and Sport 2011).

The third sector

In the UK, interventions for supported holidaymaking come primarily from the third sector. One example of a not-for-profit organization offering supported tourism services is Tourism for All. Originally established as the Holiday Care Service by the English Tourist Board in 1981, this UK charity works to enable holidaymaking by older people and those with disabilities, the latter group having been identified as being discriminated against by the 'mainstream leisure industry' (Carr 2004). Funded mostly by private individuals and the industry, Tourism for All offers no financial support to individuals, but:

- Makes travel and other arrangements for those less able to do so by themselves.
- Provides information about accessible holiday destinations and activities.
- Publicizes holidays, accommodation and attractions discounted for these groups.
- Produces a guide to obtaining financial support for holidaymaking from charities and trusts.

Some of the charities and trusts referenced by Tourism for All allow direct applications to be made; others may only be approached via a referral from a social worker, health visitor, or family doctor. In an effort to ensure realistic expectations on the part of its client group, Tourism for All is careful to advise those seeking support for holidaymaking that demand for financial support from the various funding bodies substantially exceeds their available resources.

The Family Holiday Association (FHA) is another charity established with the goal of enabling holidaymaking for disadvantaged groups. The FHA assists about 2,000 British families to take a domestic holiday each year, manages its own small accommodation stock of 12 family caravans located around the British coast and offers modest grants towards holiday costs. A further indication of the level of demand for supported holidays are the FHA criteria that applicant families must be living on relatively low incomes and have had no holiday for a four-year period prior to application. The charity also acts in the political sphere, lobbying in an effort to put social tourism on the national policy agenda.

The private sector

Any enterprise which serves the goal of making travel and tourism more accessible may be numbered amongst the social tourism movement. With a wide range of facilities and capabilities within its range, the commercial tourism sector has a potentially major role to play in the provision of supported holidaymaking opportunities. Perhaps the best-known example of market-based provision of relatively low-cost domestic holidays is the family-oriented 'holiday camp' founded by the tourism entrepreneur Billy Butlin. At nine sites, built around the UK coastline from 1936, Butlin promised 'a week's holiday for a week's pay'. By the late 1960s, his holiday centers had become a national institution. Changing tastes and competition from overseas destinations led to a decline in demand, and only three of Butlin's centers now remain. That Butlin's organization has a continuing role in the provision of low-cost domestic vacations is confirmed by the socioeconomic profile of their visitors: in 2009, 93 percent were from drawn from social groups C1/C2/D/E.

In addition, discounted low-season vacations are frequently offered by low-cost domestic holiday operators via the medium of the national press. In 2011, for instance, the popular British daily newspaper *The Sun* advertised a readers' offer of four-night midweek holidays for less than ten pounds per person. However, barriers remain in the case of families with children at school, for instance. In addition, market-based holidays for those with the very lowest incomes and other disadvantaged groups (including those with disabilities and illnesses) is not generally a commercially viable proposition.

The role of individuals acting outside the commercial sector should not be overlooked, however. Options for those with the very smallest budgets include holidays based around visits to friends and relatives – which may account for as much as 19 percent of 'mainly holiday' trips and nights spent away from home in the UK (TNS-RI Travel and Tourism 2010). Day excursions may substitute for more conventional holidays to a degree. However, the costs associated with even these least-expensive options often still exceed the ability of the most disadvantaged groups to pay.

Need, demand and poverty

At present, a substantial proportion of the UK population does not take an annual holiday. And while not everyone wishes to holiday away from home, very many more would do so if they were able. Precise figures are difficult to determine, but about 40 percent of the UK population does not take a holiday of longer than three days in any single year, a proportion which has remained constant since the mid-twentieth century (Seaton 1992). Furthermore, more than one-third of the population never takes a holiday (Coalter 2001). These broad indicators fail to differentiate between those who cannot afford a holiday and those who simply elect not to take one. However, 'non-traveler' groups were differentiated by Haukeland (1990) into the constrained and the unconstrained, the latter comprising those who elect not to travel despite having the resources to do so. In the UK, about one-third of families are unable to take a one-week holiday for financial reasons, and one-fifth – amounting to about two-and-a-half-million children – are unable to afford even day excursions (Family Holiday Association 2009; McCabe *et al.* 2007). Overall, 60 percent of the members of D/E social groups don't take holidays, while by contrast 60 percent of the wealthier A/B social group take two or more, and 20 percent three or more.

Elsewhere in Europe, growth in holiday participation in terms of the proportion of the population who can take vacations in any year has halted in certain wealthier European countries in recent decades, notably at 75 percent in the Netherlands, for instance (Richards 1998). This may indicate that markets for commercially based holidaymaking may be at or approaching saturation. At the same time, however, about 40 percent of all European citizens do not take a holiday (VisitBritain 2008), though this proportion varies dramatically between the richer and poorer countries considered. Growth trends in the number of holidays taken in recent decades have not been the outcome of an extension of consumption to all social classes but have predominantly benefited those in wealthier socioeconomic groups (Richards 1998). Overall, it is difficult not to conclude that the situation of excluded social groups in the UK and elsewhere is obscured by the generally high levels of holiday participa-tion across Europe as a whole, and particularly in wealthier countries characterized as time-rich and money-rich, where much of the population enjoys a broad range of holidaymaking options. More precise assessments of the likely magnitude of demand for supported day trips and holidays are difficult to find, but it is likely to be substantial. There is some evidence from Belgium to indicate that expressed demand for supported holidays is increasing much more rapidly than is supply as more of those on low incomes become aware of their availability, a trend which seems likely to continue into the future (Tourism Flanders and Brussels 2009). Consideration of social class provides a further dimension here. Some limited evidence suggests that class may influence people's attitudes and values towards tourism participation, with middle-class individuals seemingly placing a higher priority on holidaymaking than members of C2/D/E socioeconomic groups (Seaton 1992).

The holiday is regarded by many in Western societies as essential, and the lack of an annual vacation has been considered a contributor to 'material deprivation'

(MacInnes *et al.* 2009). The benefits of holidaymaking in terms of individuals' quality of life seem clear to the majority of the UK population which devotes time, effort and often substantial financial resources to an annual holiday. People appreciate the value of a break from routine and neighbourhood and reconnect with their family and friends in novel and perhaps exciting settings. What about those with little or no effective choice about holidaymaking? While the incidence of non-holiday-taking is distributed across all social classes, and there are numerous reasons why people are unable or unwilling to go on holiday, the most common is a lack of financial resources (Eurobarometer 2009; Smith and Hughes 1999). Income inequalities inevitably create leisure inequalities (Richards 1998) and, to re-state a point, those with the lowest holiday-taking propensity are heavily distributed towards less wealthy and older age groups (Smith and Hughes 1999).

Many countries define poverty as a very low income level at which a range of state welfare benefits become payable. Determining this often uses the relative income standard of poverty of an income less than 50 percent of the average, and conventional social welfare support measures are calculated to meet a range of what are judged basic needs. However, once the most basic needs have been met, what tends to determine whether individuals, families and population groups are more or less happy derives not upon absolute levels of consumption but people's assessment of their level relative to that of others in society. The degree to which they are able to participate in, or are excluded from, the ordinary living patterns and activities customary in the society in which they live, is a relativistic definition of poverty (Dresner 2002; Townsend 1979). Couched in terms of relative deprivation, Townsend's classic work on the definition and economics of poverty included an index of deprivation (some key indicators of which now seem somewhat quaint, including ownership of a domestic refrigerator and whether people ate a cooked breakfast most days of the week), but an annual week's holiday away from home was also included. Townsend's list of indicators still retains some validity as an indicator of a certain level of social normality, and in 2012 the lack of 'a family holiday for children away from home at least one a week a year' remains one of the UK Department for Work and Pensions indicators of material deprivation employed in assessments of child poverty.

Of all items that might be judged essential, the annual week-long holiday is that most likely forgone by children of households living in poverty, while only about 20 percent of those in non low-income households do not take holidays (MacInnes *et al.* 2009). In the latter 20 years of the twentieth century, Britain was becoming an increasingly polarized nation, with the proportion of households living in poverty in terms of both low income and multiple deprivation of necessities increasing from 14 percent in 1983 through 21 percent in 1990 to over 24 percent in 1999 (Gordon *et al.* 2000). After an interim period of some improvement, both child poverty and income inequality were rising again in the UK from the middle of the first decade of the new millennium (Brewer *et al.* 2009). The significance of the temporary escape from routine and the injection of excitement and spectacle offered to economically and socially disadvantaged families by the supported vacation is 'undoubtedly different' to that experienced by the general holiday-making population (Smith and Hughes 1999). If holidays are a coping mechanism for people living with the harsh realities of poverty, those unable to enjoy the quality of life benefits gained from vacation experiences even occasionally may consider themselves doubly deprived relative to others.

Holidaymaking and welfare – social welfare perspectives

Despite a historic research focus in tourism upon the costs to society associated with tourism, including pollution and loss of culture, for instance (Hazel 2005), there exists a body of literature examining the benefits of tourism, including linkages between holidaymaking and personal health. One common and fairly predictable theme running throughout the literature is that holidaymaking has positive impacts upon people's wellbeing, although any causal relationship between tourism and health is yet to be elucidated (Sonmez and Apostolopoulos 2009). Health and social welfare benefits to individuals and families derived from holidaymaking may include:

- Benefits for physical health.
- Improved social and spiritual wellbeing.
- Enhanced self-competence and an improved sense of self-esteem, self-reliance and self-confidence.
- The ability to feel greater joy from life.
- An enhanced perceived quality of life.
- Reduced personal sense of social alienation.
- Leisure has been identified as functioning as a coping mechanism, and a preventive role is adduced to the activity.
- The mental health benefits of leisure participation are claimed to include a perceived sense of freedom, independence, and autonomy.
- Social tourism opportunities have been found to increase family capital in the short term, and social capital – social networks, related proactive behavior and self-esteem – in the medium term.
- Value may lie not only in the inherent benefits of the holiday but also in support of other interventions.
- Overall, leisure participation has been found to add to a general sense of well-being and, in some cases, increased feelings of happiness (English Tourism Council 2000; Minnaert *et al.* 2009; Sonmez and Apostolopoulos 2009).

Some consider that the very quality of time spent on holiday is different – better and special perhaps, by virtue of the respite gained from two of the most powerful constraints of everyday life: time and place (Richards 1999), and the act of provision of supported holidaymaking has been termed an 'intervention' in the same sense as the term is employed in the provision of social welfare and health-related services. Research into the effects of supported holidays has found 'overwhelming evidence' that families' quality of life is improved by a short break away from home. Relatively small amounts of money invested in quality time for families yield long-term results; the benefits are considered to extend from individuals and families to communities and employers, and thence to wider society (McCabe 2009). If it is accepted that tourism is an essential element of the quality of life (Richards 1999), there is a debate to be had about the ethics of leaving the ability to participate in holidaymaking purely to market forces (Minnaert *et al.* 2006).

The focus of much of the literature addressing the moral and ethical dimensions of tourism and sustainability issues is firmly centered upon the population, the society, and the culture at the destination (see for instance Donoghue 2009; UNEP 2005). While such a focus upon the impacts of tourism borne by 'hosts' in environmental and social terms is appropriate and consistent with a basic interpretation of the issues involved, it is also only a partial interpretation. Any balanced ethical consideration of equity issues associated with holidaymaking should be extended to the populations of countries generating tourists too, but these are frequently excluded from consideration. A clear ethical case may be made for the extension of holidaymaking opportunities to people in difficult circumstances (one based primarily upon principles of social justice), including a concern for equity within generations and the meeting of basic human needs, something at the heart of some concepts of sustainable development. This equity- or fairness-based case may be extended by reference to normative considerations: extending the ability to enjoy the wellbeing benefits and satisfactions of what is increasingly regarded as normal, an element of citizenship and a common way of life according to standards prevailing in the developed world (Richards 1998; Smith and Hughes 1999). Such an approach puts the discussion onto a needs-focused basis rather than simply a meritocratic one. Some people may deserve a holiday because they work hard, but others perhaps need a holiday by virtue of need or circumstance.

The political dimension of social welfare perspectives, attitudes and policies towards the concept and practice of social tourism have been related to the characteristics of national welfare state regimes and have been linked with how states organize tourism (Webster *et al.* 2011). Differing political goals are rooted in differing ideologies or value sets. Some governments consider, explicitly or otherwise, that the provision of holidays and participation in holidaymaking – 'social' or otherwise – and the organization of individuals' leisure time is not a matter for state intervention. Greg Richards (1999) cited the work of Esping-Andersen (1990), who differentiated welfare state regimes into three broad types, with reference to individuals' entitlements to holidaymaking as a social right, going on to identify that both social democratic regimes and conservative-corporatist states like France and Italy are more likely to recognize tourism consumption as a social right. Under the social democratic welfare regime model in the Netherlands and Scandinavian countries, equality is geared more to the standards of the middle class and the provision of supported holidays seen as a desirable form of social intervention. Liberal regimes, by contrast, tend to be associated with the 'equality of minimal needs' (Richards 1998), often comprising limited vacation entitlements and relatively greater inequalities in the social distribution of leisure time. On the subject of social tourism, Hazel (2005) posits that the UK falls somewhere in between the two positions of social democratic and liberal. However, even in countries with liberal welfare regimes some limited provision may be made for certain particularly disadvantaged social groups, including the chronically sick, those with disabilities, and children 'in need' and their families.

Linked to the above, the concept of social exclusion, which gained currency in the European Union's poverty-focused programs of the later 1980s, is also of relevance here. Social exclusion subsequently developed to become an important theme of EU social policy despite there being no broadly accepted definition of the term. The 'social exclusion' concept may be extended to the issue of people's ability to participate in holidaymaking. While, in general, the populations of the richer countries of northwestern Europe enjoy more vacations than the poorer ones of southern and eastern Europe (Richards 1999), relatively poor individuals, families and social groups in all EU countries are excluded from the ability to enjoy leisure and recreation outside the home. However, despite the potential additional insights which might be gained (and the obvious caveat that the concept is to a degree simply a reformulation of earlier concepts linked to poverty and the quality of life), there seems to be little literature addressing links between the two.

International agreements and declarations

Several existing international agreements and declarations can be interpreted with reference to the social tourism issue, some relating to the field of leisure and tourism and others of a more general focus (see Table 5.1).

In general, the agreements and declarations summarized in Table 5.1 may be interpreted to indicate a consensus of international support for leisure and even

Table 5.1 International agreements and declarations

Date	Title	Body	Extract
1948	The Universal Declaration of Human Rights	United Nations	Article 24 – Everyone has the right to rest and leisure, including reasonable limitation of working hours and periodic holidays with pay
1980	Manila Declaration on World Tourism	World Tourism Organization	'World tourism can only flourish if based on equity' (Article 1, p. 2) 'The right to holidays, the opportunity for the citizen to get to know his own environment, a deeper awareness of his national identity and of the solidarity that links him to his compatriots and the sense of belonging to a culture and to a people are all major reasons for stimulating the individual's participation in domestic and international tourism, through access to holidays and travel' (Article 8, p. 2)

(*Continued on next page*)

Date	Title	Body	Extract
			'The importance that millions of our contemporaries attach to tourism in the use of their free time and in their concept of the quality of life makes it a need that governments should take into account and support' (Article 9, p. 3)
			'Social tourism is an objective which society must pursue in the interests of those citizens who are least privileged in the exercise of their right to rest' (Article 10, p. 3)
			'Bearing in mind the acknowledged value of tourism which are inseparable from it, the authorities will have to give more increased [sic.] attention to the development of national and international tourist and recreational activity, based on an ever-widening participation of peoples in holidays and travel [. . .] with a view to ensuring the orderly growth of tourism in a manner consistent with the other basic needs of society' (Article 23, p. 4)
			The Manila Declaration was 'welcomed' in a resolution (36/41) of the General Assembly of the United Nations in 1981.
1985	Tourism Bill of Rights and Tourist Code	World Tourism Organization	Article III – states should 'encourage the adoption of measures enabling everyone to participate in domestic and international tourism [. . .] and by [paying] particular attention to tourism for the young, elderly and disabled'
1989	Convention on the Rights of the Child	United Nations	Article 31 – states 'recognize the right of the child to rest and leisure, to engage in play and recreational activities [. . .] [and] shall encourage the provision of appropriate and equal opportunities for cultural, artistic, recreational and leisure activity'. The Convention requires signatory states to encourage provision for disabled children in particular (Article 23)
1989	The Hague Declaration on Tourism	World Tourism Organization	Principle 1 – Tourism has become a phenomenon of everyday life for hundreds of millions of people today [. . .] It constitutes an activity essential to the lives of human beings and modern societies, having become an important form of using the free time of individuals and the main vehicle for interpersonal relations and political, economic and cultural contact made necessary by the internationalization of all sectors of the life of nation [. . .] It is both a consequence and a decisive factor of the quality of life in contemporary society'.

(*Continued on next page*)

Table 5.1 (Continued)

Date	Title	Body	Extract
1996	European Social Charter (Revised)	Council of Europe	Article 15 – 'The right of persons with disabilities to independence, social integration and participation in the life of the community [. . .] 3. To promote their full social integration and participation in the life of the community in particular through measures [. . .] aiming to overcome barriers to communication and mobility and enabling access to [. . .] leisure'
1997	Manila Declaration on the Social Impact of Tourism	World Tourism Organization	'2. Improve people's standard of living through tourism by providing economic and social opportunities for wider participation'
1999	Global Code of Ethics for Tourism	World Tourism Organization	The General Assembly of the WTO 'affirm[ed] the right to tourism and the freedom of tourist movements' (p. 2) The WTO wished 'to promote an equitable, responsible and sustainable world tourism order, whose benefits will be shared by all sections of society' (p. 2) The 'Right to Tourism' – 'The prospect of direct and personal access to the discovery and enjoyment of the planet's resources constitutes a right equally open to all the world's inhabitants; the increasingly extensive participation in national and international tourism should be regarded as one of the best possible expressions of the sustained growth of free time, and obstacles should not be placed in its way' (Article 7(1), p. 5) 'The universal right to tourism must be regarded as the corollary of the right to rest and leisure' (Article 7(2), p. 5) 'Social tourism, and in particular associative tourism, which facilitates widespread access to leisure, travel and holidays, should be developed with the support of the public authorities' (Article 7(3), p. 5) 'Family, youth, student and senior tourism and tourism for people with disabilities, should be encouraged and facilitated' (Article 7(4), p. 5)

holidays as social rights, although while they may have value as political levers in practice the efficacy of all such declarations varies with the commitment and attitudes of individual governments:

- not all have committed to the various declarations outlined above;
- those that have may not implement all their provisions; and
- many are worded in a manner leaving much latitude for interpretation.

Sustainable development and the Rio Declaration

Concepts of sustainable development provide another perspective on the political dimension of social tourism. The Rio Declaration is of a different order of significance than many of those mentioned in Table 5.1, purportedly heralding a new era of 'sustainable development' for the world, and repays consideration in the current context. Its origin lay in a growth in perceptions in the later twentieth century that the negative effects of human activities were having global rather than merely local or national consequences, and that the various crises which had attracted public concern – environmental, developmental and energy – were not separate, but interrelated. More than 170 world governments participated in the 1992 United Nations Conference on Environment and Development (UNCED) – the 'Earth Summit' – held in Rio de Janeiro, and collectively adopted the Rio Declaration on Environment and Development. Entitled *Our Common Future*, the declaration comprised 27 principles intended to commit world governments to environmental protection and responsible development, to be achieved via an integrated approach to issues facing both humans and nature. The widely quoted UNCED definition of sustainable development is 'Development that meets the needs of the present without compromising the ability of future generations to meet their own needs.'

The meaning of the term 'development' is as contentious as it is central, and sustainable development may be defined in several different ways. The problem centers around obtaining agreement on the values underlying any such definition: how should physical, environmental and social criteria be prioritized relative to each other? And is development primarily about economic growth and industrialization, or non-material improvement in life, for instance? Several authors have noted that, in tourism as in other subject fields, much of the debate around the subject has focused on environmental sustainability associated with the biophysical environment, the activity, the destination and the economic dimension, while overlooking the social dimension of the concept (Butler 1999; Farrell 1999; Twining-Ward 1999). By way of explanation, the point has been made that environmental concerns have been on the public agenda for longer and are much less contentious than social justice issues (Twining-Ward 1999). An emphasis on development solely or even largely in terms of economic growth is perhaps misplaced in the twenty-first century. Furthermore, Dresner and others consider that economic growth does not necessarily seem to make people happier (Dresner 2002). Neither can terms of sustainability be defined from an exclusively environmental point of view; physical sustainability cannot be secured unless development policies pay attention to such considerations as access to resources, and the distribution of costs and benefits according to human needs.

Wellbeing is central to notions of sustainability and a major achievement of the international UNCED agreement was the extension into the political sphere of the formerly predominantly ecologically based concept of physical sustainability to the social context of development (Hediger 2000). The Commission addressed the issue of how to achieve decent human lives as part of its remit. While it is clear that the social dimension of sustainability did not receive the same level of attention as did natural resources and ecological processes (Farrell 1999; Hediger 2000) UNCED emphasized that sustainable development requires ensuring equitable opportunities for all members of society to satisfy their needs and aspirations for a better life. This is the concept of 'social sustainability', which extends notions of sustainable development significantly further than the straightforward satisfaction of physical requirements. Hediger defines 'critical social capital' as a minimum level of social cohesion beyond which the social system risks collapse (2000: 489), and social sustainability refers to a concept which seeks to maintain the stability of social and cultural systems.

Equity considerations may be considered in intra- and intergenerational terms. The Rio conference considered that even a narrow notion of physical sustainability implies a concern for social equity between generations and that this concern 'must logically be extended to equity within each generation' (World Commission on Environment and Development 1987). Successful social and cultural sustainability, in turn, require the maintenance of elements of social capital, which refers to a society's capacity to deal with social problems alongside economic and environmental ones. The definition of social capital is broad, and includes essential factors of economic production, human health and life expectancy, cultural and social integrity and social cohesion. These are all components of human wellbeing, and 'should be considered in a social welfare function' (Hediger 2000) in addition to more conventional components including incomes and environmental quality. Social capital cannot be maintained for a minority at the expense of a majority. In the present context social sustainability involves equitable access to key social welfare services, including health and education but also leisure and recreation. Improvements in social equity may result in opportunities for reductions in state resources devoted to pensions, welfare and social services, and may extend or even create new market opportunities.

From examination of the definition of 'sustainable tourism' advanced by the UN World Tourism Organization as that 'leading to the management of all resources in such a way that economic, social and esthetic needs can be fulfilled while maintaining cultural integrity, essential ecological processes, biological diversity and life support systems' (World Tourism Organization 1998), the question of exactly whose social and esthetic needs are to be fulfilled arises. The immediate subject here is the participating tourist, but issues of sustainability in tourism are closely linked to considerations of social equity (Ryan 2002), and a more nuanced interpretation of the UNWTO definition may be derived from a social welfare perspective. Such an interpretation implies a shift in consideration of the social function of holidaymaking, from being purely a private benefit enjoyed by more advantaged sections of society to a more holistic consideration of the benefits of leisure participation across the breadth of society.

While sustainable development is an inherently political concept, and one open to a range of interpretations, it is referenced as a founding principle for

EU policies and actions, and intragenerational equity is stated as a guiding principle:

> Sustainable development is a key objective for all European Community policies, set out in the treaty. It aims at the continuous improvement of the quality of life on earth of both current and future generations [. . .] It is based on the principles of democracy and the rule of law and respect for fundamental rights including freedom and equal opportunities for all.
>
> (Commission of the European Communities 2001, 2005a)

Social exclusion and childhood poverty are referenced as integral goals of European sustainable development strategy alongside more conventional concerns including environmental issues, public health and global poverty and development challenges (Commission of the European Communities 2005b), although social tourism is not mentioned.

The UK government's interpretation of sustainable development echoes that of the EU to a degree, but does not incorporate the so-called rights-based approach. The sustainable development strategy for the UK makes mention of a social dimension strand of sustainable development, relevant objectives of which include:

- ensuring a strong, healthy and just society;
- meeting the diverse needs of all people;
- promoting personal well-being;
- social cohesion and inclusion;
- creating equal opportunity for all; and
- mentions the importance of social justice and tackling inequality and social exclusion (HM Government 2005).

However, references to deprivation, social justice and wellbeing mostly refer to 'communities' and geographic areas suffering from poor environmental quality and 'degraded resources', and are expressed in terms of the biophysical environment rather than in social welfare terms.

It is important here to acknowledge that the Rio Agreement was not legally binding, and sceptics regard the UNCED report with some suspicion in its balancing of environmental 'limits' – which were not painted as posing any brake upon economic development – with endorsement of continuing economic growth. The definition of sustainable development arrived at by consensus is rather vague and 'real action [. . .] [has] tended to be much less forthcoming' (Dresner 2002). But Rio acted as a milestone towards the legitimation of a slew of extant social concerns alongside economic and environmental ones, meaning that governments and international agencies were compelled to examine the issues. The agreement remains a major landmark and one regularly referenced 20 years later. Sustainable development as a concept has succeeded at least as far as it has moved the debate forward.

Social tourism in the EU and the Barcelona Declaration

The role of the EU in tourism policy across the member states has been developing over the past few decades, and recent events indicate that the issue of social tourism has reached the European agenda. The establishment of a tourism unit within the European Commission in 1989 gave the nascent social tourism movement something to focus upon (Davidson 1992). More recently the Barcelona Declaration of 2006 (European Economic and Social Committee 2006) may represent another milestone along a policy development track which might in future lead to the Commission introducing a 'right to tourism' for citizens of the EU. An opinion paper from the European Economic and Social Committee (EESC), the Declaration is a statement of the importance of social tourism measures and a call for their adoption throughout the EU. Social tourism was described as a 'miracle' because of the diverse benefits accruing to individuals and societies – including promoting feelings of European citizenship – and 'it would be difficult to find a human economic activity that is so universally recognised and supported'. The role of the EESC is to represent the views of organized civil society (business and trade union leaders and representatives of farmers, consumers and other groups) upon economic and business policies to the European Commission and European Parliament. The European Commission and European Parliament are required to consult the EESC before making decisions but are under no obligation to follow its advice.

Subsequently, the Lisbon Treaty – 'Policies for a Better Life' – of December 2007 included objectives further committing the Union to address issues of poverty and social exclusion. In addition, it created a legal basis which would enable the European Union to develop the tourism sector for the first time. In 2010, the first meeting of EU Tourism Ministers after the signing of the Treaty approved the Madrid Declaration, a series of recommendations on European tourism policy made to the European Commission which included a recommendation for the EU to support social tourism policies (T20 Tourism Ministers 2010). The Spanish Minister for Industry, Tourism, and Trade was quoted as having said, 'The European Union commits to social tourism', tourism is a sector which 'should be an asset all citizens can enjoy', and the Vice-President of the Commission and Commissioner for Industry and Entrepreneurship was quoted as having said 'We work to turn every European citizen into a tourist.'

With new treaty powers, the EU has initiated a three-year social tourism pilot programme with a budget of €1 million per year called CALYPSO (2009–2011). While at present most supported holiday trips are made to domestic destinations in individuals' home countries, CALYPSO is a social tourism measure operating at the international level. It aims to enable EU citizens to holiday in other member countries, providing supported holidays outside the high season for four specified target groups:

- those with disabilities;
- families with low incomes;

- older people and the retired; and
- underprivileged young adults aged between 18 and 30.

Twenty-one EU and candidate countries have signed up to CALYPSO, although the UK has yet to indicate a firm interest.

Social tourism in the EU – implications and issues

Examining the concept of social tourism with reference to discourses around sustainable development inevitably entails reference to intergenerational issues and futurity. To satisfy the holidaymaking needs of current generations and in the absence of significant social redistribution measures, there is arguably a need to raise the absolute number of vacations taken each year. However, if it is accepted that compliance with the limits of critical natural capacities (or capital) is a minimum requirement of sustainable development (Hediger 2000; Pearce *et al.* 1994), widening markets for holidaymaking intragenerationally may have negative impacts in intergenerational terms. Anthropogenic climate change linked primarily to fossil fuel energy use is frequently identified as posing perhaps the greatest long-term biophysical threat to the integrity of the human environment.

The effects of more people traveling on holiday using existing transport technologies will perhaps inevitably include an increase in transport-derived emissions, which, in turn, may contribute to atmospheric and climatic impacts the effects of which future generations will have to address. This, in turn, runs counter to the need to sustain the overall integrity of the global ecosystem over the long term. and could be interpreted as meaning that long-term environmental quality goals are traded off for what may be judged short-term social ones. In the terms of the sustainability debate, then, however appropriate and ethical social tourism policies might be in terms of social sustainability, they may be characterized as examples of 'weak sustainability' measures insofar as they conflict with the need to maintain the planet's stock of critical natural capital over time. By contrast, under 'strong sustainability' principles maintenance of the overall quality of the global ecosystem is paramount and non-negotiable; so a conflict arises between the outcomes of addressing intragenerational and intergenerational equity issues. Further conflicts between environmental and social priorities might arise as a result of any future social tourism measures resulting in greater numbers of tourists massing at destinations, with potential carrying capacity implications for destination management. However, and to complicate the matter yet further, UNWTO predictions indicate that global tourist volumes will continue to increase at a roughly exponential rate for the foreseeable future, even in the absence of social tourism measures (WTO 2006).

While social tourism measures may address one dimension of intergenerational equity, they are only of real relevance to wealthier countries and regions. The prospect of introducing such measures to the less wealthy countries of the world, and especially amongst the 2.8 people living on less than €2 per day, might be desirable in a principled intergenerational sense but is otherwise wholly unrealistic and inappropriate. To offer some perspective on the matter, the eight Millennium Development Goals towards which United Nations member states have agreed to work to achieve by 2015 address far more pressing issues, including extreme poverty and hunger, child mortality, disease, universal primary education and safe drinking water. Sustainable development on a global scale probably requires the more affluent to adopt lifestyles more attuned with the planet's biophysical limits, especially with reference to discretionary activities requiring high levels of energy input (Leigh 2011). Examining the ethics of sustainability, Dresner (2002) identified instances of disagreement within the UNCED report over this issue of consumption patterns, and cites an attempt to 'paper over the divisions' about the issue, reporting the comments of a member of the Brundtland Commission secretariat largely responsible for drafting the first section of the report that the final document was 'careful' in its formulations on the issue of consumption. Specifically, some Commission members from wealthier countries had been wary of a more explicit discussion of the consumption issue, recognizing that it might imply more equal sharing of the resources of the planet, and the implication was that the 'papering over' (Dresner 2002) was necessary because there was a need to maintain consensus amongst members of the Commission.

While holidays are accepted as a social right in several EU nations, the situation is quite different in others. The distribution of state-subsidized leisure goods on a basis of need in addition to meritocratic criteria is anathema to some commentators, and perhaps particularly so with reference to certain beneficiary social groups. Many governments have developed national leisure policies often including subsidies for certain forms of arts and culture and policies to widen access to the countryside for recreation, for instance, but the tacit acknowledgement of existing socioeconomic differences by supported tourism projects and similar redistributive measures is by its very nature neither politically nor socially neutral (Shaw and Williams 2002). Indeed, the very concept of 'vacation rights' may be contentious precisely because it highlights inequality in holiday participation (Hall and Brown 2006).

Public expenditure in support of social tourism measures is a key dimension of the issue. Criticisms of social tourism measures are typically based upon the viewpoint that an individual enjoying a private benefit should be required to defray its full cost. This focus, however, fails to take the potentially significant collective social benefits into account (if we can accept that vacations are a merit good, as suggested earlier). The cost of social tourism measures can be interpreted as an investment which may serve to reduce certain costs borne by society, including a reduction in health care and social welfare costs. Supported holiday-making expenditure can also act to complement other, more expensive, forms of intervention (Minnaert *et al.* 2009). In addition, there is some evidence to suggest that state expenditure on social tourism provision can be revenue-neutral or even revenue-positive. The IMSERSO project supports holiday-taking by older Spanish people at domestic coastal resorts in the 'shoulder seasons', and one evaluation of the economics of the programme concluded that, for every euro of subsidy to the scheme, up to an additional 1.8 euros was generated through income and savings – via additional economic activity and employment, and the extension of the employment season for employees in the tourism and other sectors (Price Waterhouse Coopers 2004). Governments may conceivably achieve revenue savings from health service budgets as a result of the collective benefits derived from the enjoyment of holidays by such a large group of senior citizens (now more than one million annually in Spain), and estimates suggest that IMSERSO created about 7,000 direct and several thousand more indirect jobs.

Despite the emphasis on reducing child poverty and social exclusion in the later 1990s and the early years of the new millennium, when the political environment for lobbyists was a fertile one, holidays remain a contested element of social rights. In the UK, the Barcelona Declaration and subsequent declarations on social tourism have made very little impact upon popular and political consciousnesses. Political support for social tourism as a policy tool is influenced by national cultural attitudes towards work and leisure in the UK and elsewhere, and many elements of the concept, rationale and practice will inevitably conflict with certain shades of opinion. There is some limited evidence on the degree to which the public accepts that the holiday is a necessity at all, suggesting that about 43 percent of the British population consider a 'domestic holiday away from home once a year not staying with relatives' is *not* a necessity, a proportion which may have increased over the previous twenty years (Gordon *et al.* 2000).

In the UK, social tourism is generally seen as beyond the limits of welfare, and the social care agenda has not embraced the provision of family holidays. Unlike other Western European countries, provision for supported holidays has not benefited from legislation, and it is not considered a national economic priority given the range of alternative uses to which the resources could be devoted. The rights-based language of social exclusion and social cohesion employed by the EU and the Council of Europe stands in marked contrast to that employed in the UK. The UK tends to eschew references to rights: 'fundamental rights' are defined in a relatively narrow sense as those involving the welfare of children, or persons at serious risk of loss of life or liberty, for instance. The UK government has acknowledged the role of charities including the FHA in the provision of supported holidays, but does not regard holidays as a right and considers that subsidy would be 'unaffordable', particularly at a time of economic recession when there are competing priorities for state expenditure (House of Commons HC Deb 2010–2011). Perverse disincentives may be created, potentially penalizing individuals in low-income groups who have managed to save money for holidaymaking. There is also the concern that enhanced levels of social welfare provision may act as a disincentive to work and foster 'welfare dependency'. Other than in the case of provision for those with disabilities, the very limited justification expressed for national policy development in the field of social tourism has tended to express the rationale for increasing participation for the economic benefit of the tourism industry and domestic destinations, including coastal towns, rather than for social welfare reasons.

Despite the potential target groups eligible for supported holidaymaking under any future EU measures having been carefully circumscribed, the issue of reconciling the likely budgetary costs of any 'right to tourism' in relation to the potential levels of demand for supported holidays is a formidable one. The number of people in the EU-27 of working age with long-standing health problems or disabilities is about 46 million, for instance, of whom about 26 million are unemployed. In addition, an estimated 16 million young adults aged between 18 and 30 are classed as 'underprivileged'. Some less wealthy countries and regions of the Union may be characterized as being 'time and money poor' in terms of holidaymaking constraints (Richards 1998) and may therefore have a stronger claim on supported holidaymaking budgets than others, including the former centrally planned countries of central Europe and some southern European countries (Klein 2003). Finally, individual EU member states have discretion over which social measures they wish to adopt and which they do not.

Implications and issues – the industry

The response from the tourism industry about the implications of any European 'right to tourism' has been very limited. Supported holidaymaking measures would produce an expansion of demand at the budget end of the market, an opportunity which in turn would presumably be met by the industry with an expansion in supply. This might be particularly significant in wealthier countries like the UK and the Netherlands, where popular markets for holidaymaking are at or approaching saturation (Richards 1999). In Belgium, the motivations and attitudes of the private sector in supporting the Holiday Participation Centre were found to be based upon goodwill and humanitarian motivations, alongside a more commercially oriented recognition of the benefits of the collaboration, including extra advertising, greater name recognition, improved image and reputation, alongside additional out-of-season revenue. The issue of whether subsidies might constitute unfair competition with businesses may be an important consideration for certain sections of the private sector, however (see for instance Ryan 2002) and projects like 'Europe Senior Tourism', a recent initiative to attract older tourists to Spain with subsidized low-season holiday offers, may antagonise tourism industry stakeholders in their home countries if they perceive their low-season customer base is being attracted abroad for subsidized breaks.

The advent of corporate social responsibility (CSR) in the tourism industry may deliver a means for achieving social tourism goals. CSR has been defined as 'the continuing commitment by business to behave ethically and contribute to economic development while improving the quality of life of the workforce and their families as well as of the local community and society at large' (Business for Social Responsibility, quoted in Swarbrooke 2003: 75). Driven by the incorporation of ethical and environmental values into companies' operations, the concept has been current for about twenty years, its linkage with sustainable development has been recognized at the EU level (Council of the European Union 2009) and CSR has been identified as a useful means for involving the tourism industry in the broader sustainable development agenda (Henderson 2007; Swarbrooke 2003).

The debate on CSR in tourism has paralleled that on the Fairtrade movement to some degree, with a focus on environmental and social impacts associated with outbound tourism from the UK to less-developed countries. A few major UK outbound tourism companies appear to have started to formally recognize what might be defined as their obligations to wider society, including TUI Travel plc (the Thomson brand in the UK), a major tour operator which espouses a corporate commitment to sustainable development and states it is 'giving a fair deal to [destination] communities', amongst other measures. While references to the social dimensions of CSR in TUI's sustainable development policy relate to only to culture, people and communities at destinations (TUI Travel 2010), the company's 'nominated charity' for the last 15 years has been the FHA. Donations through TUI account for approximately one-quarter of the income of the FHA, indicating that CSR could have positive implications for the provision of supported holidays in future if more sections of the tourism industry adopt such policies. Social inclusion has been identified as one of several issues to be addressed by the UK tourism industry under CSR policies (Swarbrooke 2003), but CSR is presently relatively poorly developed in the UK domestic tourism industry. While the principles of CSR are as relevant for small companies as for large ones, the British domestic tourism industry is not nearly as dominated by large companies with CSR agendas as many other industrial sectors are.

CSR has been derided as being tokenistic and cosmetic, a cynical means of attracting additional customers while stalling any attempts at industry regulation (Henderson 2007; Swarbrooke 2003). While in the third millennium public displays of sympathy might be considered essential to improving corporate image, profitability will inevitably remain the key driver of tourism companies' actions. Sustainable development implies a level of commitment probably beyond all tourism businesses, and CSR covers only a limited range of well-defined and voluntary aspects of companies' activities. As a result, it has been identified as occupying a position near the weaker pole of the sustainability spectrum and should be assessed within that context (Henderson 2007). Realistically, any contribution made to supported holidaymaking under tourism industry CSR policies is likely only to be relatively marginal and contingent on the continuing commercial success of individual companies and the overall economic environment.

The future

There is good potential for the expansion of social tourism as a segment of the wider tourism industry over the early decades of the twenty-first century. However, whether the provision of supported holidays will become more common as a component of social welfare measures will depend upon broader political, economic, social and environmental trends, and the welfare and tourism organization regimes of states and supranational groupings. The social tourism sector seems to account for only a small proportion of tourism flows at present, although no estimates appear to be available. The scale of the task necessary to make a significant difference seems daunting, and a central issue is that the concept of social tourism is unglamorous, boasts very few champions, and is at root a contested concept. Social tourism measures may provide social benefits but they are not cost free: the average holiday provided by the UK FHA costs US$1,200 (Minnaert *et al.* 2009).

Partnership working involving various combinations of government, the not-for-profit sector and, crucially, the tourism industry, seems essential for implementing social tourism measures. Several European countries operate successful schemes utilizing such structures, though for some the management of demand has proven problematic. However, in a climate of economic recession and fiscal retrenchment, future priorities for state intervention may be dominated by primary health care and concerns about the provision of pensions, for instance. Outside the more economically developed world, the concept of social tourism may essentially be meaningless, too.

Conclusions

Holidaymaking is increasingly regarded as a social norm in many countries, and a case for making provision for supported holidaymaking for disadvantaged social groups may be constructed employing arguments based upon ethics, social equity and inclusion, health and social welfare, sustainability and related concerns. Social tourism measures have been a feature of social welfare policies in several European nations for many years, although debate on the matter has barely begun in others. There is some limited evidence to suggest that expenditure on supported holidaymaking for disadvantaged groups may be revenue-neutral or even revenue-positive. It seems clear that supported holidays will not solve the health and social welfare issues experienced by many disadvantaged groups, any more than market-based holidaymaking is a panacea for the majority of the population. However, the benefits of an annual break are sufficient to make the activity a priority for many in terms of discretionary household expenditure, and a clear case may be made for provision for supported holidays to be made an integral part of social welfare and social inclusion policies. But the issues associated with implementing any future European 'right to tourism' seem formidable, and promoting the provision of supported holidaymaking opportunities against a background of declining social welfare budgets and liberalization of social welfare regimes is likely to prove much more difficult than many alternative intervention measures. For the present, in what is perhaps the world's wealthiest region, the personal, family and broader social welfare benefits enjoyed by those able to participate in holidaymaking remain unattainable by a substantial proportion of the population.

Further research needs to be conducted into the cost-effectiveness of a range of social tourism measures and also into their efficacy in terms of their collective social welfare benefits across the breadth of society, for which there needs to be a basis of evidence. Determining the attitudes of and potential contributions from the commercial tourism sector would yield useful indications for the future, as would consideration of the prospects for expanding the role of the not-for-profit sector and social enterprise in the coproduction of supported holidaymaking opportunities.

References

Bray, R. (2000) *Flight to the Sun*, London: Continuum.

Brewer, M., Muriel, A., Phillips, D. and Sibieta, L. (2009) *Poverty and Inequality in the UK: 2009*, London: Institute for Fiscal Studies.

Butler, R.W. (1999) 'Sustainable Tourism: A State-of-the-art Review', *Tourism Geographies*, 1(1): 7–25.

Carr, L. (2004) 'Leisure and Disabled people', in J. Swain, S. French, C. Thomas and C. Barnes (eds.) *Disabling Barriers, Enabling Environments*, London: Sage, pp. 183–188.

Coalter, F. (2001) *Realising the Potential of Cultural Services: The Case for Tourism*, London: LGA Publications.

Commission of the European Communities (2001) *A Sustainable Europe for a Better World: A European Union Strategy for Sustainable Development*, Brussels: CEC, COM (2001) 264 final.

—— (2005a) *Communication from the Commission to the Council and the European Parliament: Draft Declaration on Guiding Principles for Sustainable Development*, Brussels: CEC, COM (2005) 218 final.

—— (2005b) *On the Review of the Sustainable Development Strategy: A Platform for Action*, Brussels: CEC, COM (2005) 0658 final.

Council of the European Union (2009) *2009 Review of the EU Sustainable Development Strategy*, Brussels: CEC, 16818/09.

Davidson, R. (1992) *Tourism in Europe*, London: Pitman.

Davolio, M. (2003) 'TICA: A Partner for the Development of Social Tourism in Asia and Africa', *Le Tourisme Social dans le Monde/Social Tourism International*, 141: 22.

Department for Culture Media and Sport (1999) *Tomorrow's Tourism – A Growth Industry for the New Millennium*, London: DCMS.

—— (2004) *Tomorrow's Tourism Today*, London: DCMS.

—— (2011) *Government Tourism Policy*, London: DCMS.

Donoghue, B. (2009) *Achieving the Full Potential of the Visitor Economy*, London: VisitBritain.

Dresner, S. (2002) *The Principles of Sustainability*, London: Earthscan.

English Tourism Council (2000) *Just What the Doctor Ordered: The Health Benefits of Holidays, Research & Intelligence, GP Omnibus 2000*, London: English Tourism Council.

Esping-Andersen, G. (1990) *The Three Worlds of Welfare Capitalism*, Princeton, NJ: Princeton University Press.

Eurobarometer (2009) *Survey on the Attitudes of Europeans Towards Tourism: Analytical Report Wave 2*, Budapest: The Gallup Organisation.

European Economic and Social Committee (2006) 'Opinion of the European Economic and Social Committee on Social Tourism in Europe', *Official Journal of the European Union*, 2006/C 318/12.

Family Holiday Association (2009) *Giving Families a Break!*, London: Family Holiday Association.

Farrell, B.H. (1999) 'Conventional or Sustainable Tourism? No Room for Choice', *Tourism Management*, 20(2): 189–191.

Gordon, D., Adelman, L., Ashworth, K., Bradshaw, B., Levitas, R., Middleton, S., Pantazis, C., Patsios, D., Payne, S., Townsend, P. and Williams, J. (2000) *Poverty and Social Exclusion in Britain*, York: Joseph Rowntree Foundation.

Hall, D. and Brown, F. (2006) *Tourism and Welfare: Ethics, Responsibility and Sustainable Well-being*, Wallingford: CABI Publishing.

Haukeland, J.V. (1990) 'Non-travelers: The Flip Side of Motivation', *Annals of Tourism Research*, 17(2): 172–184.

Hazel, N. (2005) 'Holidays for Children and Families in Need: An Exploration of the Research and Policy Context for Social Tourism in the UK', *Children & Society*, 19(3): 225–236.

Hediger, W. (2000) 'Sustainable Development and Social Welfare', *Ecological Economics*, 32(3): 481–492.

Henderson, J.C. (2007) 'Corporate Social Responsibility and Tourism: Hotel Companies in Phuket, Thailand, after the Indian Ocean Tsunami', *International Journal of Hospitality Management*, 26(1): 228–239.

HM Government (2005) *Securing the Future: The UK Government Sustainable Development Strategy*, London: The Stationery Office, CM6467.

House of Commons HC Deb (2010–2011) 19 November 2010 vol. 518 c1249, online. Available at www.parliament.uk/briefing-papers/SN06096.pdf (accessed 15 October 2011).

Jolin, L. (2003) 'Le tourisme social, un concept riche de ses évolutions', *Le Tourisme Social dans le Monde/Social Tourism International*, 141: 6–8.

Klein, R. (2003) Untitled, *Le Tourisme Social dans le Monde/Social Tourism International*, 141: 16.

Leigh, J. (2011) 'New Tourism in a New Society Arises from Peak Oil', *Turismos*, 6(1): 165–191.

MacInnes, T., Kenway, P. and Parekh, A. (2009) *Monitoring Poverty and Social Exclusion 2009*, York: Joseph Rowntree Foundation.

McCabe, S. (2009) 'Who Needs a Holiday? Evaluating Social Tourism', *Annals of Tourism Research*, 36(4), 667–688.

McCabe, S., Foster, C. and Urbino, M. (2007) *Briefing Paper for Policymakers: Evaluating Stated Needs for Support for Holidays*. Nottingham: Christel DeHaan Tourism & Travel Research Institute Paper, Nottingham University Business School.

McCabe, S., Joldersma, T. and Li, C. (2010) 'Understanding the Benefits of Social Tourism: Linking Participation to Subjective Well-being and Quality of Life', *International Journal of Tourism Research*, 12(6): 761–773.

Minnaert, L. (2008) 'Social Tourism in Flanders', *Tourism Insights*, online. Available at www.insights.org.uk/articleitem.aspx?title=Social%20Tourism%20in%20Flanders (accessed 15 October 2010).

Minnaert, L., Maitland, R. and Miller, G. (2006) 'Social Tourism and its Ethical Foundations, *Tourism, Culture & Communication*, 7(1): 7–17.

—— (2009) 'Tourism and Social Policy: The Value of Social Tourism', *Annals of Tourism Research*, 36(2): 316–334.

Pearce, D.W., Atkinson, G.D. and Dubourg, W.R. (1994) 'The Economics of Sustainable Development', *Annual Review of Energy and the Environment*, 19: 457–474.

Price Waterhouse Coopers (2004) *Estudio sobre el programa de vacaciones para mayores, del IMSERSO* (Study of the program holidays for the elderly), online. Available at fhaonline.org.uk/Documents/Prog08IMSERSO_PWC_Translation_0.24Mb.pdf (accessed 4 March 2011).

Richards, G. (1998) 'Time for a Holiday?' *Time & Society*, 7(1): 145–160.

—— (1999) 'Vacations and the Quality of Life: Patterns and Structures', *Journal of Business Research*, 44(3): 189–198.

Ryan, C. (2002) 'Equity, Management, Power Sharing and Sustainability – Issues of the 'New Tourism', *Tourism Management*, 23(1): 17–26.

Seaton, A. (1992) 'Social Stratification in Tourism: Choice and Experience since the War: Part 1', *Tourism Management*, 13(1): 106–111.

Shaw, G. and Williams, A.M. (2002) *Critical Issues in Tourism: A Geographical Perspective*, 2nd edn, Oxford: Blackwell.

Smith, V. and Hughes, H. (1999) 'Disadvantaged Families and the Meaning of the Holiday', *International Journal of Tourism Research*, 1(2): 123–133.

Sonmez, S. and Apostolopoulos, Y. (2009) 'Vacation Travel as Preventive Medicine', in Bushell, R. and P. Sheldon, (eds.) *Wellness and Tourism: Mind, Body, Spirit, Place*, London: Cognizant Communication Corporation, pp. 37–51.

Swarbrooke, J. (2003) 'Corporate Social Responsibility and the UK Tourism Industry', *Insights*, November: 75–83.

T20 Tourism Ministers (2010) *Declaration of Madrid within the Scope of the Informal Ministerial Meeting for Tourism under the Spanish Presidency in April 2010 in Madrid under the Motto 'Towards A Socially Responsible Tourism Mode'*, online. Available at ec.europa.eu/enterprise/sectors/tourism/files/madrid_stakeholders_conference/declaration_madrid_en.pdf (accessed 02 January 2011).

TNS-RI Travel & Tourism (2010) *The UK Tourist: Statistics 2009*, London: VisitEngland.

Tourism Flanders & Brussels (2009) *Holidays are for Everyone*, Brussels: Tourism Flanders & Brussels.

Townsend, P. (1979) *Poverty in the United Kingdom: A Survey of Household Resources and Standards of Living*, London: Penguin.

TUI Travel (2010) *Group Sustainable Development Policy*, online. Available at www.tuitravelplc.com/tui/pages/sustainabledevelopment/strategy1/policy (accessed 03 November 2010).

Twining-Ward, L. (1999) 'Towards Sustainable Tourism Development: Observations from a Distance', *Tourism Management*, 20(2): 187–188.

UNEP (2005) *Making Tourism more Sustainable: A Guide for Policymakers*, Paris: UNEP.

United Nations (1989) *Convention on the Rights of the Child*, General Assembly resolution 44/25 of 20 November 1989, New York: United Nations.

VisitBritain (2008) *A Sustainable Future for Tourism: British Tourism Framework Review Sustainability Annex*, online. Available at www.visitbritain.org/Images/BTFR%20 sustainability%20annex_tcm139-168552.pdf (accessed 03 January 11).

Walton, J.K. (2000) *The British Seaside: Holidays and Resorts in the Twentieth Century*, Manchester: MUP.

Webster, C., Ivanov, S. and Illum, S. (2011) 'The Paradigms of Political Economy and Tourism Policy: NTOs and State Policy', in J. Mosedale (ed.) *Political Economy of Tourism: A Critical Perspective*, London: Routledge, pp. 55–73.

World Commission on Environment and Development (1987) *Our Common Future: Report of the World Commission on Environment and Development*, Oxford: Oxford University Press.

World Tourism Organization (1998) *Sustainable Tourism*, Madrid: WTO.

—— (2006) *Tourism: 2020 Vision* (summary), Madrid: WTO.

6 Shapers and shifters for the future of travel and tourism

Susanne Becken

Introduction

In the past four decades leisure time has increased substantially in many countries. A recent study of the American population, for example, shows that while the number of 'market hours worked' per working age adult remained stable between 1965 and 2003, the amount of leisure time has increased substantially by 7.9 hours for men and by 6.0 hours for women (Aguiar and Hurst 2006). Alongside increases in leisure time more generally, time spent on travel for leisure (i.e. holidays) has also increased. Statistics by the United Nations World Tourism Organisation highlight the phenomenal growth that tourism has experienced since the 1950s. The year 2009, following the financial meltdown of 2008, was the second time in which growth of international tourist numbers has been negative (the other one was after September 2001), since such statistics have been collected. In 2009, international arrivals decreased from over 900 million to about 880 million (UNWTO 2010).

Much of the growth in leisure has been facilitated by increasingly accessible and affordable mobility and technology. The observed changes in leisure behavior have been associated with an increasing demand for energy and other resources, and questions about the sustainability of today's leisure and tourism have been asked (Aal 2007). In response to an increased commodification, intensification and acceleration of leisure and tourism, a new movement of 'slow travel' is emerging. This antithesis to the common way of excess consumption (Urry 2010) promotes carbon-light transport modes, slow travel speed and localized activities under the banner of simultaneously enhancing the tourist experience and minimizing footprints (Dickinson 2009).

Understanding some of these social trends and integrating them with wider economic predictions and prognoses of technological advancements is a major challenge for those involved in 'predicting' the future of tourism and travel (for an early piece see Emery 1981). All too often, however, exercises to prepare for the future fall victim to the tempting approach of simply extrapolating current trends within dominant paradigms of economic growth and neoliberalism. Such narrow-mindedness might blur the view to more rapid shifts, transformations, or tipping points that may entail a new world order within a short period of time. It is important to avoid 'wishful' prediction, especially in the light of tourism's 'promise to promote economic development and stability, peace, poverty reduction, and sustainable development' (Cole and Razak 2009: 335). It is the goal of this chapter to critically discuss trend provisions made for tourism and provide a structure for assessing systematically different drivers of change in future analyses. Drivers of change will be discussed, amongst others, in relation to the magnitude of change they induce, and whether they represent '*shifters*' (i.e. moderate change or transition) or '*shapers*' (radical transformations).

What are the key trends?

An abundant number of tourism forecasts, either at national or global levels, are available. Most countries try to predict their tourist arrivals at least for the next 5 to 10 years (e.g. New Zealand Ministry of Tourism 2010). In their 2020 vision, the UNWTO (2001) provided a forecast for global international tourism. Projections are slightly less certain than forecasts, and focus on likely trends or scenarios (Yeoman *et al.* 2009). In scenario-based projections, users are often encouraged to form their own opinion on which scenarios are more or less likely to eventuate. There are few analyses that truly explore different, yet equally plausible scenarios for tourism (e.g. Draper *et al.* 2009; Urry 2008).

Most studies provide so-called 'trend analyses', which are based on an inherent assumption of what is likely to happen in the future. These tend to focus on Western society, are short-term in nature (e.g. 2020) and base their trend on an analysis of historic data. Long-term analyses or those that consider rapid changes have not been identified for tourism. In the following, the main trends, as available in the tourism literature, will be discussed.

Economic

Many trend analyses assume ongoing economic growth and rising incomes (Dwyer *et al.* 2008; European Travel Commission 2004) that create a mass upper class of people that are able to travel and spend prolifically (Scottish Enterprise 2004). Accordingly, Mintel predicts that in 2020, tourist trips from the top 15 countries of origin will almost double (from 433 million to 837 million per annum) (Amadeus 2009). A growing middle class is expected in China and India (Draper *et al.* 2009; Yeoman *et al.* 2009), and often also in the other two BRIC countries, Brazil and Russia (Dwyer *et al.* 2008). It has been estimated that in 2020, 40 percent of the Chinese population will be middle class with an income between US$18,137 and US$36,275 per year (Amadeus 2009).

Globalization is expected to continue with an environment of improved macroeconomic policies that enable liberalization and widespread growth. In accordance with neoliberalism, the private sector will become increasingly dynamic and dominant (Dwyer *et al.* 2008). Business travel is predicted to grow rapidly, at least in the Asia Pacific region, according to a mega trend analysis by the UNWTO in 2006. The market segment of 'global executives' has been identified as the most affluent of segments, with high expectation of service and luxury (Amadeus 2009).

Most of the future trend analyses acknowledge that there are risks associated with downturns in key economies, disagreement over global trade rules, and growing disparity between rich and poor (e.g. Amadeus 2009; Dwyer *et al.* 2008; Tourism Victoria no date). Few studies put such major challenges at the core of their future development. A notable exception is the Tourism 2023 scenarios, where both climate change and energy constraints are seen as the key defining dimensions of the future of tourism (Draper *et al.* 2009).

Demographic/social/cultural

The world population is increasing and it is also getting older, at least in the wealthier countries (Dwyer *et al.* 2008). In the United Kingdom, in 2020 the number of those over 50 will outnumber those aged younger than 50 (Scottish Enterprise 2004). Most trend analysts are in agreement that overall the population is getting healthier (especially the elderly) (Amadeus 2009), and that older people will take more trips. However, a trend towards increasing obesity has also been observed, and noted as an important factor in shaping leisure and tourism (Scottish Enterprise 2004). The search for health and wellbeing has been identified as a key consumer trend that provides new business opportunities (Amadeus 2009).

Family composition is likely to change with older parents, more single house-holds and an increasing number of grandparents traveling with their grandchildren (Bosshart and Frick 2006; Scottish Enterprise 2004, Tourism Victoria no date). Children will become increasingly important in consumption decisions and parents see holidays as an opportunity for their children to learn new skills (Scottish Enterprise 2004). Some believe that the trends towards more but shorter holidays will continue (European Travel Commission 2004).

There seems to be some uncertainty around future changes in the amount of leisure time. Some studies predict it to increase, while others note that people are increasingly stressed for time and require products that accommodate a sense of escape from their intense everyday life, especially managers and professionals (Tourism Victoria no date) (Dwyer *et al.* 2008; Yeoman *et al.* 2009). A Scottish study on lifestyles reported that leisure time in the UK has declined since the 1990s (Scottish Enterprise 2004). Similarly, despite trends indicating that people are wealthier, it has been observed that people are more conscious of their spending and actively engaging in bargain-hunting (Amadeus 2009), and questions have been raised about how affordable travel will be for the growing segment of elderly (Draper *et al.* 2009).

Tourists are becoming more interested in a balanced lifestyle (Tourism Victoria no date) and at the same time they are becoming increasingly experienced travelers (European Travel Commission 2004). They will be more demanding in their travel experiences, which are believed to become more activity than place-based. One consequence of this is that there are more and more specialized products that serve niche markets. Some analysts also predict a trend towards more luxury products (European Travel Commission 2004) as well as those that contain some educational or spiritual components (Scottish Enterprise 2004). A greater demand for authenticity is anticipated (European Travel Commission 2004; Yeoman *et al.* 2009).

Technological

The key technological advancements are seen in the information technology sector, facilitating new forms of networking, communication and even virtual travel (Bosshart and Frick 2006; Dwyer *et al.* 2008). For the Asia Pacific region, the UNWTO (2006) predicts a continued growth in online transactions and a transformation of travel agents into travel consultants. A study on traveler tribes by Amadeus (2009) foresees that customers will travel as 'digital personal identities' that require personalized and up-to-date information, delivered with an increasing sophistication of visual technologies.

Another technological trend that has been noted as important for travel and tourism is a potential breakthrough in the commercialization of biofuel production from algae (Draper *et al.* 2009). Whether transport costs generally will increase or decrease remains ambiguous. Some authors argue that the model of low-cost carriers will increase in its market penetration and lead to more affordable travel (Amadeus 2009; Bosshart and Frick 2006; UNWTO 2006; Yeoman *et al.* 2009), whereas others point to increasing transport costs due to rising oil prices and carbon policies (Draper *et al.* 2009). Amadeus (2009) also points to new developments in aircraft technology that increase fuel efficiency substantially, and also comments on the coming into the market of space tourism. The increasing competitiveness of high-speed trains has been noted (European Travel Commission 2004).

Environmental

The impacts of climate change are seen by many as the greatest environmental challenge in the next century (Draper *et al.* 2009). Climate change will directly affect tourists through increased risks to safety and health (e.g. exposure to extreme events and diseases) and also impact on tourist infrastructure, destinations and major environmental assets (e.g. beaches and world heritage sites) (UNESCO 2007). Existing issues of water scarcity are likely to be exacerbated by climate change, and conflicts over water are expected to increase (Dwyer *et al.* 2008). Changes in climatic conditions are also increasing pressure on already stressed ecosystems, with the risk of growing losses of biodiversity.

Another increasingly pressing challenge is the depletion of natural resources, in particular 'cheap oil', but also other resources such as gas, phosphorous and food (Bosshart and Frick 2006; Draper *et al.* 2009). Oil is the lifeblood of tourism because it facilitates cheap transportation. Depletion of global oil reserves and reduced global production will increase prices and also lead to extreme price volatility, hence providing a real challenge for businesses (Becken *et al.* 2010;

Draper *et al.* 2009). While Amadeus (2009) argues that consumers have been remarkably resilient to fuel surcharges imposed by airlines, it has been argued that major and long-lasting increases in oil prices will have major implications for tourism and society as a whole (Becken 2011).

At the same time, most analysts state that people from developed countries are increasingly conscious of the social and environmental implications of their consumption behaviors (Dwyer *et al.* 2008; European Travel Commission 2004). In particular, the carbon footprint associated with travel is seen to pose an increasing constraint on people's willingness to engage in 'binge flying' or other intense forms of carbon consumption (Draper *et al.* 2009). Scottish Enterprise (2004) recognized a trend of British consumers 'downshifting' in the search for an easier life. However, more generally it as has been pointed out that increasing awareness may not necessarily lead to changes in actual reductions in travel, with tourists traveling despite a feeling of guilt, or opting for carbon offsetting mechanisms (Becken 2007; DEFRA 2007). Notwithstanding, tourist destinations and businesses have been advised to improve environmental standards in the face of more environmentally conscious customers (European Travel Commission 2004).

Political factors and other risks

Political prognoses address questions of geopolitical power and world order. There seems agreement that while the USA will be less powerful in the future it will remain a major player, and China and India will emerge as key forces in the geopolitical landscape. With respect to Russia, Dwyer *et al.* (2008) note 'Russia has an international potential due to its gas and oil, but will be limited by social and political challenges' (p. viii).

A major trend is an increase in the threat of terrorism – even cyber terrorism (Bosshart and Frick 2006; Dwyer *et al.* 2008) – and regional conflicts amongst less developed countries. This is believed to be fueled by overpopulation and growing pressure on resources, although it is unclear to what extent these pose challenges to outbound travel from rich countries (Draper *et al.* 2009).

Increased international travel is seen as a key factor in the spread of infectious diseases and the risk of a global pandemic (Dwyer *et al.* 2008). A general climate of fear may restrain people's willingness to travel in the future (Amadeus 2009, see the notion of American angst in Yeoman *et al.* 2009), and there is a recognized need to provide safety measures for tourists (which will increase costs of travel) and prepare for periods of crisis (European Travel Commission 2004).

Nature of change

While the trends identified above are likely to provide guidance for destinations and enterprises (Dwyer *et al.* 2008), more value can be added by considering the specific nature of change against four criteria: (i) the elements of the tourism system that are changing, (ii) the degree of certainty associated with a driver of change, (iii) the timescale with which change will manifest and (iv) the magnitude and irreversibility of change. It will be argued that the magnitude of change is fundamental because it determines whether a system is merely shaping towards a new state or whether it has to shift radically.

Elements of the tourism system

The most basic approach to tourism as a system goes back to Leiper (1995) and describes tourism as comprising three elements: tourists (country of origin), a transit route and destinations (host countries). Each of these can be usefully further disaggregated into key dimensions, for example motivational and economic aspects of tourist behavior, the operation of transportation systems and their economics and businesses at the destination alongside natural resources.

Table 6.1 provides an overview of a selected number of drivers of change, and indicates the elements to which they relate most prominently, i.e. tourism demand, transportation and tourism supply. While all drivers are likely to relate to all parts of the tourism system, some can clearly be linked to specific elements more than others. Demographic change, for example, clearly affects the motivational and economic aspects of tourism demand, and it may – to some extent – shape how transportation systems operate and what kinds of products and services tourism businesses offer. The structure, choice of drivers and interactions presented in Table 6.1 have to be seen as exemplary for alternative ways of approaching tourism futures in a differentiated way that enables a focused analysis of drivers and impacts.

Uncertainty

> The growth in international travel will continue to rise as the globalization of business and growing migration fuel the need to travel abroad, and rising consumer affluence coupled with a reduction in the cost of travel brings it into the reach of more people. However, a number of critical uncertainties, such as growing concern about environmental issues and the rising price of oil, may apply brakes to this trend.
>
> (Amadeus 2009: 4)

This quotation highlights that different trends or drivers of change are associated with different degrees of (un)certainty. Only few analyses explicitly acknowledge this. The Tourism 2023 study from the United Kingdom (Draper *et al.* 2009) was identified as the only exercise that explicitly outlined those influences that are more certain than others. Climate change impacts, water scarcity, cost of resources (including oil), growth in visitor numbers, aging population and political insta-bility were the more certain factors. How environmental attitudes affect mobility, future legislation and how expensive oil would be were perceived as less certain (amongst others).

In the absence of certainty, there is a risk that analysts focus on those aspects that appear more certain, that is following established patterns, failing to recognize the

Table 6.1 Major drivers of change as they relate to the different components of the tourism system

		Peak Oil	Climate change impacts	Climate change policy	Environmental awareness	Demographic change	Global economy	Terrorism	Technology/ innovation	Pandemic
Tourism demand	Motivation		✓		✓	✓		✓	✓	✓
	Economic	✓		✓		✓	✓			
Transit provision	Operational	✓	✓	✓	✓	✓		✓	✓	✓
	Economic	✓					✓			
Tourism supply	Business	✓	✓	✓	✓	✓	✓		✓	
	Environmental resource	✓	✓		✓					

less certain events as potentially equally plausible factors of change. In fact, some would argue that unexpected or non-linear changes are more likely in the complex tourism system than the simple continuation of linear trends during times of (temporary) equilibriums (Farrell and Twining-Ward 2005). The problem of uncertainty has been identified by Butler (2009) as a major dichotomy within tourism, presenting itself as a tension between inertia and dynamism. As such, Butler argues for both evolutionary and revolutionary predictions for tourism destinations.

Timescales

Change can manifest incrementally or as a rapid shift. Rapid shifts may still follow relatively predictable linear patterns, or present themselves in the form of chaos, where periods of relative stability are ended abruptly and the system changes from one state to another within a very short period of time. The terminology from chaos theory is that a system moves toward 'the edge of chaos' until a trigger throws it into disarray and requires it to reorganize in a possibly very different way (Faulkner and Russell 1997). There are many examples of such chaotic changes within tourism, evident from individual businesses to whole destinations. The impact of a natural disaster could be a trigger to lead to a complete reorganization of a tourism destination. Running out of fossil fuels could be another factor that pushes tourism – or certain subsystems within tourism – over the edge of chaos, requiring restructuring as a very different system.

As a result of chaotic upheaval, it is possible that new properties of the tourism system will emerge. These might not have been foreseen under the previous conditions. For example, the introduction of jet engines triggered unprecedented movements of tourists around the globe to distant destinations, with irreversible effects on local communities and environments in the destination (often developing) countries. At the same time those global tourist flows made tourism one of the largest redistributors of wealth between industrialized and developing countries.

Climate change is commonly presented as a long-term problem with timescales of decades or centuries. Projections of sea-level rise, for example by the Intergovernmental Panel on Climate Change (2007), usually refer to a time span between the present and 2100 (predicted increases of 18–59 cm). Such longer-term changes are relevant for the environmental resources (see Table 6.1 within tourism supply) on which tourism is based, for example beaches. However, it is important to note that there is increasing debate about so-called tipping points and catastrophic changes in the climatic systems, such as a sudden change in ocean currents or the melting of Arctic ice. Also, other effects associated with climate change, such as consumer perceptions (see 'motivations' within tourism demand, Table 6.1), can become relevant much sooner than the actual biophysical effects (Scott and Becken 2010).

Magnitude

Drivers of change that appear more certain or predictable than others and manifest incrementally (e.g. the aging of the population) are easier to manage and are unlikely to impact at a magnitude that would impede tourism from operating. These drivers will moderately change the development of tourism but do not require major transformations. For this reason, they are referred to as *shapers*. Environmental awareness and climate change policies ('motivations' and 'policy' within tourism demand in Table 6.1) are examples of shapers (Scott and Becken 2010).

In contrast, some drivers of change pose a severe risk to tourism because they are able to almost fully constrain its functionality. These drivers are called *shifters* – often they are the less certain factors and preparation for their occurrence is limited. Table 6.1 highlights those drivers that are seen as shifters in their effect on specific elements of the tourism system. Peak Oil and its manifestation in rapidly increasing oil prices is seen as a major risk for tourism demand, the economics of transportation and tourism businesses. A large number of studies have linked oil prices to economic productivity, showing that higher prices lead to lower gross domestic product and disposable income, and thereby significantly affect tourists' propensity to travel (summarized in Becken *et al.* 2010). The transit route, i.e. transportation systems, is the weakest link in the system. Aviation costs in particular are likely to increase substantially, affecting those destinations for which no substitutes are available. Increased operational costs and reduced demand will affect airlines to the point of bankruptcy, as already experienced to some extent during the high oil prices of 2008 (Becken 2009). Hence, Peak Oil is seen as a shifter in relation to the transit element of the tourism system. Businesses involved in tourism will also be affected by Peak Oil, be it as a result of increasing operational costs, a worsening economic environment or reduced demand.

Impacts of climate change are also likely to force some destinations to shift to a new state. The Great Barrier Reef in Australia, for example, is recognized as the key attraction for visitors to Queensland. Yet there is a real risk that due to warming of sea temperatures and other factors, the reef will be gone in the foreseeable future, possibly as soon as 2030 (Turton *et al.* 2009). The consequences for the tourism destinations along the Queensland coast could be significant. Similarly, a growing body of literature highlights the likely changes for many alpine resorts that – under present climate conditions – provide opportunities for ski tourism (e.g. Dawson *et al.* 2009; Hennessy *et al.* 2008). Under climate change scenarios, many of the resorts, especially the low-lying ones, will face less snow, increasing snow lines and warmer temperatures that will make snowmaking uneconomical or impossible. Hence, a rapid restructuring (a shift) of the existing infrastructure may be required to adapt to these major changes.

Other shifters are the condition of the global economy, technological advancements for transportation and the occurrence of a global pandemic. The financial crisis in 2009 has shown how fragile Western countries have become with the increasing complexity of their finances and economic activities. In response to massive government-funded stimulation packages the recession was minimized, but in the longer term it is conceivable that similar events might happen again and that developed countries will not recover from them. With respect to technology it is theoretically possible that dramatically different systems evolve that allow for a continuation of individual mobility, but at the expense of personal freedom. Urry (2008) describes a future scenario of 'digital panopticum' based on the 'good intentions' scenario in the British Foresight Programme (Foresight 2006). In this scenario a new 'architecture of technologies and practices' (Foresight 2006: 270) emerges in the form of smart and digitized transport systems that provide an alternative to the automobile-driven society of today. Finally, as recent epidemics of SARS (severe acute respiratory syndrome) and swine flu demonstrated, the occurrence of a global pandemic has the potential to shift tourism to a new state of extremely reduced travel and minimal exchange between countries.

Conclusion

This chapter provided an overview of existing 'future' studies for tourism. Clearly, there is a demand for understanding possible changes in the future and preparing for them. Investors make decisions based on anticipated demand, destinations prepare for the future through product development and marketing and businesses – while often operating under shorter timeframes – also benefit from information that assists their planning for the future.

However, this chapter also criticized the fact that many of the tourism forecasts, projections and scenarios are based on false assumptions of certainty, by simply following historic trends and extrapolating them into the future. This linearity does not always exist and in reality, there is great uncertainty around timescales and the magnitude of changes. It has been argued in this chapter that the present approach might pick up on shapers, but is likely to underestimate the importance of so-called shifters – drivers of change that have the potential to substantially revolutionize tourism or eradicate components of it irreversibly. Part of the failure to grasp the implications of the occurrence of shifters is a common tendency to understand tourism systems as equilibriums, when really they are dynamic systems that are constantly changing and adapting to change (Urry 2008).

The imminence of Peak Oil is the most prominent example where analyses fail to fully integrate its effects on the future of tourism. While some analyses mention the depletion of (cheap) oil resources as a factor, they still – paradoxically – believe that the current trends of economic growth, increasing wealth and global connectedness will prevail. Whether the root cause of this omission lies in collective denial (Cohen 2001), lack of understanding, technophilia, a tendency to deliver a positive message to those who fund the analysis in question, or simply our inability to imagine a society so different to the one we live in today remains unresolved. It is suggested, though, that future studies for tourism are approached in a more critical manner, for example by using a risk-management framework that allows for inclusion of low probability–high-impact events, or for those events that are probable but uncertain in their ramifications (such as Peak Oil). More 'realistic' scenarios for the future are likely to generate the greater long-term benefit for tourism because they allow participants to make informed decisions for their own risk management.

References

Aal, C. (2007) 'Leisure Time and Sustainable Development: Results from a Norwegian Survey', paper presented at the ESF workshop on changing housing and leisure time cultures, Minorca, Spain 21–23 March 2007, online. Available at www.slideshare.net/anskaar/leisure-time-and-sustainable-development (accessed 5 January 2012).

Aguiar, M. and Hurst, E. (2006) *Measuring Trends in Leisure: The Allocation of Time over Five Decades*, Working Paper No. 6–2, Federal Reserve Bank of Boston, online. Available at www.bos.frb.org/economic/wp/wp2006/wp0602.pdf (accessed 5 January 2012).

Amadeus (2009) *Future Traveller Tribes 2020. Report for the Air Travel Industry*, online. Available at www.amadeus.com/amadeus/documents/corporate/TravellerTribes.pdf (accessed 5 January 2012).

Becken, S. (2007) 'Tourists' Perception of International Air Travel's Impact on the Global Climate and Potential Climate Change Policies', *Journal of Sustainable Tourism*, 15(4): 351–368.

——— (2009) 'Global Challenges for Tourism and Transport: How will Climate Change and Energy affect the Future of Tourist Travel?', in S. Page (ed.) *Transport and Tourism – Global Perspectives*, 3rd edn, Essex: Pearson Education Limited, pp. 328–342.

——— (2011) 'A Critical Review of Tourism and Oil', *Annals of Tourism Research*, 38(2): 359–379.

Becken, S., Ngyen, M. and Schiff, A. (2010) 'Developing an Economic Framework for Tourism and Oil', *LEaP Report 12*, online. Available at www.lincoln.ac.nz/leap (accessed 5 January 2012).

Bosshart, D. and Frick, K. (2006) *The Future of Leisure Travel – Trend Study*, Kuoni, online. Available at www.gdi.ch (accessed 5 January 2012).

Butler, R. (2009) 'Tourism in the Future: Cycles, Waves or Wheels?', *Futures*, 41(6): 346–352.

Cohen, S. (2001) *States of Denial. Knowing about Atrocities and Suffering*, Cambridge: Polity Press.

Cole, S. and Razak, V. (2009) 'Tourism as Future', *Futures*, 41(6): 335–345.

Dawson, J., Scott, D. and McBoyle, G. (2009) 'Analogue Analysis of Climate Change Vulnerability in the US Northeast Ski Tourism', *Climate Research*, 39(1): 1–9.

DEFRA (2007) 'Public Understanding of Sustainable Leisure and Tourism', research report completed for the Department for Environment, Food and Rural Affairs by the University of Surrey, online. Available at www.defra.gov.uk (accessed 20 March 2008).

Dickinson, J. (2009) *Slow Tourism Travel for a Lower Carbon Future*, Bournemouth University, online. Available at www.bournemouth.ac.uk/icthr/PDFs/rgsnontech.pdf (accessed 5 February 2010).

Draper, S., Goodman, J., Hardyment, R. and Murray, V. (2009) *Tourism 2023. Four Scenarios, a Vision and a Strategy for UK Outbound Travel and Tourism*, Forum for the Future, online. Available at www.forumforthefuture.org/projects/travel-and-tourism (accessed 15 January 2010).

Dwyer, L., Edwards, D., Mistilis, N., Roman, C., Scott, N. and Cooper, C. (2008) *Megatrends Underpinning Tourism to 2020. Analysis of Key Drivers for Change*, Gold Coast, Australia: CRC for Sustainable Tourism.

Emery, F. (1981) 'Alternative Futures in Tourism', *International Journal of Tourism Management*, 2(1): 49–67.

European Travel Commission (2004) *Tourism Trends for Europe*, online. Available at www.etc-corporate.org (accessed 20 October 2010).

Farrell, B. and Twining-Ward, L. (2005) 'Seven Steps Towards Sustainability: Tourism in the Context of New Knowledge', *Journal of Sustainable Tourism*, 13(2): 109–122.

Faulkner, B. and Russell, R. (1997) 'Chaos and Complexity in Tourism: In Search of a New Perspective', *Pacific Tourism Review*, 1(2): 93–102.

Foresight (2006) *Intelligent Information Futures. Project Overview*, London: Department for Trade and Industry.

Hennessy, K.J., Whetton, P.H., Walsh, K., Smith, I.N., Bathols, J.M., Hutchinson, M. and Sharples, J. (2008) 'Climate Change Effects on Snow Conditions in Mainland Australia and Adaptation at Ski Resorts through Snowmaking', *Climate Research*, 35(3): 255–270.

Intergovernmental Panel on Climate Change (2007) *Fourth Assessment Report (AR4). Summary for Policymakers. Synthesis Report*, Contribution of Working Groups I, II and III to the Fourth Assessment Report of the Intergovernmental Panel on Climate Change. Geneva, Switzerland, online. Available at www.ipcc.ch/publications_and_data/ publications_ipcc_fourth_assessment_report_synthesis_report.htm (accessed 5 January 2012).

Leiper, N. (1995) *Tourism Management*, Melbourne: RMIT Press.

New Zealand Ministry of Tourism (2010) *New Zealand Tourism Forecasts 2010–2016. Summary Document*, Wellington: New Zealand Ministry of Tourism.

Scott, D. and Becken, S. (2010) 'Adapting to Climate Change and Climate Policy: Progress, Problems and Potentials', *Journal of Sustainable Tourism*, 18(3): 283–295.

Scottish Enterprise (2004) *Future Trends in Lifestyle and Leisure. Getting Ready for Tomorrow's Tourism Today*, online. Available at www.scottish-enterprise.com (accessed 5 January 2012).

Tourism Victoria (no date) *Trends affecting the World Tourism Industry. Strategic Plan 2002–2006*, online. Available at www.tourism.vic.gov.au/strategicplan/plan2002_2006/1_ introduction/assets/intro_graph2.pdf (accessed 5 January 2012).

Turton, S., Hadwen, W. and Wilson, R. (eds.) (2009) *The Impacts of Climate Change on Australian Tourism Destinations: Developing Adaptation and Response Strategies – a Scoping Study*, Gold Coast, Australia: CRC for Sustainable Tourism.

UNESCO (2007) *Case Studies on Climate Change and World Heritage*, Paris: UNESCO World Heritage Centre.

UNWTO (2001) *Tourism 2020 Vision*, Madrid: World Tourism Organization.

—— (2006) *Mega-trends of Tourism in Asia Pacific*, Madrid: World Tourism Organization.

—— (2010) 'World Tourism Barometer', 8(1), online. Available at unwto.org/facts/eng/ pdf/barometer/UNWTO_Barom10_1_en_excerpt.pdf (accessed 5 January 2012).

Urry, J. (2008) 'Climate Change, Travel and Complex Futures', *The British Journal of Sociology*, 59(1): 261–279.

—— (2010) 'Consuming the Planet to Excess', *Theory, Culture & Society*, 27(2–3): 1–22.

Yeoman, I., Greenwod, C. and McMahon-Beattie, U. (2009) 'The Future of Scotland's International Tourism Markets', *Futures*, 41(6): 387–395.

7 Tourism and quality of life

Nicos L. Kartakoullis, George Karlis,
Kostas Karadakis, Amanda Sharaf and
Craig Webster

Introduction

The new millennium has witnessed major changes in tourism. The changes have been driven by a number of factors – the threat of terrorism, the global economy, the changing needs of travelers, the need to be entertained and the desire to have the ultimate tourism experience to enhance one's quality of life (Karlis 2011). Tourism service providers today are thus posed with more challenges than ever, ultimately to ascertain that the tourist experience is one that leads to an enhanced quality of life. In an ever-competitive world with a mixture of expanding tourism markets (for example, Turkey and India) and traditional tourism markets (for example, Greece and Italy), it has now become more important than ever for service providers to enhance awareness of quality of life and its relationship to tourism. This chapter purports to contribute to the limited research that exists in this area.

Specifically, the intent of this chapter is to depict the relationship between tourism and quality of life through the overview of selected existing theories and literature. To fulfill this intent, this chapter commences with an understanding of tourism and an understanding of quality of life. It then proceeds to overview two social theories linked to tourism and quality of life – social exchange theory, and expectancy value theory. Then it proceeds to the relationship between tourism and quality of life articulated through two dimensions: (1) quality of life and tourism impacts, and (2) quality of life and the satisfaction with the tourism experience. Finally, it comments on the trends in tourism and quality of life and what challenges this poses for tourism in the next few decades.

Understanding tourism

Tourism is understood to be the temporary movement of people outside of their places of work and residence (Mathieson and Wall 1982). According to Kelly (1996), tourism is distinguished from any other activity in that it requires an overnight stay or a distance to be traveled of over 100 miles. Regardless of how tourism is defined objectively, it is primarily a subjective and intrinsic experience. Similar to leisure, tourism relates to both leisure and recreation. According to

Butler (1999), tourism is considered a part of leisure, in the sense that it takes place during leisure time or when a person is 'at leisure'. Tourism is also understood to be a part of recreation, in that it consists of traveling amongst other activities (Butler 1999). Mieczowski (1981) illustrates this relationship in his conceptualization of the relationship among leisure, recreation and tourism. His conceptualization implies that tourism is an aspect of recreation, which in turn comprises a portion of leisure (Mieczowski 1981).

Like leisure, tourism maintains similar properties, including a number of motivations and satisfactions. According to Kelly (1996), tourism produces satisfactions intrinsic to the experience itself. For the most part, tourism involves some degree of freedom and self-determination when engaging in travel. Satisfactions in companionship, including opportunities to reconnect and re-establish connections with others, are also part of the experience. Finally, satisfactions in reaching the destination, as well as satisfactions in learning and understanding different and new regions and cultures, are some of the motivating factors associated with the experience.

Reasons for choosing to travel vary depending on the motivations and preferences of the individual along with other demographic and life-cycle factors. Plog's (1974) typology may provide some understanding explaining how individual personalities determine travel interests. It consists of a continuum ranging from psychocentric tendencies to allocentric tendencies. Psychocentric tendencies are characterized by self-centeredness and predictable leisure patterns, while pure allocentric tendencies are focused on things beyond the self, involving an interest in experimenting outside of the individual's own realm. For the most part, Plog (1974) identified that most people fall somewhere in between the two tendency types, consisting of both psychocentric and allocentric characteristics. Both of these typologies may be linked to the ultimate of experience of travel – that is, enhanced quality of life.

Quality of life

Quality of life is a people-centered notion. The emphasis of quality of life is on people – those directly affected by an experience and those indirectly affected by an experience. Tourism is an experience that tends to be self-selected for the ultimate goal of pleasure, satisfaction and relaxation (Karlis 2011). The link between tourism and quality of life is an obvious one, yet little research exists in tourism to articulate this relationship. Tourism is an experience that can have either a positive and/or negative effect on an individual or a group (community) of individuals and on quality of life.

Research suggests that quality of life refers to individuals' multi-attribute assessment of their lives and includes a threefold structure, consisting of one cognitive element (life satisfaction) and two affective elements: (a) the existence of positive effect, and (b) the lack of negative effect. These elements describe different characteristics of quality of life, but are not completely separate (Suh *et al.* 1996), and are assumed to represent a single characteristic. Thus quality of life is influenced by the positive and negative impacts associated with either hosting an event and tourism development or the experience as a tourist.

Literature shows that there are many definitions of subjective wellbeing. Diener (1994) describes subjective wellbeing as the extent to which a person evaluates their overall quality of life in a positive way. For Diener and Lucas (1999) subjective wellbeing is a complex notion that encompasses: (1) an individual's emotional responses (pleasant–unpleasant affects), (2) an individual's overall satisfactions, and (3) an individual's global judgments of life satisfaction.

For Stathi *et al.* (2002), understanding quality of life is a complex phenomenon. Specifically, for Stathi *et al.* (2002) it is a self-expression, self-understanding and self-evaluation conducted by the individual of their quality or state of existence. This state of existence is related to behavior, in particular the outcome of a behavior or experience. From a tourism perspective, the quality of a tourism experience may be shaped by the social exchanges resulting from the experience – social exchange theory – or by the expectancies one has from the tourism experiences – expectancy-value theory.

Social exchange theory

Social exchange theory has been an effective theory in order to gain an understanding of residents' perceptions of tourism (Ap 1992). The advantages of using social exchange theory are that it can help explain positive and negative attitudes, and investigates exchanges at the individual or communal level (Ap 1992). Social exchange theory states that residents are more inclined to engage in exchange with others if they believe they will receive benefits without acquiring intolerable expenses (Gursoy and Kendall 2006). Social exchange theory is a behavioral theory that aims to understand and predict individuals' reactions in an interactive process (Ap 1990). It is a social interaction theory examining the individual or community's willingness to take part in an exchange with others if the individual or community believes that they will benefit from the exchange (Deccio and Baloglu 2002). Social exchange theory is useful in the study of resident attitudes towards tourism because it may clarify residents' motives and reasons for engaging into an exchange process with tourists or their lack of support for such an exchange (Deccio and Baloglu 2002). The common theme is that individuals or communities tend to partake in an exchange with tourists if they recognize that the exchange will result in a gain. Therefore, if individuals or community members feel that their quality of life improves or there is a perceived improvement to their quality of life from engaging in tourist exchanges or tourism development, the individual or community will continue to support tourism development. The literature indicates that the economic, tourism/commercial, physical/environment and social/cultural impacts are expected to influence residents' quality of life and their motivation to be involved in an exchange and to support tourism development or hosting an event in their community (Yoon *et al.* 2001).

It is important to note that the exchange theory is not stagnant; residents constantly reassess the exchange operation (Waitt 2003). Social exchange theory is more complex than is suggested in the literature mentioned above. It involves not only an assessment of immediate perceived benefits and costs, but also of longer-term benefits and costs. Also, the theory includes prior experience as a component in determining residents' expectations. For example, if a resident has experienced negative outcomes (disruption from everyday life associated with construction) from previous interactions with hosting the event or from tourism development, this affects their assessment of a beneficial outcome from future interactions and vice versa. Before any initial exchange occurs, perceptions about the event are established and serve as a benchmark for future assessments about the importance of exchange. Post-event or once tourism has been developed, residents will re-examine the exchanges that occur and the results observed to be above the benchmark will be seen as positive impacts, with the opposite for outcomes below the benchmark. The results that are seen as positive impacts on the residents' quality of life will be considered a gain for the residents which will in turn provide positive views or support toward future tourism initiatives. This will also set a new standard that will be used by the residents in order to evaluate support for future events and future tourism development (Yoon *et al.* 2001). As can be seen, using social exchange theory can help identify which factors influence positive support for an event through the exchanges that they experience.

A challenge with using social exchange theory is that over time, the exchange process discussed above may not be important for the residents because the exchange process is not closely related to the event or tourism and the tangible outcomes the event or tourism activities brings about. Another challenge with using social exchange theory is that it has a tendency to assume rational information processing which does not consider responses that are established in personal and social values (Fredline 2005).

Expectancy-value theory

Broadly speaking, this theory speculates that a person's expectancies for success and the value they have for success indicate motivation to perform tasks for success (Wigfield 1994). Expectancy-value theory implies that a person familiarizes themselves to a community through expectations (beliefs) and evaluations (Palmgreen 1984). Within this approach behavior and attitudes can be viewed as a function of (1) expectancy (or belief) – the chance that an object is seen to have a specific attribute or that a behavior will have a specific outcome; and (2) evaluation – the level of affect linked to a characteristic or behavioral outcome, whether it be positive or negative (Palmgreen 1984).

The expectancy-value theory has been advanced in the tourism literature by Lindberg and Johnson (1997a) to help explain social behaviors (Eagly and Chaiken 1993). According to Fredline (2005) there is a relationship between the importance residents put on specific outcomes (values) and how much they believe a tourism event adds to these outcomes (expectancy). Expectancy-value theory is fairly new in the tourism literature, but is very helpful in identifying motivating factors that can help determine support for a tourism event. Knowing what residents value and expect out of an event can help organizers plan for improvements within the community that in turn can improve the quality of life for the residents. Furthermore, this theory can help maximize positive impacts and minimize negative impacts experienced by the community, ultimately enhancing quality of life, thus creating support for future events and tourism development.

Quality of life and tourism impacts

The importance of studying quality of life and the impacts tourism has on a community's quality of life is to evaluate both the physical design and the individuals' subjective perspectives (Morrison Institute for Public Policy 1997). As the literature above suggests, defining quality of life is difficult, although there is agreement that quality of life consists of multiple dimensions comprised of an individual's life and environment (Andereck *et al.* 2007). According to Andereck *et al.* (2007: 484) quality of life 'refers to one's satisfaction with life, and feelings of contentment or fulfillment with one's experience in the world. It is how people view, or what they feel about, their lives.' Although it is important to note that individuals experience and interpret similar situations and circumstances differently (Taylor and Bogdan 1996), the tourism industry can serve as a catalyst in order to build infrastructure that improves a community's quality of life (Andereck *et al.* 2007).

According to Mattson (1990) in order to improve a community's quality of life the community needs to ensure that their economic development strategies are in line with the community's central character. This can be achieved through conserving their landmarks, heritage sites and the unique destination characteristics that attract tourists and businesses (Andereck *et al.* 2007). This strategy has been linked with tourism development initiatives. These developments and the tourism industry have increasingly been credited with increasing the quality of life for residents by developing and attracting festivals, restaurants, natural and cultural attractions, outdoor recreation opportunities and sporting events which residents, the community and tourists can participate and enjoy (Andereck *et al.* 2007). Andereck *et al.* (2007: 485) suggests that quality of life:

> is improved through tourism developments if a community and the residents experience an increase in the standard of living, increased tax revenues, increased employment opportunities and economic diversity, all of which may create a positive impact on a resident's perception of quality of life.

However, negative impacts to quality of life must be considered, and studies suggest that negative impacts can include crowding, traffic congestion, an increase in crime, cost of living, tension between residents and tourists and a disruption in residents' everyday life (Andereck *et al.* 2007; Ap and Crompton 1993; McCool and Martin 1994).

Studying the impacts of tourism on residents and a community's quality of life is important because it assists in examining residents' attitudes and perceptions with regard to tourism, and helps identify which factors lead to resident support for tourism development (Perdue *et al.* 1999). Studies have found that the factors that influence quality of life that are associated with tourism impacts and development are often categorized as: (1) economic, such as tax burdens, inflation and job availability; (2) sociocultural, such as community image, the availability of festivals and museums and awareness of cultural heritage; and (3) environmental, such as crowding, air, water and noise pollution, wildlife destruction and litter (Andereck *et al.* 2007; Andereck and Vogt 2000; McGehee and Andereck 2004).

Other studies that have measured perceptions of quality of life impacts associated with tourism have looked at the net economic gain, minimal impact to everyday life, having recreation infrastructures in place, beautiful environments, positive interactions between residents and tourists, an understanding and tolerance for community/culture and inclusion of local residents in the decision-making process (Andereck *et al.* 2007; Lindberg and Johnson 1997b). Furthermore, Liu and Var's (1986) study found that residents' attitudes towards tourism are influenced by economic, sociocultural and environmental impacts, with residents indicating that it was economic and cultural impacts providing benefits to the community, while the social and environmental costs were not seen as negative impacts of tourism.

In a subsequent study, Andereck *et al.* (2007) found that tourism impacts that were self-valued were important for quality of life. Quality of life is 'essential for residents' satisfaction with their community, personal lives, activities and environment', according to Andereck *et al.* (2007: 498). The empirical findings indicate that residents view tourism development as having both positive and negative impacts on quality of life (Andereck *et al.* 2007: 498).

In sum, the impacts of tourism are closely linked with quality of life, particularly from the perspective of enhancing the positive and reducing the negative. Research by Kreag (2001) provides a comprehensive overview of the types of impact of tourism from a positive and negative perspective. Each of these impacts of tourism can have a direct or indirect effect on the quality of life of an individual and/or group of individual (community).

Tourism provides a number of benefits and costs to both the tourist and the host community. From an economic perspective, tourism contributes to a region's economy. Tourism, like leisure, is linked to a region's level of economic development. The extent to which individuals have opportunities for leisure depends upon the money they have available to spend, the leisure goods and services available for purchase, how much time they have available and the availability of leisure good and services (Russell 2005). The relationship between the economy, leisure and tourism is reciprocal in nature, in that the economy creates shifts in leisure and tourism, and vice-versa (Russell 2005). The economic benefits for the host community are the most significant in promoting tourism within a specific region (Kim 2002). For the most part, tourism plays a substantial role in providing jobs for individuals within the host communities. In addition to the creation of jobs, the development and improvement of infrastructure also contributes significantly to a region's economy (Kelly and Freysinger 2000). In addition to some of the direct benefits, there are secondary benefits accrued to the local businesses supporting the tourists within the region, through the provision of goods and services required by tourists. The extent of economic cooperation that takes place within a region is also a significant benefit to the community, involving the collaboration between developers and local host communities (Kelly and Freysinger 2000).

Tourism also produces a number of social and cultural benefits. It can create opportunities to develop indoor and outdoor facilities and parks and other infrastructure, which can be beneficial to the locals within the community (Lankford and Howard 1994; Liu and Var 1986). Other social developments are evident with the development of ecotourism and cultural tourism, where tourists are exposed to the real authenticity of a region, all while minimizing negative impacts to the environment (Kelly and Freysinger 2000). Additionally, both the local people within the host community as well as tourists experience different lifestyles and cultures, enabling greater cross-cultural understanding (Belisle and Hoy 1980; Kelly 1996; Kelly and Freysinger 2000).

Environmental benefits as a result of tourism have also been discussed. Tourism can help preserve the environment through increased investments in its infrastructure (Kelly and Freysinger 2000). Through the use of ecotourism, tourists are able to experience and appreciate natural environments in environmentally sustainable ways that promote their preservation (Kelly and Freysinger 2000).

In addition to some of the benefits, there are economic costs associated with tourism. The development of jobs within the region may be low-wage or exploitative in nature. As a result of foreign investment and domination within the region, the interests of capitalist investors are supported first and foremost, and workers' wages are kept low to produce the greatest profit. Additionally, the hiring of managers and from outside the host community means that professional opportunities are not available for local people, producing economic losses amongst the host community (Kelly and Freysinger 2000).

Social and cultural costs are also a result of tourism. For the most part, the local community may experience a loss of leisure resources due to the influx of tourists as well as tourists' greater purchasing power in utilizing certain leisure resources and facilities (Kelly and Freysinger 2000). Additionally, the costs of tourism include congestion and crowding in public spaces, as well as other social costs such as prostitution, drugs and other activities affecting the host community. Mass tourism also impacts traditional ways of living, where tourists who are unaware of local culture, may disrupt local traditions and cultures to obtain certain experiences (Kelly and Freysinger 2000).

Although tourism can enhance the preservation and appreciation of a locale though increased awareness among tourists, there are negative environmental impacts. Some of these are a result of the development of infrastructure to support capitalist interests. For the host country, the costs may include damage and destruction to the environment in order to accommodate new developments (Kelly

1996). Other sources of environmental degradation include pollution, over-crowding and waste to natural environments (Kim 2002). The increase in concern over the environmental impacts of tourism has led to growth in alternative forms of tourism, such as nature tourism and ecotourism (Butler 1999). Understanding the benefits and costs of tourism are essential for planners and developers interested in developing a tourist destination within a community and ultimately enhancing the quality of life of tourists and residents. It is the residents within the community who are most affected by the effects of tourism, and obtaining their support will be integral to successful tourism planning and development.

Quality of life and travel and tourism

Understanding the level of tourist satisfaction with travel and tourism services may be dependent upon the individual's overall reflection on the trip itself (Neal *et al.* 1999). Although tourism plays a part of the leisure experience, satisfaction with the travel and tourism experience may directly affect life satisfaction, rather than contribute to leisure satisfaction (Neal *et al.* 1999). According to Neal *et al.* (1999), satisfaction with instrumental indicators include: (1) the physical conditions associated with a travel experience, and (2) expressive factors characterized by feelings associated with the travel experience. Both of these are significant in determining overall satisfaction with the travel experience.

From the tourist's perspective, overall satisfaction with the travel experience is greatly dependent upon the satisfaction derived from the overall reflection on the trip, as well as the levels of satisfaction with each stage of the trip (Neal *et al.* 1999). According to Clawson and Knetsch (1971) there are stages to travel which include: (1) preparation for the trip, such as motivations, gathering information and making arrangements, (2) transportation services used en route to the destination, (3) the use of destination services through travel and tourism service providers, and (4) the use of services to return home from the destination. Satisfaction with each of the stages of travel contributes to overall satisfaction with travel services and the quality of life of travelers (Neal *et al.* 1999).

Subjective measures in determining satisfaction with the overall trip experience can also lead to an understanding of tourism's relationship to quality of life. Reflections on the trip characteristics of leisure, such as freedom, level of involvement, level of arousal, level of mastery and spontaneity may also lead to one's perceived quality of life (Unger and Kernan 1983). Trip reflections are significant in producing long-term satisfaction for travelers (Neal *et al.* 1999). For travel planners within the tourism industry, ensuring that travelers are satisfied with their services is a significant aspect of building a successful tourism and travel industry within their region.

Conclusion

The experience of tourism for both tourists and the people of the community (travel destination) may lead to an enhanced quality of life. This analysis has identified how quality of life may be enhanced through the impacts of tourism on the community and the individual and the satisfaction with the tourism experience. Indeed, the relationship between tourism and quality of life is evident though the potential of the tourism experience to bring joy, satisfaction and pleasure and feelings of accomplishment to tourists and to those impacted by tourism.

Those responsible for the provision of tourism services and for the marketing of tourism products would benefit from an enhanced understanding of the relationship between tourism and quality of life. Quality of life is the ultimate goal of tourism, particularly for a tourism experience that is driven by pleasure. Tourism practitioners, administrators and service providers should ultimately seek to understand and examine means to enhance the quality of life not only of tourists but those in the community that may benefit from the tourism experience.

In terms of the future, those who deal with issues linked with tourism would be wise to investigate the link between how individuals experience tourism and their quality of life. There are, for example, global changes that are occurring that would likely play an important role in this. For example, with the growth of Asian economies, it would be wise for researchers to look into how tourists in the future, many more of whom will be from Asia, consider the relationship between tourism and quality of life. Will the newly wealthy classes in developing countries consider the quality of life issues and tourism in the same way as the traditional tourists from the more developed countries? This is an issue to be looked into, since the perception of tourism and its relationship with quality of life may not follow the Western model.

There are other global changes that may influence how people consider tourism and its relationship with quality of life. For example, if the future is an expansion of free markets and post-World War Two growth, we would expect that the entire tourism industry globally would continue to benefit from the continuation of affluence and will merely have to adjust to cultural dimensions linked with the new tourists from newly wealthy countries (not entirely Asian). However, if the future is less rosy and is linked with declining access to food and natural resources, as those who are most pessimistic about the future suspect, then a whole new thinking about what the role of tourism will be is most likely. Indeed, if there is a shrinking middle class that has the means to enjoy mass tourism, it may be that there will be a return to a 'plantation' vision of tourism. All will be done to appeal to the shrinking pool of persons who can afford tourism with little or no concern for the costs of the host community, apart from getting access to cash from the tourist class.

References

Andereck, K.L. and Vogt, C. (2000) 'The Relationship Between Residents' Attitudes Toward Tourism and Tourism Development Options', *Journal of Travel Research*, 39(1): 27–36.

Andereck, K.L., Valentine, K., Vogt, C. and Knopf, R. (2007) 'A Cross-cultural Analysis of Tourism and Quality of Life Perceptions', *Journal of Sustainable Tourism*, 15(5): 483–500.

Ap, J. (1990) 'Residents' Perceptions Research on the Social Impacts of Tourism', *Annals of Tourism Research*, 17(4): 610–616.

—— (1992) 'Resident Perceptions on Tourism Impacts', *Annals of Tourism Research*, 19(4): 665–690.

Ap, J. and Crompton, J.L. (1993) 'Residents' Strategies for Responding to Tourism Impacts', *Journal of Travel Research*, 32(1): 47–50.

Belisle, F.J. and Hoy, D.R. (1980) 'The Perceived Impact of Tourism by Residents. A Case Study in Santa Marta, Columbia', *Annals of Tourism Research*, 7(2): 83–101.

Butler, R.W. (1999) 'Understanding Tourism', in E.L. Jackson and T.L. Burton (eds.) *Leisure Studies: Prospects for the Twenty-first Century*, State College, PA: Venture Publishing, pp. 97–116.

Clawson, M. and Knetsch, J.L. (1971) *Economics of Outdoor Recreation*, Baltimore, MD and London: The Johns Hopkins Press.

Deccio, C. and Baloglu, S. (2002) 'Nonhost Community Resident Reactions to the 2002 Winter Olympics: The Spillover Impacts', *Journal of Travel Research*, 41(1): 46–56.

Diener, E. (1994) 'Assessing Subjective Well-being: Progress and Opportunities', *Social Indicators Research*, 31(2): 103–157.

Diener, E. and Lucas, R.E. (1999) 'Personality and Subjective Well-being', in D. Kahneman, E. Diener and N. Schwarz (eds.) *Well-Being: The foundations of Hedonic Psychology*, New York: Sage Foundation.

Eagly, A. and Chaiken, S. (1993) *The Psychology of Attitudes*, Orlando, FL: Harcourt Brace Jovanovich.

Fredline, E. (2005) 'Host and Guest Relations and Sport Tourism', *Sport in Society*, 8(2): 263–279.

Gursoy, D. and Kendall, K.W. (2006) 'Hosting Mega Events: Modeling Locals' Support', *Annals of Tourism Research*, 33(3): 603–623.

Karlis, G. (2011) *Leisure and Recreation in Canadian Society: An Introduction*, 2nd edn, Toronto: Thompson Educational.

Kelly, J.R. (1996) *Leisure*, 2nd edn, Needham Heights, MA: Allyn and Bacon.

Kelly, J.R. and Freysinger, V.J. (2000) *21st Century Leisure: Current Issues*, Needham Heights, MA: Allyn and Bacon.

Kim, K. (2002) *The Effects of Tourism Impacts upon Quality of Life of Residents in the Community*, Doctoral dissertation, Virginia Polytechnic Institute and State University, online. Available at scholar.lib.vt.edu/theses/available/etd-12062002-123337/unrestricted/Title_and_Text.pdf. (accessed 12 February 2011).

Kreag, G. (2001) *The Impacts of Tourism*, Duluth, MN: University of Minnesota.

Lankford, G. and Howard, D. (1994) 'Developing a Tourism Impact Attitude Scale', *Annals of Tourism Research*, 21(1): 121–139.

Lindberg, K. and Johnson, R.L. (1997a) 'The Economic Values of Tourism's Social Impacts', *Annals of Tourism Research*, 24(1): 90–116.

—— (1997b) 'Modeling Resident Attitudes Toward Tourism', *Annals of Tourism Research*, 24(2): 402–424.

Liu, J.C. and Var, T. (1986) 'Resident Attitudes Toward Tourism Impacts in Hawaii', *Annals of Tourism Research*, 13(2): 193–214.

Mathieson, A. and Wall, G. (1982) *Tourism, Economic, Physical and Social Impacts*, London: Longman.

Mattson, G.A. (1990) 'Municipal Services and Economic Policy Priorities among Florida's Smaller Cities: A Comparison by Public Officials', *National Civic Review*, 79(5): 436–445.

McCool, S. and Martin, S. (1994) 'Community Attachment and Attitudes Towards Tourism Development', *Journal of Travel Research*, 32(3): 29–34.

McGehee, N. and Andereck, K.L. (2004) 'Factors Predicting Rural Residents' Support of Tourism', *Journal of Travel Research*, 43(2): 131–140.

Mieczowski, Z.T. (1981) 'Some Notes on the Geography of Tourism: A Comment', *The Canadian Geographer*, 25(2): 186–191.

Morrison Institute for Public Policy (1997) *What Matters in Greater Phoenix: 1997 Indicators of our Quality of Life*, Tempe, AZ: Arizona State University.

Neal, J.D., Sirgy, M.J. and Uysal, M. (1999) 'The Role of Satisfaction with Leisure Travel/ tourism Services and Experience in Satisfaction with Leisure Life and Overall Life', *Journal of Business Research*, 44(3): 153–163.

Palmgreen, P. (1984) 'Uses and Gratifications: A Theoretical Perspective', in R. N. Bostrom (ed.) *Communication Yearbook 8*, Beverly Hills, CA: Sage Publications.

Perdue, R., Long, P. and Kang, Y.S. (1999) 'Boomtown Tourism and Resident Quality of Life: The Marketing of Gaming to Host Community Residents', *Journal of Business Research*, 44(3): 165–177.

Plog, S.C. (1974) 'Why Destination Areas Rise and Fall in Popularity', *Cornell Hotel and Restaurant Administration Quarterly*, 14(4): 55–58.

Russell, R. (2005) *Pastimes: The Context of Contemporary Leisure*, 3rd edn, Champaign: IL: Sagamore Publishing.

Stathi, A., Fox, R. and McKenna, J. (2002) 'Physical Activity and Dimensions of Subjective Well-being in Older Adults', *Journal of Aging and Physical Activity*, 10(1): 76–92.

Suh, E., Diener, E. and Fujita, F. (1996) 'Events and Subjective Well-being: Only Recent Events Matter', *Journal of Personality and Social Psychology*, 70(5): 1091–1102.

Taylor, S.J. and Bogdan, R. (1996) 'Quality of Life and the Individual's Perspective', in R. L. Schalock (ed.) *Quality of Life Volume 1: Conceptualization and Measurement*, Washington, DC: American Association on Mental Retardation.

Unger, L.S. and Kernan, J.B. (1983) 'On the Meaning of Leisure: An Investigation on Some Determinants of the Subjective Leisure Experience', *Journal of Consumer Research*, 9(4): 381–392.

Waitt, G. (2003) 'Social Impacts of the Sydney Olympics', *Annals of Tourism Research*, 30(1): 194–215.

Wigfield, A. (1994) 'Expectancy-value Theory of Achievement Motivation: A Developmental Perspective', *Educational Psychology Review*, 6(1): 49–78.

Yoon, Y., Gursoy, D. and Chen, S.J. (2001) 'Validating a Tourism Development Theory with Structural Equation Modeling', *Tourism Management*, 22(4): 363–372.

8   Through a glass darkly

The future of tourism is personal

C. Michael Hall

Introduction

This is a chapter about the future of tourism and tourism studies. Both are considered because they are inextricably linked, although the degree of real influence that academics have on the trajectory of tourism development is a moot point. The focus of the chapter is on the forces that shape contemporary tourism. It is also a personal view. Indeed, it has to be because from a social constructionist perspective the selection of method, epistemology, approach, ontology, problem definition and what you say in publications and where you choose to say it reflects the values of the author. Therefore, rather than hide behind a thin veneer of empiricist rationality, the author has decided to be much more intellectually honest.

Playing the futurist

I do not claim to be a futurist. I particularly do not proclaim to be the world's only professional crystal ball-gazer or a futurologist specializing in travel and tourism, especially when there are numerous other people who write on the future of travel and tourism. However, I am interested in tourism futures and futures generally, and am even willing to write about them (e.g., Hall 2000, 2005) and make predictions (see Hall 2000). Indeed, it is hard to finish off a publication, especially a book, without saying something about the future (e.g., Gössling and Hall 2006a; Hall and Härkönen 2006; Hall and Sharples 2008), even if only in terms of the future research agenda that might exist.

This is not to decry the efforts of those who do make a professional living out of predicting the future. Gambling is after all one of the world's largest industries – legal or otherwise. Unfortunately, the search for profit via educated gambling (educated because the proponents have usually undertaken an MBA or at least a finance course at a business school) has very much become integral to the global financial and economic system. We are now enveloped, as Susan Strange wrote in 1997, by 'casino capitalism', whereby:

> The Western Financial System is rapidly coming to resemble nothing as much as a vast casino. Every day games are played in this casino that involve

sums of money so large that they cannot be imagined. At night the games go on at the other side of the world.

(Strange 1997: 1)

Unfortunately, such games have real consequences for individual livelihoods and wellbeing, including those of academics. Clearly, a rise in interest rates or the loss of a job or a market for one's product and services has an economic impact, but these also have social effects as well as, in the longer run, environmental implications. Not that, of course, for most people working in the business of tourism research these are more than mere abstractions, given that such writing is usually employed by and middle-class academics with reasonably secure jobs (so long as you have met the university demands for increased productivity in teaching, research, services and fulfilled the latest variation of the RAE, or, as in the case of the present author, been working in a university which has had its student numbers drop because of the impacts of earthquakes, with the government and/or university council refusing to guarantee staff employment in the immediate future so that they can fulfill their neoliberal objectives of efficiency and relevancy). In fact, being able to deal with abstractions is an advantage in tourism. The study of tourism is usually the study of the well-off (because an individual must have a surplus of time and money to be able to engage in leisure travel).

Such abstractions are also essential to the political economy of contemporary neoliberal capitalism in which tourism and the university is embedded. It is essential to the daily abstractions of stock and currency exchange, financial, economic, social and unemployment statistics that are the cards on the gaming, sorry – financial institutions', table. And in which universities invest. Such abstractions help you absolve yourself (if you actually were ever concerned in the first place) that your decision-making will actually harm a real person. Instead, you can take comfort in knowing that in promoting tourism you have done your little bit for gross domestic product (GDP), job creation in the service sector (thanks to you that 'nice little waitress' down the road has a part-time job as well as the sourced-out part-time cleaning staff) and helped further the attractiveness of the city for business by supporting yet another regeneration through tourism effort. Of course, such abstractions are also increasingly common in the military, where it is possible to divorce the results of actions via remotely controlled weapons and a computer screen. This is not a facetious or ironic comparison. The actions of financial analysts and economists (including those at universities) working at their computer screen can cause just as much misery as the military, and perhaps even more personal, community and collective damage at times. But for some reason it seems to be more acceptable.

Casino capitalism, power and luck

Strange (1997: 2) argues that:

The financial casino has everyone playing the game of Snakes and Ladders. Whether the fall of the dice lands you on the bottom of a ladder, whisking you up to fortune, or on the head of a snake, precipitating you to misfortune, is a matter of luck [. . .] This cannot help but have grave consequences.

While it is certainly possible to agree as to the significance of the grave consequences of casino capitalism, the issue of luck is much more of a moot point. Lukes and Hagland (2005), among others (Barry 1980a, b; Dowding 1996), closely connect issues of luck with issues of power. As Lukes and Hagland (2005: 46) query:

> The question is: are we sometimes mistaken for conceptual reasons when we (whether as social scientists or as social actors) suppose that some individuals and groups have power over others? Should we sometimes rather say that the former are beneficiaries of good and the latter victims of bad luck? And if so, when should we speak of power and when of luck?

Dowding's (1996: x) response is:

> [When] we model the power structure we find that we need to introduce a separate concept – that of luck – which enables some to get what they want without trying. Luck is not power and it is the failure to understand luck that led much of the earlier debate [on power] astray.

For Dowding power is 'The probability of getting what you want if you act in all possible worlds which are the same as the actual one with the exception of the preferences of all other actors' (1996: 53).

Therefore, 'The decisiveness and luck of an actor vary according to the preferences of other actors, but an actor's power remains the same. It is a disposition, analyzable counter[f]actually by taking into account possible preference changes' (Dowding 1996: 53).

Barry (1980a: 184) takes an individual's power to be the 'ability to change outcomes from what they would otherwise have been in the direction he desires'. Although Barry also argues that it should be apparent that, 'the likelihood that outcomes will correspond to his desires does not depend solely on his power', but also 'depends on what the outcome would have been in the absence of his intervention'. This Barry calls luck. 'Someone with a little power (or no power) but a lot of luck may thus consistently be able to obtain more preferred outcomes than someone who has a lot of power but only a little luck' (1980a: 184). For Barry (1980b: 348) 'power' is 'an inherently counterfactual notion' whereby 'an actor's power is his ability to overcome resistance – not his probability of overcoming resistance' (which may or may not occur). So Barry calls 'the probability of getting the outcomes you want success' with success being defined as 'the sum of luck and decisiveness. Luck is the probability of getting what you want without trying and decisiveness is the increase in the probability of getting what you want that occurs if you try' (1980b: 350). According to Barry, power is therefore 'a capability rather than a probability. An actor has more power the greater the range of unfavourable distributions of preferences within which he is decisive, in other words the more opposition he can overcome' (Barry 1980b: 350).

Barry (1980a, b) regards power as being attributable to agents, rather than structures (Lukes 2005). Similarly Dowding (1996: 28) states it is 'a mistake to think that because we are mapping the structure of power, that structures have power'. Nevertheless, Dowding does acknowledge that the distribution of luck in society is 'not mere happenstance' (1996: 71), but is systematic. Because of this the 'powerless may be impersonally oppressed by the logic of situations as well as by the directed social power of others':

> Some groups of people are lucky: they get what they want from society without having to act. Some groups are systematically lucky: they get what they want without having to act because of the way society is structured. It may seem odd to think that luck can be systematic; but it denotes the fact that people may get what they want without trying and this property attaches to certain locations within the social and institutional structure. Luck in this sense is closer to fortune or destiny than to simple chance.
>
> (Dowding 1996: 71)

The systematic luck of capitalists

In support of his arguments, Dowding discusses what he describes as the systematic luck of capitalists. According to Dowding (1996: 74), capitalists have no need to intervene with respect to a shift towards a more socialist economy. This is 'because they are lucky, and partly because the politicians may be afraid to act in ways contrary to the interests of business lest businessmen do intervene'. Likewise, in response to the 'growth machine' thesis (Jonas and Wilson 1999; Logan and Molotch 2007; Molotoch 1976), that focuses on the significance of alliances of pro-growth interests in urban development and which has been widely utilised in reference to tourism development (Canan and Hennessy 1989; Gill 2000; Hall 2006; Harrill 2004), Dowding argues that it is the 'systematic luck' that allows pro-growth coalitions to act 'with the acquiescence of the majority of the local population [. . .] The cards are stacked in developers' favour. The structure of capitalist society makes capitalists systematically lucky' (1996: 79–80, 82). In an earlier work Dowding (1991: 154) similarly commented that capitalists are lucky because they are:

> Capitalists within a capitalist system with a competitive party structure [. . .] They may be powerful as well, but there is an empirical difference between the two. If they are systematically lucky and not powerful, then when their interests are challenged they will not be able to respond; if they are powerful then they can respond.

As Lukes and Haglund (2005: 50) argued in response to Dowding:

To argue baldly that capitalists are systematically lucky is to leave unconsidered the non-random political choices that have given capitalists more or less power in specific historical and geographical contexts. Not only does such an approach cloud these issues; it has the further effect of depoliticizing inequality and political power by taking them out of the realm of human action, laws and institutions.

In contesting Dowding's claims Lukes and Haglund (2005: 50–53) provide a number of observations with respect to the problems of collective action that highlight how 'luck' may benefit some, while simultaneously disfavoring others:

1 *Recognition of interests* is in part shaped by powerful actors who – through hegemonic beliefs, pervasive ideologies and media access, to name only a few resources – can, through a variety of mechanisms, induce and encourage people to have beliefs that serve the interests of the powerful while subverting their own.
2 *Relative costs of participating in collective action* may also be affected by powerful actors who, explicitly or implicitly, block actual and potential efforts at collective action, often via regulatory means or non-decision-making.
3 *Opposition* can also be influenced by power, usually via encouraging division of interests.
4 There is unequal access to *state processes*, usually as a result of lobbying and networks.
5 Failure to *advertise* effectively may have much more to do with who controls media messages than with lack of an effective media campaign by the group attempting to organize or with underlying interests of the target population. In particular media messages that challenge hegemonic practices are usually ignored.
6 Finally, even if collective action problems are *overcome* and subordinate groups 'win', this does not imply that those in opposition to their doing so did not deploy what power they had to make winning very costly for the victorious.

Such issues are critical in seeking to understand the future of tourism. They force us to consider the way in the future is not simply the result of the chance interaction of random individual processes that will provide lucky results for some, but that *structure matters* (Lukes 2005). Furthermore, structure matters not only in consideration of the future outside of the academy but also within it, as structures exist not just 'out there', but also 'in here'. This is not to suggest a somewhat paranoid perspective on the future and who and what shapes it, i.e. 'the *assumption* that states of affairs held to be undesirable [. . .] are always and everywhere the result of the machinations of the powerful'. But it is to suggest that 'power can produce its effects in a remarkable variety of ways, some of them indirect and some hidden' (Lukes and Haglund 2005: 55). Indeed, if power, as Lukes and Haglund assume:

Either favours or does not disfavour the interests of the powerful and either favours or disfavours the interests of those subject to their power, then the power of the powerful may be either institutional or brute power, or a mixture of the two.

(2005: 60)

This chapter does not focus on the role of brute power in shaping the future. That role should be clear enough to anyone who watches the evening news, even if it's the Fox Network or Sky News (or perhaps not if that is all you watch). Instead, it argues that institutional power plays a critical role in shaping agendas *and* how to examine them.

Institutions, ontologies, and the rules of the game

An institution represents a social order or pattern that has attained a certain state and which help establish the 'rules of the game' (Hotimsky *et al.* 2006: 41). They are 'production systems, enabling structures, social programs or performance scripts' (Jepperson 1991: 145). Searle (1995, 1998) distinguished between 'institutional' and 'brute' facts. The former are those that 'can only be identified in terms of the rules that constitute the institutional reality'; brute facts 'can be identified without any reference to constitutive rules'. Therefore, 'constitutive rules create "institutional power", that is, the power that agents have or exercise by virtue of their compliance with constitutive rules' (Lukes and Haglund 2005: 60), and, as Searle (1998: 131) maintains, 'the whole point, or at least much of the point, of having institutional facts is to gain social control of brute facts'. Such a perspective is consistent with Schattschneider's (1960) concept of the 'mobilization of bias'. According to Schattschneider (1960: 71) 'all forms of political organization have a bias in favour of some kinds of conflict and the suppression of others because organization is the mobilization of bias. Some issues are organized into politics while others are organized out'. In considering the future we therefore need to be aware of what is being institutionalized in and out, including what is accepted as appropriate forms of knowledge and what form non-decision-making takes.

Ontologies condition the ways of seeing, creating and understanding not only different forms of knowledge but also their acceptability. Ontologies are therefore not just academic concerns but also determine how problems are defined and how they should be understood. Bhaskar (2008) has suggested that there are three main ontological traditions within science: classical empiricism, transcendental idealism and transcendental realism. Classical empiricism recognizes 'the ultimate objects of knowledge' as 'atomistic events' in which 'knowledge and the world may be viewed as surfaces whose points are in isomorphic correspondence or, in the case of phenomenalism, actually fused' (Bhaskar 2008: 14, 15). The positivist account, which is usually associated with the scientific method of the natural sciences, presupposes an ontology of empirical realism, whereby the world consists of 'experience and atomistic events constantly conjoined' (Bhaskar

2008: 221–222) in which there is a dichotomous and oppositional division between humans (or the individual) and the environment. Such an approach has a strong relationship to the role of reductionism and mechanism as distinguishing features of Western natural science, ontological reduction being the thesis 'that the properties of any entity may be understood by knowing the properties of its parts, because nothing can be explained about the entity without reference to its parts' (Keller and Golley 2000: 172).

The classical empiricist approach has been extremely significant in teaching and research on tourism but the framework it provides is often taken for granted without consideration of the 'assumptions that organise and, importantly, circum-scribe the field of analysis' (Castree 2002: 116–117). For example, consider the use of the metaphor of tourism or tourist impact on the environment that has become strongly embedded in tourism and wider discourse (Hall and Lew 2009), so much so that 'the metaphor of human impacts has come to frame our thinking and circumscribe debate about what constitutes explanation' (Head 2008: 374). This metaphor is derived from the material realist ontology of classical empiri-cism and has several features:

1   The emphasis on *the moment(s) of collision between two separate entities* (e.g. the 'impact' between tourism and the environment) has favored explanations and methods that depend on correlation in time and space (Weyl 2009) to the detriment of the search for mechanisms of connection and causation rather than simple correlation (Head 2008).
2   The emphasis on the moment(s) of impact *assumes a stable natural, social or economic baseline* (Hall and Lew 2009), *and an experimental method in which only one variable is changed* (Head 2008). This approach is inappro-priate for understanding complex and dynamic socio-environmental systems (Hall and Lew 2009; Head 2008).
3   Perhaps most profoundly influential (Head 2008), is the way the terms 'tourism impacts' or 'tourist impacts' ontologically *positions tourism and tourists as 'outside' the system under analysis*, as outside of nature (or what-ever it is that is being impacted) (Hall and Lew 2009). This is ironic given that research on global climate and environmental change demonstrates just how deeply entangled tourism is in environmental systems (Gössling and Hall 2006b; Gössling *et al.* 2010; Hall 2010a; Hall and Saarinen 2010), yet the metaphor remains in widespread use.
4   Placing a significant explanatory divide between humans and nature requires the *conflation of bundles of variable processes* under headings like 'human', 'climate', 'environment' and 'nature' (Head 2008).
5   Dichotomous explanations are characterized by their *veneer of simplicity and elegance*. Yet, 'the view that causality is simple takes many more assump-tions than the view that it is complex' (Head 2008: 374).

Ontologically and epistemologically there is relatively little critique in tourism because the classical realist empiricism (Bhaskar 2008) that underlies much research is strongly driven by a materialist and mechanistic orientation that artificially divides facts and values. Yet ontological differences raise fundamental questions about how future trends and even desired futures can actually be understood; the ethical relationships between humans and the environment given the influence of ontology on values toward nature; and as criticism of natural science. Geuss (1981) held that critical theories were fundamentally different from theories in the natural sciences, because while the natural sciences claim to be objective, critical theories are reflective. In addition, critical theories are also distinguished by the extent to which they provide guides for human action by being inherently emancipatory; having cognitive content; and being forms of knowledge in themselves. Habermas (1978) for example, placed great theoretical emphasis on what he termed cognitive or knowledge-constitutive interests, in order to explain the connections between knowledge and action. Habermas' critique of the relationship between theory and practice in modern science has been especially influential given that he believed that science had divorced itself from the means of understanding its social context (Unwin 1992). For Habermas (1978: 63) both material scientism and absolute idealism eliminate 'epistemology in favour of unchained universal "scientific knowledge"'. Yet in spite of these criticisms the hegemony of the long dominant positivist outlook, with its strongly quantitative and instrumentalist approach, has 'usurped the title of science' (Bhaskar 2008: 7) and fashions its popular image and understanding (Bhaskar 2008).

Constructing the academy

The mobilization of bias needs to be placed within an institutional context. As research on the history of science has indicated, institutions play an extremely important role in determining the trajectories of research and how the future is constructed. Several reasons can be provided from an institutional perspective for the continued strength of positivism in tourism research as well as the overall standing of interdisciplinary and more critical and qualitative work. First, successive governments in many developed countries support a research and tertiary education agenda that is increasingly focused on supposedly apolitical economic and market-oriented research deliverables (Demeritt 2000). 'Positivist science, with its apparent capacity to explain, solve and predict, but most of all serve those in power, has not surprisingly continued to find favour' (Unwin 1992: 153). Second, pressure from university administrations to 'obtain grants for high cost research projects [. . .] frequently reflect[s] the technical interest of logical positivism to maintain the social and political order' (Unwin 1992: 153). Third, the growth in the role of journal rankings and research performance appraisals as part of the formal assessments of academic research has become part of the 'rules of the game' within which research is conducted and published:

> At a macro level structures and reviews define what constitutes 'good' research by prescribing the means by which it is analysed, who does the

analysis, what is included in the analysis, where tourism studies lies as a body of knowledge and what the implications of the analysis will be.

(Hall 2011a: 17)

Such assessment therefore acts to not only measure the quality of research output but also influence academic hiring and rewards and has favored certain positivist approaches and methods as well as problem definition over others (Wells 2010; Hall 2011a).

According to the Business and Management Studies sub-panel of the British 2009 Research Assessment Exercise (RAE) (2009: 5):

> Some submissions received contained research output that seemed to sub-panel members to be of little or no relevance to business and management studies and sub-panel members were concerned that some submissions were an overeclectic mix of outputs. In a very limited number of cases, such left-field outputs were given low grades because of their lack of relevance.

Although tourism is not specifically mentioned in this case, tourism studies is clearly an area of research that feeds into a number of different epistemological and methodological approaches, such as post-colonial studies, cultural and heritage studies and visual consumption, that are not mainstream business and management theory (Hall 2011a). (In the case of the 2009 RAE approximately 40 percent of the tourism related publications were submitted to the business panel, compared to the Sport-Related Studies panel, 21 percent; Art and Design, 9 percent; Geography and Environmental Studies, 8 percent; and 22 percent elsewhere; Hall 2011a). Furthermore, the strong qualitative tradition in tourism research may also not be fully accepted by a Business and Management panel. Indeed, the panel later reports, with specific reference to hospitality and tourism:

> Some of the outputs submitted had limited relevance to Business and Management. As in the last RAE [. . .] research in this field lags behind the development of mainstream management theory. Moreover, as identified in the previous RAE, many outputs were purely conceptual, often based on literature reviews, or what the authors described as 'exploratory studies', which lacked rigour and/or significance.

(RAE 2009: 8–9)

Fourth, the combination of the above has served to institutionalize positivist science within universities and research institutions and structures (Unwin 1992; Hall 2011a).

Constructing the science of global environmental change

One of the best examples of the institutionalization of instrumentalist science approaches to environmental issues is global climate and environmental change

(Bryant 1998). The need to integrate social and biophysical perspectives in environmental change research is widely recognized (Conrad 2009; Demeritt 2009; Füssel and Klein 2006; O'Brien 2011; Yearly 2009), including with respect to the need for ontological shifts (Turnpenny *et al.* 2011), and the production of local knowledge (Slocum 2010). However, given the institutional nature of universities, research and forecasting bodies some types of social science assessment will be acceptable and other will not. For example, in the expert review of the first draft of the Intergovernmental Panel on Climate Change's (IPCC) Working Group II Fourth Assessment Report on Climate Change Impacts, Adaptation and Vulnerability, Karen O'Brien of the University of Oslo commented, 'Methodologies that incorporate social science perspectives such as institutions and social networks, or that include human behaviour, such as agent based modelling and actor network theory, are excluded from this assessment of assessment methodologies' (Intergovernmental Panel on Climate Change 2005: 15). In response the writing team noted:

> Addressed – we can understand the reviewer's perspective, and have tried to address those concerns, though they seem to reflect a very structured view of what different methods are and are not, which is not very amenable to the treatment that we have developed here.
>
> (Intergovernmental Panel on Climate Change 2005: 15)

Demeritt's (2001a, b) examination of the construction of climate change and the politics of science is particularly informative (see also the response of Schneider 2001). Demeritt retraces the history of climate modeling and associated climate science to identify tacit social and epistemic communities that are characterized by the technocratic and reductionist inclinations of climate change science. It is important to emphasize, however, that Demeritt was not denying the existence of climate change (as neither is the present author) but rather the way in which climate change science is constructed and how this leads into issues of the politics of the dominant natural science-led formulation of the climate change problem as well as issues of public trust.

Demeritt (2001a, b, 2006) argues that climate change has been constructed in narrowly technical and reductionist scientific terms by the IPCC and other international and national scientific bodies on climate change and that this promotes certain kind of knowledge at the expense of others. 'For the most part, climate change model projections have been driven by highly simplistic business-as-usual scenarios of human population growth, resource consumption, and [greenhouse gas] (GHG) emissions at highly aggregated geographic scales' (Demeritt 2001a: 312), that operate at a global scale, rather than framing the problem in terms of alternative, and no less relevant forms, such as the structural imperatives of the capitalist economy that drives emissions (Wainwright 2010); the north–south gap in terms of emissions; or regionalized conceptions that focus on issues of poverty and deprivation (Gössling *et al.* 2010). As Demeritt (2001a: 316) argues, 'by treating the objective physical properties of [greenhouse gases] in isolation from the surrounding social relations serves to conceal, normalize, and thereby reproduce those unequal social relations'.

The dominant scientific positions within the IPCC process has also led to the physical reductionism of simulation modeling becoming the most authoritative method for studying the climate system (Demeritt 2001a, b). Yet the appeals of formal quantitative evaluation methods are social and political as much as technical and scientific. Just as significantly, it also makes them more credible from a public perspective of natural science:

> Insofar as adherence to rigidly uniform and impersonal and in that sense 'procedurally objective' [. . .] rules limits the scope for individual bias or discretion and thereby guarantees the vigorous (self-)denial of personal perspective necessary to make knowledge seem universal, trustworthy and true.
>
> (Demeritt 2001a: 324)

Issues surrounding how climate change research is constructed scientifically are clearly significant for understanding tourism's relationship to global change, and therefore the future of tourism (and the planet) for a number of reasons. First, it helps explain why anthropogenic climate change has primarily been defined in environmental rather than political terms (Gössling *et al.* 2010), or one that requires framing in terms of the imperatives of the capitalist economic system and its alternatives (Hall 2009, 2011b). Secondly, even though, as noted above, there has been a call for greater social science information to be brought into the climate change assessment process, this has primarily been assessed in terms of neoclassical economic contributions (e.g. Stern 2007), which have themselves been greatly influenced by the ontology of natural science. Perhaps ironically, neoclassical economic accounts of climate change and the justification for action to minimize the effects of climate change are also dominated by formal modeling (Dietz and Stern 2008). For example Hamilton *et al.* (2005), which was the only tourism-related paper cited in the 2007 Stern Review (Hall 2008), was based on a simulation model. Yet as Gössling and Hall (2006c) and Scott *et al.* (2012) indicate, there are a number of major weaknesses in such models with respect to predicting travel flows as a result of climate change (also see Bigano *et al.* 2006; Gössling and Hall 2006d). Moreover, the neoclassical economic belief that the social and economic value of things can be expressed in terms of aggregate individual willingness to pay or in monetary terms at all is open to substantial criticism. As Demeritt and Rothman (1999: 404) noted, such a utilitarian view of value has been subjected to a number of different philosophical and moral critiques:

- It is anthropocentric and ignores intrinsic value.
- The world cannot be broken down into discrete and alienable entities to which monetary values might meaningfully be attached.
- It confuses values and preferences.

- Its narrow decisionist framework artificially abstracts information about human values and preferences from an ongoing and multidimensional social process of (re)expressing them.
- Money conceals a profound asymmetry in the apparent equality of the exchange relation.

Therefore, the choice of valuation procedure, like the definition of value itself as used by governments and supranational authorities such as the UNWTO, World Travel and Tourism Council and the World Economic Forum in relation to the future of the planet's environment (and therefore the planet), is part of a mediated and embodied social construction of knowledge and is ultimately personal and political rather than objective and rational (Demeritt and Rothman 1999; Hall 2011b). However, they may not know it. Or, if they do, they choose to publically ignore it, as otherwise it would cast doubt on the objectivity and strength of their pronouncements.

Brute reductionism and the economization of everything

Whether it be Dowding's analysis of luck and power, the decision-making of research assessment committees, or the simulation modeling of the IPCC or the Stern Review, we are faced with could be described as 'brute reductionism'. This term is used in a narrow sense by Lukes and Haglund (2005) with respect to Dowding's work on rational choice theory; it is here used in a broader context to refer to the wider dominance of natural science ontology and neglect of the social (and political) construction of knowledge and truth statements. Such a situation is also indicative of the process of economization, which refers to the assembly of actions, behaviors, devices, institutions, objects and analytical/ practical descriptions which are tentatively and sometime controversially quali-fied as 'economic' by scholars, lay people and/or market actors (Çaliskan and Callon 2009). As Callon's (1998) earlier work on the competition between calculative agencies noted:

> Imposing the rules of the game, that is to say, the rules used to calculate decisions, by imposing the tools in which these rules are incorporated, is the starting point of relationships of domination which allow certain calculating agencies to decide the location and distribution of surpluses. The extension of a certain form of organized market, an extension which ensures the domination of agents who calculate according to the prevailing rules of that particular market, always corresponds to the imposition of certain calculating tools.

> (Callon 1998: 46)

So we come full circle. In order to understand the future and how it will be made we need to understand the rules of the game and the role of institutions and power structures in the making of those rules. Tourism is embedded in the rules of the game in terms of both its consumption and production and an area of academic knowledge (Hall 2010b). Many tourism academics seem to ignore that they are placed within the increasingly dominant neoliberal discourse of academic capitalism, competitiveness and the entrepreneurial university. Academic publishing and performance and perhaps the discourse is itself embedded in 'a particular industrial actor-network of academic knowledge production, circulation and reception' (Gibson and Klocker 2004: 425).

Tourism is therefore also embedded in contemporary capitalism. Strange (1997) regarded the characteristics of casino capitalism as being linked to interconnected innovations in the way in which financial markets work; the sheer size of markets; commercial banks turned into investment banks; the emergence of Asian nations as players; and the shift to self-regulation by banks. Similarly, Harvey (2000) identified four recent shifts in the dynamics of globalization: financial deregulation, technological change and innovation, media and communications and the cost and time of moving commodities, all of which impact tourism. These are important points. We should no longer go on treating the future of tourism and even contemporary tourism as if capitalism isn't there. Not only are the more substantial changes of the global environment coincident with the emergence of global capitalism but the recent rapid transformation of the global environment, with respect to population growth, growing food and water insecurity, biodiversity loss, deforestation, desertification, Peak Oil and climate change is also coincident with casino and neoliberal capitalism. If the future of tourism is to be addressed then it needs to be done in the context of capitalism's role in consumption and production and hence accumulation, and in its contribution to producing inequalities of wealth and power (Wainwright 2010).

Unfortunately, however, I do not think tourism studies and the tourism academy are geared for this. Business as usual is far safer. For some it is much easier going to free or subsidized conferences and meetings in China even though it is an authoritarian and repressive state with an appalling record in human rights, than having the ethical courage to say no. Or maybe it never even crosses the academy's mind because members of the academy consider such activities as contributing to 'international understanding'. There is far more reward for writing yet more papers on branding, image, consumer behavior, market segmentation, tourism economics and authenticity, than there is for pointing out how unequal it all is and how tourism might actually contribute to further inequality and yet further environmental degradation. Ecotourism has not saved the environment and tourism is less sustainable than it ever was (Hall 2010c, 2011b). There is an alternative development paradigm and alternative futures are possible (Hall 2009, 2011c). However, unless we understand the role of institutions and power we are doomed to repeat previous failures to change economic and environmental course. We may chide multinational corporations about the ethics of their international behavior and their contribution to wellbeing, but the academy does not chide itself.

Conclusion: the alternative is outside the rules of the current game

As a result of oil and other economic and environmental shocks substantial concerns were expressed in the late 1960s and early 1970s with respect to an over-concentration in government policies on economic growth without consideration of the limits of natural resources (e.g. Daly 1974; Meadows *et al.* 1972; Mishan 1967). These were also discussed with respect to the implications for tourism. For example Mishan (1970), in concluding his evaluation of the Commission on the Third London Airport, commented:

> Equity is wholly ignored. If indeed, the business tycoons and the Mallorca holiday-makers are shown to benefit, after paying their fares, to such an extent that they could more than compensate the victims of aircraft spillover, the cost-benefit criterion is met. But compensation is not paid. The former continue to enjoy the profit and the pleasure; the latter continue to suffer the disamenities.
>
> (Mishan 1970: 234)

Similarly, in an article entitled "Slow is beautiful" Gleditsch (1975: 91) noted 'the severe environmental problems involved in an unlimited or uncontrolled further growth in aviation' as well as the uneven structure of personal mobility. In a prescient observation of what would now be described as the 'hypermobile' (Gössling *et al.* 2009), Gleditsch (1975: 91):

> hypothesized [. . .] that topdogs will secure a disproportionately high share of the advantages and a disproportionately low share of the disadvantages of any new transportation system [. . .] With resources such as education and income, topdogs are in a position to make use of new transportation technology – and avoid its cost.

An accurate assessment of both the present and the future.

So, what then of the future? Do I embrace a happy smiling future for tourism? Well, only with luck. Tourism will continue in some shape or form as long as the human race survives. However, with respect to the future I am more concerned as to what type of future there might be in general. And on this I am much more sanguine. On current trends the likelihood is that many of the major primates and mega-fauna will not exist in the wild in 20 years from now, there will be major conflict over resources, food, and water security, and we will still be discussing how to make a destination competitive. To quote an Australian saying, 'This is complete and utter bullshit', yet we still have American academics sending out emails on TRINet every year naming 'the ten most important issues facing tourism', and others believing that this is meaningful. How facile and ridiculous can critique and debate in tourism studies actually get?

So yes, the future is personal. I will probably having a conversation with my son on his twenty-first birthday starting 'dad – dad what did you do?' Perhaps bearing witness is a start but it is likely not enough, instead there is a real need for action for change. A good start would be to acknowledging that all is not green in the garden of tourism. But then, if it's not in an A* journal, the result of quantitative analysis and contributes to the next round of research assessment that allows you to keep your job, then you probably don't care anyway.

Acknowledgements

This paper represents a coming together of three different works, Hall (2011a) on journal rankings and their influence, Hall (2011b) on policy learning and policy failure in sustainable tourism, and a draft of a chapter on 'natural science ontology' for *A Handbook of Tourism and the Environment*, edited by A. Holden and D. Fennell, together with a long-standing interest in power and institutions. I would note though that this is by far the blackest account of where we are going.

References

Barry, B. (1980a) 'Is it Better to be Powerful or Lucky? Part 1', *Political Studies*, 28(2): 183–194.
—— (1980b) 'Is it Better to be Powerful or Lucky? Part 2', *Political Studies*, 28(3): 338–352.
Bhaskar, R. (2008) *A Realist Theory of Science*, 2nd edn, Abingdon: Routledge.
Bigano, A., Hamilton, J.M., Maddison, D.J. and Tol, R.S.J. (2006) 'Predicting Tourism Flows under Climate Change. An Editorial Comment on Gössling and Hall (2006)', *Climatic Change*, 79: 175–180.
Bryant, R.L. (1998) 'Power, Knowledge and Political Ecology in the Third World: A Review', *Progress in Physical Geography*, 22: 79–94.
Çaliskan, K. and Callon, M. (2009) 'Economization, Part 1: Shifting Attention from the Economy Towards Processes of Economization', *Economy and Society*, 38: 369–398.
Callon, M. (1998) 'Introduction: The Embeddedness of Economic Markets in Economics', in M. Callon (ed.) *The Laws of the Markets*, Oxford: Blackwell.
Canan, P. and Hennessy, M. (1989) 'The Growth Machine, Tourism, and the Selling of Culture', *Sociological Perspectives*, 32(2): 227–243.
Castree, N. (2002) 'False Antitheses? Marxism, Nature and Actor Networks', *Antipode*, 34: 111–146.
Conrad, J. (2009) 'Climate Research and Climate Change: Reconsidering Social Science Perspectives', *Nature and Culture*, 4(2): 113–122.
Daly, H.E. (1974) 'The Economics of the Steady State', *American Economic Review*, 64(2): 15–21.
Demeritt, D. (2000) 'The New Social Contract for Science: Accountability, Relevance, and Value in US and UK Science and Research Policy', *Antipode*, 32: 308–329.
—— (2001a) 'The Construction of Global Warming and the Politics of Science', *Annals of the Association of American Geographers*, 91(2): 307–337.
—— (2001b) 'Science and the Understanding of Science: A Reply to Schneider', *Annals of the Association of American Geographers*, 91(2): 345–348.
—— (2006) 'Science Studies, Climate Change and the Prospects for Constructivist Critique', *Economy and Society*, 35(3): 453–479.

—— (2009) 'Geography and the Promise of Integrative Environmental Research', *Geoforum*, 40(2): 127–129.

Demeritt, D. and Rothman, D. (1999) 'Figuring the Costs of Climate Change: An Assessment and Critique', *Environment and Planning A*, 31(3): 389–408.

Dietz, S. and Stern, N. (2008) 'Why Economic Analysis Supports Strong Action on Climate Change: A Response to the Stern Review's Critics', *Review of Environmental Economics and Policy*, 2(1): 94–113.

Dowding, K.M. (1991) *Rational Choice and Power*, Aldershot: Edward Elgar.

—— (1996) *Power*, Minneapolis, MN: University of Minnesota Press.

Füssel, H-M. and Klein, R.J.T. (2006) 'Climate Change Vulnerability Assessments: An Evolution of Conceptual Thinking', *Climatic Change*, 75(3): 301–329.

Geuss, R. (1981) *The Idea of a Critical Theory: Habermas and the Frankfurt School*, Cambridge: Cambridge University Press.

Gibson, C. and Klocker, N. (2004) 'Academic Publishing as "Creative" Industry, and Recent Discourse of "Creative Economies": Some Critical Reflections', *Area*, 36(4): 423–434.

Gill, A. (2000) 'From Growth Machine to Growth Management: The Dynamics of Resort Development in Whistler, British Columbia', *Environment and Planning A*, 32(6): 1083–1104.

Gleditsch, N.P. (1975) 'Slow is Beautiful. The Stratification of Personal Mobility, with Special Reference to International Aviation', *Acta Sociologica*, 18(1): 76–94.

Gössling, S. and Hall, C.M. (2006a) 'Conclusion: "Wake Up – This is Serious"', in S. Gössling and C.M. Hall (eds.) *Tourism and Global Environmental Change: Ecological, Economic, Social and Political Interrelationships*, London: Routledge, pp. 305–320.

—— (eds) (2006b) *Tourism and Global Environmental Change*. London: Routledge.

—— (2006c) 'Uncertainties in Predicting Tourist Flows under Scenarios of Climate Change', *Climatic Change*, 79(3–4): 163–73.

—— (2006d) 'Uncertainties in Predicting Travel Flows: Common Ground and Research Needs. A Reply to Tol *et al.*', *Climatic Change*, 79(3–4): 181–183.

Gössling, S., Ceron, J-P., Dubios, G. and Hall, C.M. (2009) 'Hypermobile Travellers', in S. Gössling and P. Upham (eds.) *Climate Change and Aviation*, London: Earthscan, pp. 131–139.

Gössling, S., Hall, C.M., Peeters, P. and Scott, D. (2010) 'The Future of Tourism: A Climate Change Mitigation Perspective', *Tourism Recreation Research*, 35(2): 119–130.

Habermas, J. (1978) *Knowledge and Human Interests*, 2nd edn, London: Heinemann.

Hall, C.M. (2000) 'The Future of Tourism: A Personal Speculation', *Tourism Recreation Research*, 25(1): 85–95.

—— (2005) 'The Future of Tourism Research', in P. Burns, C. Palmer and B. Ritchie (eds.) *Tourism Research Methods: Integrating Theory with Practice*, Wallingford: CABI, pp. 221–230.

—— (2006) 'Urban Entrepreneurship, Corporate Interests and Sports Mega-events: the Thin Policies of Competitiveness within the Hard Outcomes of Neoliberalism', *Sociological Review*, 54(Supp. 2): 59–70.

—— (2008) 'Tourism and Climate Change: Knowledge Gaps and Issues', *Tourism Recreation Research*, 33(3): 339–350.

—— (2009) 'Degrowing Tourism: Décroissance, Sustainable Consumption and Steady-state Tourism', *Anatolia: An International Journal of Tourism and Hospitality Research*, 20(1): 46–61.

—— (2010a) 'Tourism and Biodiversity: More Significant than Climate Change?', *Journal of Heritage Tourism*, 5(4): 253–266.

—— (2010b) 'Academic Capitalism, Academic Responsibility and Tourism Academics: Or, the Silence of the Lambs?' *Tourism Recreation Research*, 35(3): 298–301.

—— (2010c) 'Crisis Events in Tourism: Subjects of Crisis in Tourism', *Current Issues in Tourism*, 13(5): 401–417.

—— (2011a) 'Publish and Perish: Bibliometric Analysis, Journal Ranking and the Assessment of Research Quality in Tourism', *Tourism Management*, 32(1): 16–27.

—— (2011b) 'Policy Learning and Policy Failure in Sustainable Tourism Governance: From First and Second to Third Order Change?', *Journal of Sustainable Tourism*, 19(4–5): 649–671.

—— (2011c) 'Consumerism, Tourism and Voluntary Simplicity: We all Have to Consume, but do we Really Have to Travel so Much to be Happy?', *Tourism Recreation Research*, 36(3): 298–303.

Hall, C.M. and Härkönen, T. (2006) 'Research Agendas and Issues in Lake Tourism: From Global to Local Concerns', in C.M. Hall and T. Härkönen (eds.) *Lake Tourism: An Integrated Approach to Lacustrine Tourism Systems*, Clevedon: Channelview Press, pp. 223–233.

Hall, C.M. and Lew, A. (2009) *Understanding and Managing Tourism Impacts: An Integrated Approach*, London: Routledge.

Hall, C.M. and Saarinen, J. (eds.) (2010) *Polar Tourism and Change: Climate, Environments and Experiences*, London: Routledge.

Hall, C.M. and Sharples, L. (2008) 'Future Issues and Trends: Food Events, Festivals and Farmers' Markets', in C.M. Hall and L. Sharples (eds.) *Food and Wine Festivals and Events Around the World: Development, Management and Markets*, Oxford: Butterworth Heinemann, pp. 331–348.

Hamilton, J.M., Maddison, D.J. and Tol, R.S.J. (2005) 'Climate Change and International Tourism: A Simulation Study', *Global Environmental Change*, 15(3): 253–266.

Harrill, R. (2004) 'Residents' Attitudes Toward Tourism Development: A Literature Review with Implications for Tourism Planning', *Journal of Planning Literature*, 18(3): 251–266.

Harvey, D. (2000) *Spaces of Hope*, Berkeley, CA: University of California Press.

Head, L. (2008) 'Is the Concept of Human Impacts Past its Use-by Date?' *The Holocene*, 18(3): 373–377.

Hotimsky, S., Cobb, R. and Bond, A. (2006) 'Contracts or Scripts? A Critical Review of the Application of Institutional Theories to the Study of Environmental Change', *Ecology and Society*, 11(1): 41, online. Available at www.ecologyandsociety.org/vol11/iss1/art41/ (accessed 30 December 2011).

Intergovernmental Panel on Climate Change (2005) *IPCC WGII Fourth Assessment Report, Climate Change Impacts, Adaptation and Vulnerability, Expert Review of First Order Draft*, Specific Comments, Chapter 2, December 5, 2005, online. Available at ww.ipcc-wg2.gov/AR4/FOD_COMMS/Ch02_FOD_comments.pdf (accessed 30 December 2011)

Jepperson, R.L. (1991) 'Institutions, Institutional Effects, and Institutionalism', in R.W. Powell and P.J. DiMaggio (eds.) *The New Institutionalism in Organizational Analysis*, Chicago, IL: University of Chicago Press, pp. 143–163.

Jonas, A.E.G. and Wilson, D. (eds.) (1999) *The Urban Growth Machine: Critical Perspectives, Two Decades Later*, Albany, NY: State University of New York Press.

Keller, D.R. and Golley, F.B. (eds.) (2000) *The Philosophy of Ecology. From Science to Synthesis*, Athens, GA: University of Georgia Press.

Logan, J.R. and Molotch, H.L. (2007) *Urban Fortunes: The Political Economy of Place, 20th Anniversary Edition, With a New Preface*, Berkeley, CA: University of California Press.

Lukes, S. (2005) *Power: A Radical View*, 2nd edn, London: Palgrave Macmillan in association with the British Sociological Association.

Lukes, S. and Haglund, L. (2005) 'Power and Luck', *Archives européennes de sociologie*, 46(1): 45–66.

Meadows, D.H., Meadow, D.L., Randers, J. and Behrens, W.W. (1972) *The Limits to Growth. Report to the Club of Rome*, New York: Universe Books.

Mishan, E.J. (1967) *The Costs of Economic Growth*, New York: Frederick A. Praeger.

—— (1970) 'What is Wrong with Roskill?' *Journal of Transport Economics and Policy*, 4(4): 221–234.

Molotch, H. (1976) 'The City as a Growth Machine,' *American Journal of Sociology*, 82(2): 309–355.

O'Brien, K. (2011) 'Responding to Environmental Change: A New Age for Human Geography?' *Progress in Human Geography*, 35(4): 542–549.

Research Assessment Exercise (RAE) (2009) *RAE2008 Subject Overview Reports: UOA 36 Business and Management Studies*, online. Available at www.rae.ac.uk/pubs/2009/ov/ (accessed 30 December 2011).

Schattschneider, E. (1960) *Semi-sovereign People: A Realist's View of Democracy in America*, New York: Holt, Rinehart and Wilson.

Schneider, S.H. (2001) 'A Constructive Deconstruction of Deconstructionists: A Response to Demeritt', *Annals of the Association of American Geographers*, 91(2): 338–344.

Scott, D., Hall, C.M. and Gössling, S. (2012) *Tourism and Climate Change: Impacts, Adaptation and Mitigation*, London: Routledge.

Searle, J.R. (1995) *The Construction of Social Reality*, New York: Simon and Schuster.

—— (1998) *Mind, Language and Society*, New York: Basic Books.

Slocum, R. (2010) 'The Sociology of Climate Change: Research Priorities', in J. Hagel, T. Dietz and J. Broadbent (eds.) *Workshop on Sociological Perspectives on Global Climate Change*, Arlington: National Science Foundation and American Sociological Association, pp. 135–139. Available at ireswb.cc.ku.edu/~crgc/NSFWorkshop/Readings/NSF_WkspReport_09.pdf.

Stern, N. (2007) *The Economics of Climate Change: The Stern Review*, Cambridge: Cambridge University Press.

Strange, S. (1997) *Casino Capitalism*, Manchester: Manchester University Press.

Turnpenny, J., Jones, M. and Lorenzoni, I. (2011) 'Where Now for Post-normal Science? A Critical Review of its Development, Definitions, and Uses', *Science Technology Human Values*, 36(3), 287–206.

Unwin, T. (1992) *The Place of Geography*, Harlow: Longman.

Wainwright, J. (2010) 'Climate Change, Capitalism, and the Challenge of Transdisciplinarity', *Annals of the Association of American Geographers*, 100(4): 983–991.

Wells, P. (2010) *The ABS Rankings of Journal Quality: An Exercise in Delusion*, Working Paper, The Centre for Business Relationships, Accountability, Sustainability and Society, Cardiff Business School, online. Available at www.brass.cf.ac.uk/uploads/010610_ABS_Rankings.pdf (accessed 30 December 2011)

Weyl, H. (2009) *Philosophy of Mathematics and Natural Science*, revised and augmented English edition based on a translation of Olaf Helmer. Princeton, NJ: Princeton University Press.

Yearley, S. (2009) 'Sociology and Climate Change after Kyoto: What Roles for Social Science in Understanding Climate Change?', *Current Sociology*, 57(3): 389–405.

Part III

Managerial issues and future tourism

9 Tourism in a technology-dependent world

Ulrike Gretzel

Introduction

Much has been written about the intricate relationship between tourism and technology, and specifically information technology (IT), stressing the importance of technological progress for tourism development, competitive tourism industries, greater global mobility and ever-more sophisticated tourism experiences (Buhalis and Law 2008; Gretzel and Fesenmaier 2009; Hall 2005; Poon 1993; Sheldon 1997; Werthner and Klein 1999). Recent advances in mobile technologies, social media, pervasive computing and artificial intelligence suggest that tourism's dependency on IT is bound to increase, with tourism experiences being mediated by an ever greater array of devices that provide opportunities to interact with information, services, things and other human beings before, during and after a vacation (Jansson 2007; Tussyadiah and Fesenmaier 2009; Wang, Park and Fesenmaier 2011). Tomorrow's prototypical tourist is probably not one with a Hawaiian shirt and a huge camera around the neck awkwardly gazing at natives or distant landscapes but an individual with a personal digital device connected to a myriad of information sources, allowing for interactions with a global social network and supporting touristic gazes at an augmented reality that facilitates interactions with the environment in new forms (Gretzel 2010). Thus, the question concerning technology is an important one to ask to understand the future of tourism and to envision the nature of tourists in such a technology-dependent world (Gretzel and Jamal 2009).

Reflections on the technology-based future of tourism, however, are usually not very critical and generally colored by 'all progress is good' thinking. Discourse on technological impact in tourism often focuses on greater efficiencies, increased accessibility and transparency of information, enhanced services and experiences, greater connectivity, positive impacts on mobility, the leveling of playing fields and power shifts in favor of tourism consumers (Buhalis 1997, 2003; Buhalis and Law 2008; Gretzel and Fesenmaier 2009; Joo 2002; Pühretmair and Nussbaum 2011; Stamboulis and Skayannis 2003; Werthner and Klein 1999). While such discussions are important and valid, they present an incomplete picture of the future. A more holistic view needs to acknowledge that tourism and technology exist within broader environmental, political, economic and social contexts that will simultaneously shape and be shaped by technological advances. Technological progress brings with it technological dependence, and such dependence is closely linked to power issues that then infiltrate all areas of life. It opens up avenues for inequalities and abuses of technological advantages. This chapter will address specific areas of technological developments with significant implications for tourism, and will discuss opportunities as well as drawbacks connected to these. As such it will provide the basis for critical envisioning of possible futures in tourism that will require interventions to create a desired future.

Pervasive technology availability and use

Technology has not only become cheaper but also more mobile. Advances in wireless technologies further contribute to more ubiquitous access and use, affecting all stages of the tourism experience, from dreaming to planning to enacting and remembering. Many of the current and future technological developments will further strengthen this trend, but one area of recent technological advances warrants particular mention, namely wearable and surface computing. Wearable and surface computing will not only facilitate pervasive availability and use of technology, but will make it increasingly difficult to distinguish technology from its surroundings and to discriminate technology use from non-use. Ultimately, this will completely change the way tourists will retrieve/provide information and communicate with other individuals and tourism providers.

Developments in the areas of wearable and surface computing imply that anything can become an interface. Therefore, technology as a device and clearly defined object will increasingly become a thing of the past. Efforts in these areas also challenge traditional modes of input. Gesture-interaction devices, wearable motion sensors in clothing and devices that can infer the user's context based on scent are only some of the latest developments in wearable computing (Smailagic and Kenn 2011). Full-size projection keyboards (Tomasi *et al.* 2003) can turn anything from airplane tray tables to reception counters into interactive devices. Such natural user interfaces are seen as the next big evolution in computing (Seow *et al.* 2009) and have of course enormous use potential in tourism, where mobility is extremely high, contextual information is needed and technological objects can disturb pristine views and optimal experiences such as flow. Ultimately, the human body itself will become an interface. Human augmentics (Kenyon and Leigh 2011) refers to bionic devices which will enhance human abilities to visually, aurally, cognitively and physically interact with environments, such as contact lenses delivering augmented reality displays or implanted microchips and muscle stimulation devices. In the case of cognitive implants this means that information will be delivered directly to the brain, eradicating what we typically consider to be an interface.

Tourism is essentially a mediated activity with various stakeholders (travel agents, tour guides, mass media, destination marketing organizations, family and friends, etc.) playing formal and informal mediating roles (Jennings and Weiler 2004). In recognition that mediation (both formal and informal) is central to tourism experiences, one has to ask how ubiquitous technology will impact the nature and quality of the sensory and emotional aspects of tourism experiences, and the meaning derived from them (Gretzel *et al.* 2011). Tussyadiah and Fesenmaier (2009) and Wang *et al.* (2011) illustrate the importance of considering technology not only as a communication tool for traditional mediators but as a mediator itself. One can expect that future tourism experiences will be fundamentally different in nature and significance because of the increased mediation through and by information and communication technologies. Indications of such change can already be sensed today when tourists broadcast their experiences live to known others and the world through tweets and Facebook posts, let location-based services direct them to nearby attractions, and use augmented reality apps on their smart phones to obtain additional information about a historic building instead of following a tour guide's or guidebook's interpretation. While this mediation is very visible today, it might not be in the future when natural user interfaces dominate or interfaces in the traditional sense do no longer exist. Mediation is not neutral. It means direction of attention to certain things and not others and appropriation of contents to fit the medium, but very often also framing of messages to advance a specific agenda. Therefore, the questions of what stories future tourists will be told and what experiences will be promoted to them and by whom are important ones to be addressed from a societal point of view.

Credibility, responsibility and privacy

Web 2.0 technologies have changed the way tourists and tourism providers communicate and share information (Sigala *et al.* 2012). First, ever more information about tourism experiences is created and widely shared with known and unknown others; secondly, this information is increasingly created and promoted by tourists and other entities outside of the traditional tourism industry; thirdly, the information can be instantly evaluated and sometimes even manipulated by others. This means that the touristic information space has not only expanded tremendously but now also includes different types of information and new sources of information. In addition, the information is now often highly personalized and with greater technological capabilities and more sophisticated algorithms developed in the future, this will increasingly be the case. Personalization through context-aware systems involves the capturing and processing of information about the user and her location, time of use, weather conditions, etc. (Adomavicius and Tuzhilin 2011). The user usually consciously enables such features and typically has to provide explicit input. However, more and more information is also created implicitly through interactions with technologies: mobile phone traces, digital data points in search engines, emails and social networks, credit card use data, etc. When systematically analysed, and especially when combined, these digital traces provide comprehensive profiles of users, their preferences and behavioral patterns. Information has economic value and companies are already increasingly taking advantage of data explicitly or implicitly supplied by users of technologies. As Dwyer (2011: 59) points out, 'Google studies the context of *you*', so that it can sell its advertising products effectively. Like Google, Facebook also tracks everything users do within its social networking site to be able to provide its advertising clients with targeted marketing opportunities. According to Dwyer (2011), both companies continue to invest in new ways to collect ever-greater amounts of increasingly personalized information without the knowledge and direct consent of the user. There is also a growing number of technology companies emerging that focus on the mining of data available through social media to provide businesses with market intelligence. Some of them are specifically focused on the tourism industry (e.g. Revinate.com).

Moreover, information is increasingly stored and processed outside of the use device. Cloud computing has become a household word recently and its growth suggests that it will dominate information storage and Web services provision in the future. Cloud computing refers to software and hardware that allows users to tap into services and resources that exist in distributed data centres (Armbrust *et al.* 2009). This means that rather than installing hardware or downloading software, technology users now access information, applications and services remotely through the Internet. This provides great advantages as, for example, small tourism businesses do not have to maintain a lot of technological infrastructure, business travelers have greater access to important documents and applications on the go, and devices in general can become even lighter and thus more mobile because they only need processing but not storage capacities. However, at the same time, this also implies a substantial need for constant connectivity to the Internet and greater vulnerability to data theft or misuse.

These technological trends have several implications for the future of tourism and need to be critically evaluated. Tourism is an information-intense industry, and changes in technology with accompanying changes in the information ecology have tremendous effects on its structure and processes (Werthner and Klein 1999). First, if Facebook and Google and their likes know more about who takes vacations, which destinations are popular and how tourism experiences are remembered, then the question of where the boundaries of the tourism industry lie becomes critical. Bringing together the various stakeholders to discuss tourism issues is seen as essential to sustainable tourism management (Getz and Jamal 1994). It is not clear how such collaborative planning can work if major stakeholders are unknown or do not identify with tourism. Secondly, credibility of information is especially important in tourism because of the risks involved in traveling. If it is no longer clear where information resides and who owns it, then it is hard to assign responsibilities. Traditional information brokers in tourism such as destination marketing organizations and tour operators are known entities that work hard to establish trust within the tourism value chain. They assume responsibilities not only for information collection but also for verification and maintenance. Due to the fluidity and increasingly distributed nature of online information, with contents being posted and re-posted and retrieved from information clouds, it will be a challenge for Internet users of the future to clearly identify sources of tourism information and judge their credibility. Thirdly, massive data collection and the selling of such data raise issues of control and privacy. Both Google and Facebook are constantly in the news because of privacy violations and seem to have inept privacy management strategies in place (Dwyer 2011). They also create an illusion of control for the users by letting them set privacy controls while in the background, everything is captured and analysed. Privacy issues are particularly prominent in the context of location-based services in tourism (Anuar and Gretzel 2011), as they can not only identify a particular user based on characteristics and preferences but can also pinpoint the physical location and geographic patterns of the individual. Establishing trust with the providers of such applications is especially challenging in a tourism context because it involves greater needs for location-based support that might encourage privacy trade-offs and transactions that are more characterized by one-off relationships due to variety-seeking and increasingly shorter vacations. Tourism is also a use context that involves fun and liminality (Ryan 2002), leading tourists to engage in behaviors that might not be seen as acceptable in daily life and probably also leading to decreasing motivation to think about privacy issues. The often international nature of tourism experiences adds another layer of complexity to problems of credibility, responsibility and privacy. In general, technological advances are much faster than changes in legal systems and social norms, leading to dangerous gaps in the protection of rights, as well as in what is possible and what is deemed to be acceptable behavior.

New interactional frameworks

Because of the increasing use of social media and mobile technologies, Mascheroni (2007) argues that sociality has become mobile. This phenomenon has been widely discussed in the tourism literature in the context of backpackers and their respective virtual communities (Paris 2009; Young and Hanley 2011). It however now applies to a broad range of social interactions in tourism. As stressed by Litvin *et al.* (2008), accounts of personal experiences are critical for informing tourism-related decision-making processes due to the experiential nature of tourism. Because of technological advances, such personal exchanges of tourism information are increasingly taking place online, creating a wealth of electronic word-of-mouth that is often intended for communication beyond one's personal social circle. Digital tourism experience accounts serve important psychological and social functions throughout all stages of the tourism experience (Gretzel and Fesenmaier 2009), for instance status display and meaning creation. They have also widened the possibilities of communication with different groups across the different experience stages. Rosh White and White (2007) describe increased communication with families and friends at home. Platforms such as Virtualtourist.com and WAYN.com support exchanges with potential travel companions and also with local residents. Mobile phone apps that instantly translate conversations facilitate direct interactions with locals and tourism provider staff when on vacation. Moreover, it is now very common to befriend travel acquaintances through social networks to exchange photos and stories after the vacation. On the other hand, Gretzel (2010) points out that technology also limits interactions.

Instead of asking locals one can now consult the mobile phone for directions, and by popping in earphones and engaging with digital contents on a mobile device one can effectively avoid any kind of interaction with felow travellers. In the words of Turkle (2011), we can now be 'alone together', experiencing new intimacies in solitude and new solitudes in intimacy.

Progress in Web 2.0 and mobile technologies also changes the relationships travelers form with tourism destinations and service providers. Tourism consumers now often actively seek out relationships with companies through email newsletter subscriptions, 'liking' companies on Facebook, following destinations on Twitter, etc. Engagement with tourism providers and destinations is therefore much more active than in the traditional broadcast advertising world. Personalization technologies move such interactions to the next level. Tourists who enter personalized relationships with actors in the tourism industry engage in value co-creation with these companies. This requires changes in conventional customer relationship management practices and re-thinking of existing marketing models. One of the biggest advantages is the stickiness of such relationships (Novak and Schwabe 2009), as consumers invest in their profiles and companies make it difficult for them to move personalized contents. Overall, both consumers and producers of tourism experiences have much to gain from such technology-mediated relationships. However, due to the nature of tourism, many transactional relationships in tourism are short-lived and processes involved in 'breaking-up' with a tour company and 'defriending' destinations have to be discussed. Technology also allows consumers to circumvent the tourism industry to ever greater degrees. Platforms like Couchsurfing.com provide tourists with the opportunity to take advantage of the hospitality of locals in its original, non-transactional form. This is different from the disintermediation often discussed as a result of technology replacing services usually performed by specific companies in the tourism value chain. It does not simply change the procedural characteristics of a transaction but creates a new form and culture of travel.

When thinking about interactions, one has to of course also think about human–technology interactions and their effects on tourism experiences. Technology changes our actual perceptions and our motivations to process information (Gretzel 2010). It can facilitate tourism experiences as much as it can also disrupt them. As Turkle (2011) puts it, technology allows us to do anything from anywhere with anyone but also drains us as we try to do everything everywhere with everyone. It opens up new possibilities but also creates expectations that sometimes cannot be met.

Most importantly, thinking about the future of tourist–technology interactions, one has to acknowledge the shrinking distinction between humans and technology. Technology becomes increasingly human while humans become more and more technological, with cyborgs moving from science-fiction novels into reality and robotics shifting attention from industrial automation to humanoids for personal uses (Darlo *et al.* 2001). Robots do not have to be perfectly human-like in order to elicit sophisticated interactional patterns and emotions from humans; rather, they have to be 'alive enough' to become respected companions (Turkle

2011: 35). Indeed, social interactions can be triggered by rather mundane technologies such as traditional computer interfaces (Nass and Moon 2000). This raises questions of what rights cyborgs and human-like technologies have (Clarke 2011) and how human–robot interaction should be structured and governed (Thrun 2004). It requires acknowledging that technology has agency (Latour 2005) and discussing its implications. It further demands a better understanding of the qualities of interactions and their meaningfulness.

Last, but not least, it is important to recognize that technologies increasingly interact with each other. Radio frequency identification (RFID) tags talk to scanners, mobile phones interact with appliances, remote sensors feed information into databases, and so on. This of course requires interoperability among different kinds of technologies. Technological efforts such as the Semantic Web (Fensel *et al.* 2011) try to facilitate technology–technology interactions and are very much the focus of current and future developments. Efforts to build ontologies to facilitate such interactions also exist in tourism, where harmonizing contents and system languages has proven to be very important but quite difficult (Prantner *et al.* 2007). It does not take much to be able to imagine the many good things that will emerge from increased interactions among technologies, but also not much to realize the potential for abuses and the challenge of controlling such interactions with technologies gaining ever greater autonomy through advances in artificial intelligence.

Parallel worlds

The hype around technological development makes it easy to forget that there are geographic areas and individuals not connected through network technology. Existing coverage maps of Australia, for example http://www.nbnco.com.au/our network/coverage-maps.html, show that mobile phone and broadband Internet coverage can be sporadic even in industrialized nations. However, issues of digital divides are not limited to technological access but rather comprise of inequalities with respect to knowledge, education, resources, social support, language, cultural norms, information practices, etc. (Warschauer 2004). Thus, they cannot be easily eradicated through provision of technology and, even if use is achieved, might lead to different use patterns (Selwyn 2004). Therefore, visions of a future in which digital divides have been eliminated by policies focused on universal technology provision are not realistic.

Issues of digital divides have recently been addressed by the tourism literature. Minghetti and Buhalis (2010) stress the need for broader definitions of digital divides and outline their importance for tourism. They specifically argue that digital divides in tourism are even more complex than in other areas of economic and social exchanges because they happen at the interplay of demand and supply with very different digital, economic, social and cultural backgrounds, leading to a number of possible combinations of exchanges between high, upper, medium and low digital access destinations and tourists. Maurer and Lutz (2011) expand the model by adding layers of usage, skills and attitude gaps over the basic access gaps of destinations and tourists proposed by Minghetti and Buhalis. Lee and

Gretzel (2010) also show that differences in online travel planning between rural and urban US travelers cannot be explained by access divides only and very much pertain to different usage needs and attitudes.

What the current digital divide literature does not address is the question of whether a uniform world in terms of access to and use of digital technology is desirable from a touristic point of view. Tourist behavior is often motivated by desires to escape, to experience something different and to be aroused by the thrill of adventure (Pearce 2005). Growing technology dependence in daily life might mean ever greater needs to experience technology-free vacations. Indeed, tourists already increasingly seek out areas where network connectivity is nonexistent. Gretzel (2010) argues that with mobile phones providing ubiquitous safety nets, real adventures can only be had outside of network coverage. In the future, 'getting lost' will be increasingly seen as a privilege. Remoteness is already more likely defined based on lack of access to communication technologies than lack of transportation. Therefore, places free of technology might become the touristic paradises of the future. Burns and O'Regan (2008) describe the need of back-packers to drop out by not only leaving home but also leaving all technology behind. Deliberate actions to avoid technology are not only taken by tourists but also by tourism industry providers to create certain types of experiences. For instance, mobile phone blockers might be installed in hotel lobbies and spas to ensure the luxury atmosphere is not interrupted. Some eco lodges pride them-selves of being completely off the grid and off the network. Green Bank in West Virginia already markets itself as a wireless-free haven to potential tourists (Kooser 2011). This all leads one to think that in the future we might encounter parallel worlds or bubbles of high technology access and use and technology-free zones, with tourists traveling back and forth between them to take advantage of the best of both worlds. Consequently, tomorrow's tourist is as likely completely wired and equipped with the latest gadgets as completely stripped of technology. However, if, as described above, technology is merged with our bodies this will create problems for those who would like to leave it behind. Further, Gretzel (2010) argues that while physically stepping outside of the network might be possible, escaping the network culture might not be feasible (Terranova 2004).

Conclusion

The technological future of tourism is neither rosy nor gloom and doom. It is both full of opportunities and dangers, and it is essentially what we make of it. Techno-logical change is complex and not predetermined but the result of choices related to the design and use of the affordances of the technology. The above descriptions illustrate that technology can make travel simultaneously very social and extremely lonely (Turkle 2011), uniting and separating, stimulating and dull. One of the major issues is that tourism is often an application domain, but tourism stake-holders are usually not engaged in the actual technology development decisions. Tourism also serves as a catalyst of technological development in areas that might be socially or environmentally not ready as tourists increasingly take technologies with them when they travel. Further, theory building in academic tourism research lags behind in terms of acknowledging the mediated nature of tourism experiences and tourism-related transactions as well as the role of technology in sustainable tourism planning and management.

Tomorrow's tourists will certainly use technologies and they will be increasingly sophisticated and ever more blended into natural surfaces and human bodies. But it is not clear what these technologies are and what new interactional paradigms they will create. It is also not obvious who the users and non-users (both deliberate and involuntary) will be and who will own and control technologies and the digital traces they create. Most importantly, what we now conceive of as the tourism industry will likely have undergone fundamental changes and tourists will probably interact with a variety of entities, both human and technological, involving traditional economic transactions and other forms of exchanges to meet their tourism-related needs. These are important issues that this chapter raised. Addressing them requires research but also public discourse and regulatory frameworks that anticipate the changes and respective opportunities and challenges outlined above.

References

Adomavicius, G. and Tuzhilin, A. (2011) 'Context-aware Recommender Systems', in F. Ricci, L. Rokach, B. Shapira and P.B. Kantor (eds.) *Recommender Systems Handbook*, Vienna, Austria: Springer, pp. 217–253.

Anuar, F. and Gretzel, U. (2011) 'Privacy Concerns in the Context of Location-based Services Applications: Research Opportunities and Directions for Tourism', paper presented at ENTER 2011 Conference, Innsbruck, Austria, January 26–28, 2011.

Armbrust, M., Fox, A., Griffith, R., Joseph, A.D., Katz, R.H., Konwinski, A., Lee, G., Patterson, D.A., Rabkin, A., Stoica, I. and Zaharia, M. (2009) 'Above the Clouds: A Berkeley View of Cloud Computing', Technical Report No. UCB/EECS-2009-28, Berkeley, CA: University of California at Berkeley, online. Available at www.eecs. berkeley.edu/Pubs/TechRpts/2009/EECS-2009-28.pdf (accessed 9 January 2012).

Buhalis, D. (1997) 'Information Technology as a Strategic Tool for Economic, Social, Cultural and Environmental Benefits Enhancement of Tourism at Destination Regions', *International Journal of Tourism Research*, 3(1): 71–93.

—— (2003) *eTourism: Information Technology for Strategic Tourism Management*, London: Pearson.

Buhalis, D. and Law, R. (2008) 'Progress in Information Technology and Tourism Management: 20 years on and 10 years after the Internet – the State of eTourism Research', *Tourism Management*, 29(4): 609–623.

Burns, P.M. and O'Regan, M. (2008) 'Everyday Techno-social Devices in Everyday Travel Life: Digital Audio Devices in Solo Travelling Lifestyles', in P.M. Burns and M. Novelli (eds.) *Tourism and Mobilities: Local Global Connections*, Wallingford: CAB International, pp. 146–186.

Clarke, R. (2011) 'Cyborg Rights', *IEEE Technology and Society Magazine*, 30(3): 49–57.

Darlo, P., Guglielmelli, E. and Laschi, C. (2001) 'Humanoids and Personal Robots: Design and Experiments', *Journal of Robotic Systems*, 18(12): 673–690.

Dwyer, C. (2011) 'Privacy in the age of Google and Facebook', *IEEE Technology and Society Magazine*, 30(3): 58–63.

Fensel, D., Facca, F.M., Simperl, E. and Toma, I. (2011) *Semantic Web Services*, Berlin: Springer.

Getz, D. and Jamal, T. (1994) 'The Environment–community Symbiosis: A Case for Collaborative Tourism Planning', *Journal of Sustainable Tourism*, 2(3): 152–173.

Gretzel, U. (2010) 'Travel in the Network: Redirected Gazes, Ubiquitous Connections and New Frontiers' in M. Levina and G. Kien (eds.) *Post-global Network and Everyday Life*, New York: Peter Lang, pp. 41–58.

Gretzel, U. and Fesenmaier, D. (2009) 'Information Technology: Shaping the Past, Present and Future of Tourism', in T. Jamal and M. Robinson (eds.) *Handbook of Tourism Studies*, Thousand Oaks, CA: Sage, pp. 558–580.

Gretzel, U. and Jamal, T. (2009) 'Conceptualizing the Creative Tourist Class: Technology, Mobility and Tourism Experiences', *Tourism Analysis*, 14(4): 471–482.

Gretzel, U., Fesenmaier, D.R., Lee, Y.-J. and Tussyadiah, I. (2011) 'Narrating Travel Experiences: The Role of New Media', in R. Sharpley and P. Stone (eds.) *Tourist Experiences: Contemporary Perspectives*, New York: Routledge, pp. 171–182.

Hall, C.M. (2005) 'Reconsidering the Geography of Tourism and Contemporary Mobility', *Geographical Research*, 43(2): 125–139.

Jansson, A. (2007) 'A Sense of Tourism: New Media and the Dialectic of Encapsulation/decapsulation', *Tourist Studies*, 7(1): 5–24.

Jennings, G. and Weiler, B. (2004) 'Mediating Meaning: Perspectives on Brokering Quality Tourist Experiences', Department of Management Working Paper Series 20/04, Monash University, online. Available at www.buseco.monash.edu.au/mgt/research/working-papers/2004/wp20-04.pdf (accessed 5 December 2011).

Joo, J. (2002) 'A Business Model and its Development Strategies for Electronic Tourism Markets', *Information Systems Management*, 19(3): 58–69.

Kenyon, R.V. and Leigh, J. (2011) 'Human Augmentics: Augmenting Human Evolution', paper presented at IEEE Engineering Medicine Biology Conference 2011, Boston, MA, August 30–September 3, 2011.

Kooser, A. (2011) ' "Allergic" to Wi-fi? Move to West Virginia', online. Available at news.cnet.com/8301-17938_105-20106269-1/allergic-to-wi-fi-move-to-west-virginia/ (accessed 5 January 2011).

Latour, B. (2005) *Reassembling the Social: An Introduction to Actor-network-theory*, Oxford: Oxford University Press.

Lee, K. and Gretzel, U. (2010) 'Differences in Online Travel Planning: A Rural vs. Urban Perspective', 41st Annual Proceedings of the Travel and Tourism Research Association Conference, San Antonio, TX, June 20–22, 2010, Travel and Tourism Research Association.

Litvin, S.W., Goldsmith, R.E. and Pan, B. (2008) 'Electronic Word-of-mouth in Hospitality and Tourism Management', *Tourism Management*, 29(3): 458–468.

Mascheroni, G. (2007) 'Global Nomads' Network and Mobile Sociality: Exploring New Media Uses on the Move', *Information, Communication & Society*, 10(4): 527–546.

Maurer, C. and Lutz, V. (2011) 'The Impact of Digital Divide on Global Tourism: Strategic Implications of Overcoming Communication Gaps caused by Digital Inequalities', in R. Law, M. Fuchs and F. Ricci (eds.) *Information and Communication Technologies in Tourism 2011*, Vienna, Austria: Springer Verlag, pp. 265–278.

Minghetti, V. and Buhalis, D. (2010) 'Digital Divide in Tourism', *Journal of Travel Research*, 49(3): 267–281.

Nass, C. and Moon, Y. (2000) 'Machines and Mindlessness: Social Responses to Computers', *Journal of Social Issues*, 56(1): 81–103.

Novak, J. and Schwabe, G. (2009) 'Designing for Reintermediation in the Brick-and-mortar World: Towards the Travel Agency of the Future', *Electronic Markets*, 19(1): 15–29.

Paris, C.M. (2009) 'The Virtualization of Backpacker Culture', in W. Höpken, U. Gretzel, and R. Law (eds.) *Information and Communication Technologies in Tourism 2009*, Vienna, Austria: Springer Verlag, pp. 25–35.

Pearce, P.L. (2005) *Tourist Behaviour: Themes and Conceptual Schemes*, Clevedon: Channel View Publications.

Poon, A. (1993) *Tourism, Technology and Competitive Strategies*, Wallingford: CAB International.

Prantner, K., Ding, Y., Luger, M., Yan, Z. and Herzog, C. (2007) 'Tourism Ontology and Semantic Management System: State-of-the-arts Analysis', IADIS International Conference WWW/Internet 2007, online. Available at www.iadis.net/dl/final_uploads/200712C070.pdf (accessed 5 January 2011).

Pühretmair, F. and Nussbaum, G. (2011) 'Web Design, Assistive Technologies and Accessible Tourism', in D. Buhalis and S. Darcy (eds.) *Accessible Tourism: Concepts and Issues*, Bristol: Channel View Publications, pp. 274–286.

Rosh White, N. and White, P.B. (2007) 'Home and Away: Tourists in a Connected World', *Annals of Tourism Research*, 34(1): 88–104.

Ryan, C. (2002) *The Tourist Experience*, 2nd edn, London: Thomson Learning.

Selwyn, N. (2004) 'Reconsidering Political and Popular Understandings of the Digital Divide', *New Media Society*, 6(3): 341–362.

Seow, S.C., Wixon, D., MacKenzie, S., Jacucci, G., Morrison, A. and Wilson, A. (2009) 'Multitouch and Surface Computing', in D.R. Olsen Jr., R.B. Arthur, K. Hinckley, M.R. Morris, S.E. Hudson and S. Greenberg (eds.) *CHI Extended Abstracts, CHI 2009*, April 4–9, 2009, Boston, MA, pp. 4767–4769.

Sheldon, P.J. (1997) *Tourism Information Technology*, Wallingford: CAB International.

Sigala, M., Christou, E. and Gretzel, U. (eds.) (2012) *Social Media in Travel, Tourism and Hospitality*, Brookfield, VT: Ashgate.

Smailagic, A. and Kenn, H. (2011) 'New Advances in Wearable Computing', *Pervasive Computing*, 10(4): 96–100.

Stamboulis, Y. and Skayannis, P. (2003) 'Innovation Strategies and Technology for Experience-based Tourism', *Tourism Management*, 24(1): 35–43.

Terranova, T. (2004) *Network Culture: Politics for the Information Age*, Ann Arbor, MI: Pluto Press.

Thrun, S. (2004) 'Toward a Framework for Human–robot Interaction', *Human–Computer Interaction*, 19(1–2): 9–24.

Tomasi, C., Rafii, A. and Torunoglu, I. (2003) 'Full-Size Projection Keyboard for Hand-held Devices', *Communication of the ACM*, 46(7): 70–75.

Turkle, S. (2011) *Alone Together: Why we Expect More from Technology and Less from Each Other*, New York: Basic Books.

Tussyadiah, I. and Fesenmaier, D.R. (2009) 'Mediating Tourist Experiences: Access to Places via Shared Videos', *Annals of Tourism Research*, 36(1), 24–40.

Wang, D., Park, S. and Fesenmaier, D.R. (2011) 'The Role of Smart Phones in Mediating the Touristic Experience', *Journal of Travel Research*, forthcoming, first published on December 23, 2011, online. DOI: 10.1177/0047287511426341.

Warschauer, M. (2004) *Technology and Social Inclusion: Rethinking the Digital Divide*, Cambridge, MA: MIT Press.

Werthner, H. and Klein, S. (1999) *Information Technology and Tourism – a Challenging Relationship*, Vienna, Austria: Springer-Verlag.

Young, T. and Hanley, J. (2011) 'Virtual Mobilities: Backpackers, New Media and Online Travel Communities', online. Available at www.tasa.org.au/uploads/2011/01/Young-Tamara_-Hanley-Jo.pdf (accessed 10 December 2011).

10 Human resource issues in the new millennium

Scott Richardson

Introduction

The tourism and hospitality industry worldwide has been confronted with the problem of attracting and retaining quality employees, which has led to a shortage of skilled personnel to staff the large number of tourism and hospitality businesses (Deery and Shaw 1999; Dermady and Holloway 1998; Emenheiser *et al.* 1998; Ferris *et al.* 2002; Freeland 2000; Heraty and Morley 1998; Hinkin and Tracey 2000; Tourism Division 2002). This problem is complex with many different contributing factors, and it has been argued that there are a number of industry-specific characteristics that exacerbate this skills shortage. These characteristics include a young transient workforce, low levels of pay and formal qualifications, high levels of female, student, part-time and casual workers, a high proportion of low-skilled jobs, a large proportion of hours worked outside normal business hours, a negative industry image in the eyes of potential employees, a large number of migrant staff, poor utilization of student labor and high levels of staff turnover (Baum 2006; Brien 2004; Fraser 2003; Freeland 2000; Riley *et al.* 2002; Service Skills Victoria 2005; Tourism Division 2002). These characteristics all add to the complex problems associated with the recruitment and retention of quality employees for tourism and hospitality companies in the new millennium.

A number of recent reports have highlighted the issue of labor and skills shortages worldwide (de Jong 2008; International Society of Hospitality Consultants 2006). At the 2006 International Society of Hospitality Consultants (ISHC) Annual Conference held in Miami, Florida, ISHC members participated in a series of roundtable discussions to identify the top ten issues in the tourism and hospitality industry for 2007. The debate included in-depth discussions on over 100 different issues. Ultimately, the issue thought to be the greatest contemporary challenge for the tourism and hospitality industry was labor and skills shortages (International Society of Hospitality Consultants 2006). It is claimed that attracting and retaining qualified workers, once only an issue for a small number of regional, remote and niche markets, is becoming the most significant concern for all tourism and hospitality businesses globally. The International Society of Hospitality Consultants (2006) claim that demography, wage levels, failure to adequately address worker satisfaction and a reputation for long hours and low pay are all contributing factors.

Peter de Jong, the President and CEO of the Pacific Asia Travel Association, agrees, claiming that a shortage of human resources has been identified as one of four 'mega forces' which are re-shaping the demand for travel services. Mr. de Jong claims that:

> The explosive growth of tourism infrastructure globally is placing incredible strains on the travel and tourism industry to deliver sufficient levels of suitably-skilled human resources to sustain this growth. In some cases the 'hardware' is being built without concern for the 'software' needed to run the operations. This is a huge, multi-dimensional dilemma covering issues such as recruitment, education, on-the-job training, language skills, performance management, retention and the mobility of labour.
>
> (de Jong 2008: 3)

Skills shortages in the tourism and hospitality industry

There are a number of factors that will contribute to the scarcity or shortage of a particular skill (Trendle 2005). On the demand side, new products, new technology and globalization will affect the requirements for particular skills, while on the supply side the aging of the workforce, changes in the attractiveness of a particular position and changes in the number of new workers entering and completing training and education will determine the extent of skills available (Department of Employment and Workplace Relations 2002; Trendle 2005). For these reasons a shortage of skilled labor can be caused or removed by a number of factors influencing the supply and demand of skilled labor. There is evidence that skills shortages lead to firms having difficulties in providing suitable customer service, delays in developing new products and services, increased operating costs and obstacles to meeting the required quality standards (Mulcahy 1999). Understanding which of the abovementioned factors are causing the current skills shortage in the tourism and hospitality industry and being able to formulate solutions to combat this problem is extremely important to the economic performance of the industry as a whole.

On a regional basis, in an Australian context the Tourism Division (2002) state that there are a number of areas in which there are skills shortages in the tourism and hospitality industry. Some of the areas reported include a critical shortage of chefs, cooks and pastry cooks as well as food and beverage staff in the hospitality industry, while in the tourism industry there are skills shortages in particular geographic areas such as Gippsland, the Central Highland and the Great Ocean Road regions in Victoria (Service Skills Victoria 2005). It was also found that there are a number of skills gaps emerging including in the areas of e-business, customer service, small business management and risk assessment and management. The Tourism Council of Tasmania (2004) agree that chefs and food and beverage attendants with adequate skills are in short supply but add that other areas are also facing skills shortages, including candidates with gaming licenses as well as Keno and Totalisator Agency Board (TAB) experience. The report also suggests that given the developing demand for special interest tourism activities, there is also a shortage of guides with adequate interpretive skills. It has been suggested that due to the fragmented nature of the industry in Australia, it is not well equipped to respond to the future challenges presented by these skills shortages (Service Skills Victoria 2005).

On a wider basis, the World Travel and Tourism Council (cited in de Jong 2008) predicts that Asia Pacific travel and tourism will require more than 15 million directly related new jobs by 2020 just to service travel demand. This claim is underlined by the fact that there are over 1,200 new hotels under development in the Asia Pacific region and these organizations will require hundreds of thousands of experienced managers, front desk, housekeeping, food and beverage and maintenance staff, to name just a few of the positions that will be need to be filled (de Jong 2008). De Jong (2008) also claims that in China alone an estimated 4,000 new airline pilots will be required each year just to keep up with basic growth.

According to Lucas and Johnson (2003: 153) 'attracting and retaining well-educated, skilled, enthusiastic and committed workers is a chronic problem for the hospitality and tourism industries in the developed world'. This problem is highlighted by a number of studies indicating that the proportion of workers in the tourism and hospitality industry who have tertiary qualifications is much lower than most other industry sectors (ABS 2006). There are also reports of many tourism and hospitality management graduates leaving the industry or even failing to enter the industry upon graduation due to low job satisfaction, poor employment conditions and absence of motivating factors, resulting in high staff turnover and wastage of trained and experienced personnel (Doherty *et al.* 2001; Jenkins 2001). In fact, O'Leary and Deegan (2005) found that 46 percent of tourism and hospitality graduates were working in other industries.

Domonte and Vaden (1987) state that the factor that had the greatest influence on career decisions of potential hospitality employees was work experience. There has been much written recently about the benefits of work-based learning, also known as 'work-integrated learning'. Work-based learning is seen as one of the best ways of ensuring the future tourism and hospitality workforce is well trained and has an understanding of what it is like to work in the industry. This should reduce the likelihood that perceptions of the industry will keep them out, and they will gain the skills that the industry needs (Mulcahy 1999). The economic environment over the last decade, with generally low unemployment rates, means that job markets in many parts of the world are very competitive, both between companies within industries, as well as across industries. This environment, coupled with tourists in the new millennium becoming more sophisticated and demanding, has resulted in companies within the tourism and hospitality industry needing to also become sophisticated enough to handle the range of clients and circumstances with which they are faced. Therefore, in order to succeed, organizations must employ workers that have a combination of industry experience and educational qualifications to ensure the challenges and complexities of management in today's industry are met.

A widespread view is that skills shortages need to be addressed because they potentially impact on productivity, employment, and earnings (Frogner 2002;

Trendle 2005). The National Tourism Investment Strategy Consultative Group (2006) states that enterprises experiencing skills shortages will in the short term experience increased recruitment and operating costs, reduced productivity and constraints on growth: in the long term the skilled workers may leave the industry altogether. There are a number of reasons that skills shortages are appearing in the tourism and hospitality industry. The International Society of Hospitality Consultants (2006: 1) states that four of the biggest issues facing tourism and hospitality company's recruitment and retention issues in the new millennium are:

- Demographics: Population growth rates have been slowing in Europe, the US and elsewhere for decades, so the number of workers leaving the workforce now exceeds those that are entering. The aging workforce moving into retirement is creating a huge void that can only be expected to grow larger going forward.
- Lagging wage rates: Long criticized for paying salaries and wages below those common in other industries, hospitality companies are increasingly finding it difficult to attract and retain qualified candidates willing to attract standard wages.
- Industry reputation: Like it or not, the hospitality industry has not done enough to earn a reputation as a top career choice for college graduates. Notorious for long hours, night and weekend shifts our industry has Gen-X'ers and Gen-Y'ers seeking other careers with a perceived higher quality of life and better wages.
- De-emphasis on training and worker satisfaction: Following the worldwide dip in demand that followed 9/11 and the Bali bombings many hotel companies failed to fully restore training and worker enrichment programs that marked the 1980s and 1990s. This comes at a time when lodging brands are increasingly adding amenities and services in order to differentiate themselves from competitors.

These issues highlight the issues facing tourism and hospitality employers. Some of these are within the control of the industry, such as lagging wage rates, reputation and training. The industry must address these. The issue of demographics is out of the control of employers and highlights the need to understand the young workers and potential workers to ensure that their needs are being met by the industry.

New generations of employees

A further complication also arises in that in the new millennium employers have had to deal with the emergence of a new generation of worker, Generation Y, and in coming years the emergence of Generation Z. While research into the career needs of Generation Z are only just beginning, much has been written on the career requirements of Generation Y. The ways in which this group view a career are different to previous generations. The traditional work philosophy has been a job for life, with employees spending their entire careers in one industry and in many cases with just one employer (Ayres 2006). Over the past decade, coinciding with the new millennium, this philosophy has been replaced by a more uncertain career structure, with employees frequently changing employers within their industry and many also pursuing work in different industries (Ayres 2006). The Generation Y employee is not interested in a job for life, instead seeking flexibility and work–life balance (Oliver 2006). This means that this current generation of employees, as well as future generations, will be more demanding on employers than their predecessors, leading to organizations facing further recruitment and retention issues. Morton (2002) states that Generation Y employees show a tendency towards valuing equality in the workplace: they seek positions that offer reasonable wages and good opportunities for training and they respect managers who empower workers and who are open and honest with employees.

Lloyd (2005) states that in the current economic climate, with skills shortages prevalent, the Generation Y employee knows that they can pick and choose their employer: they use this power to get what they want or they will find another job. Oliver (2006) states that overall Generation Y workers are seen to have much higher expectations of a job than previous generations, including high expectations of pay, conditions, promotion and advancement. If an employer cannot meet the expectations mentioned above, the Generation Y employee will pursue other avenues for employment. If employers can better understand the psyche of the Generation Y worker it will allow them to provide greater opportunities for them based on their ideals and expectations. Barron *et al.* (2007: 122) also claim that 'given the implications of this group's features on recruitment to, and retention in, the hospitality industry, in conjunction with management and development needs, it is important for the industry as a whole that this knowledge gap is addressed'. These factors highlight the importance of studying the attitudes and perceptions of current students (Generation Y) towards working in the tourism and hospitality industry. It is thus important to understand how employers in the tourism and hospitality industry are utilizing students, as casual and part-time workers, as well as in work-based learning programs, and how the utilization of these employees is affecting decisions regarding pursuing or continuing careers in the industry.

Tourism and hospitality students' perceptions of the industry

A number of recent reports and articles by Richardson (2009a, b, 2010a, b, c) have highlighted the perceptions and attitudes of current Generation Y student's undertaking tourism and hospitality degrees in both Australia (379 respondents) and Malaysia (439 respondents). These studies have focused on two main areas: the factors these students find important when choosing a career and the extent to which they believe the tourism and hospitality industry offers these factors (Richardson 2009b, 2010a, c). This previous research was based on a study by Kyriacou and Coulthard (2000), and asked students to identify how important each of 20 chosen factors were when choosing a career and the extent to which they believed a career in tourism and hospitality offered them these factors. It is apparent from these reports that students do not believe that the industry offers them the factors they find important when choosing a career. Richardson recently conducted the same study with a smaller group of US students (258 respondents) and the findings of this aggregated study (1,076 respondents) will be discussed further in this chapter.

Overall it was found that respondents rate each of the 20 items as important, with very few respondents choosing not important for any of the factors and only three factors receiving more than 10 percent of respondents choosing not important. The most important factor identified by respondents was 'A job that I will find enjoyable', which 87.5 percent of respondents considered as very important. Based on the number of respondents who chose very important as their response, the next four most important factors in choosing a career are 'Pleasant working environment' (72.9 percent), 'A secure job' (67.6 percent), 'Good promotion prospects' (63.7 percent) and 'High earnings over length of career' (63.6 percent).

When assessing whether respondents believed the industry offered them these important factors, it was found that while more than 50 percent of respondents rate 13 factors as very important, there is only 1 factor where more than 50 percent of respondents claim the industry definitely offers these factors. For instance, while 99.8 percent of respondents claim that finding a job that is enjoyable is important, only 40.1 percent believe they will definitely find an enjoyable job in the tourism and hospitality industry. Other factors with similar responses include 'A secure job', with 98.2 percent of respondents claiming this is important, while 20.2 percent claim the industry does not offer this at all, 'Good promotion prospects' (98.9 percent important, 22.4 percent not at all offered) and 'High earnings over length of career' (98.2 percent important, 32.5 percent not at all offered), 'A job that can easily be combined with parenthood' (82.2 percent important, 38.2 percent not at all offered), and 'Reasonable workload' (96 percent important, 30.3 percent not at all offered).

To test statistically whether significant differences occur between the importance respondents place on career factors and the extent to which they believe tourism and hospitality offered these, a paired sample t-test was used. All factors, except one, 'The opportunity to travel abroad', were found to be significantly different because their p-value is less than the critical value of 0.05. For all of the 20 factors the importance factor has a lower mean than the extent to which students believe a career in tourism and hospitality offers that factor. This implies that students do not believe that a career in tourism and hospitality will offer them the factors that they find important in choosing a future career.

This study investigated undergraduate student's attitudes towards important factors in choosing a career as well as their perceptions as to the degree they believed tourism and hospitality careers offer these factors. They show that undergraduate students who are studying tourism and hospitality in Australia, the United States and Malaysia do not believe that the industry offers them the attributes that they see as important in choosing a future career. It was found that for the majority of the 20 factors examined, there is a significant difference between what the students see as important in pursuing a future career and the extent to which they feel a career in tourism and hospitality offers these in both countries. These findings highlight the fact that industry must attempt to address this imbalance if it has any chance of recruiting and retaining these very important assets.

Further to these findings, when assessing the areas that Australian students held negative views of the industry Richardson (2010b, c) found that the main areas that respondents list include poor relationships with managers, unfair promotion procedures, unclear career paths, low pay and a poor work–life balance because of the unusual hours worked. Some of the comments made by students in relation to their relationships with managers (Richardson 2009a) included:

> I worked at a Leagues club and was left in one department – even though my original employment agreement included rotating around and learning various departments. I was also expected to do shifts of up to 15 hours when a new bar was being launched. The treatment at this club was less than satisfactory and I believe this was partially to blame for the enormous turnover of staff.

There were many other responses relating to the poor treatment of staff by managers, including one respondent reporting that they were suspended for taking time off while they were sick, and another claiming that their manager was 'constantly screaming at me leaving me feeling embarrassed and unappreciated'. A number of respondents also commented that they did not believe that their managers had the expertise or knowledge to successfully manage their organization. One respondent claimed:

> I had more than one negative experience with people who were in charge and had no idea, poor people skills, no management expertise or compassion. Whilst working for one employer they decided that part-time meant that you had to be available when they wanted you not when you were available, the attitude was job first studies second, I chose studies.

Finally some respondents claimed that management did not spend enough time and effort in ensuring one of their greatest assets, their staff, had sufficient resources to carry out their jobs to a high standard. Respondents reported that in some cases their employer had no human resource department and provided very few training and development opportunities. Another commented on the fact that while they believed that they would receive better treatment and opportunities in a smaller organization they actually found bigger organizations provided them with better training and career opportunities, with one respondent claiming 'It still amazes me that my employer at a major sporting facility treats me better than many of the smaller companies that I have worked for (perhaps funding for training and HR is the key here?)'. Another respondent was also very critical of the level of HR management in the industry, commenting that:

> In general I feel HR management (or lack thereof) is the most critical aspect of these industries. Human capital is more valuable than any piece of equipment and I honestly think that employers and managers forget where their earnings come from. Quality staff (motivated, well trained, efficient) = happy customers = $$$. Seems like a pretty simple equation yet in previous

jobs I have found that to improve profits a new coffee machine was bought, table settings changed, new menu implemented etc. [. . .] rather than spending a day training and motivating staff to improve service and increase sales. The promotion of the 'team' within a hospitality business is a façade as few actually achieve this due to casualization and high staff turnover.

Another issue that was mentioned a number of times by respondents (Richardson 2009a) were working conditions in the industry. A number of respondents claimed that the conditions of their employment left them feeling unmotivated and unappreciated, and morale in the industry is negatively affected by these conditions. The main issues discussed by respondents included not getting paid for working overtime, issues with the hours worked and the pay levels offered in the industry. Some of the comments provided by respondents in relation to the excessive and unusual number of hours worked and pay issues in the industry included:

I was employed as a casual to work 20–30 hours per week though after several weeks it increased to 50 hours a week. I had to work 6–7-day weeks and was unable to choose which days I could have off.

Whilst a second respondent also commented on the unusual number of hours worked in the industry:

Unfortunately for us, we are understaffed and overworked. Working 6 days a week, 13 hour days for 3 months over summer does not boost an employee's morale! Under the previous manager staff morale was at an all time low, with many staff leaving, bitching being the most common chat among staff and staff having no reward for their hard work. The staff were forced under a new agreement (apparently a majority vote was for), giving us a base wage increase, but cutting all other penalties – including public holidays. As a high majority of our staff are students this did not go over well as we work the public holidays to make that extra money.

These factors led to a staggering 42.4 percent of respondents, who stated they had work experience in the tourism and hospitality industry in Australia, claiming it was definite that they would not pursue a career in the industry, with almost all (92.6 percent) citing working in the industry as the main reason for this decision (Richardson 2010b).

Recommendations to ensure an adequate workforce into the future

Information/communication and marketing of career opportunities

Universities need to play their part in ensuring that students are being given realistic expectations of the types of positions available in the industry. They need to also provide students with a greater awareness of the working conditions. The careers and career paths offered by the industry also need to be more adequately developed, and these paths require more extensive and comprehensive marketing and promotion. Information about the career paths available should be made easier to access for current and prospective staff in order for them to start planning their career. This information could be provided during induction with the company when students begin their casual or part-time positions while they are still studying. This will introduce students to the career paths offered and advise them of the skills and training they will require to pursue these opportunities. This will facilitate career planning whereby these students will begin to plan their career with the company from their first days on the job.

Image

The image of employment in the tourism and hospitality industry needs to be improved. This can only be achieved if the industry works collaboratively to address the issues surrounding low pay and long and unusual hours. As previously discussed, the current generation of workers (Generation Y) are looking for a career which offers them work–life balance. These employees do not want to work every weekend or on every holiday. They also do not want to work late nights or early mornings on a consistent basis. They want flexibility in their rostering and freedom to have a life outside the workplace. It is imperative that the industry works on using innovative rostering techniques to ensure these workers can get the work–life balance that they require. If this is to occur, then all parties will benefit. The employee will be happy, and therefore more productive and more likely to stay with the employer. The employer will benefit through reduced staff turnover, lower costs and higher productivity of the workforce, which all add up to greater profits for the organization. Also, as the Generation Y employee is extremely concerned with their work–life balance, if the employer can meet their needs in this area the worker is less likely to be concerned about the wages offered.

Relationship with managers/empowerment

One of the main student concerns with tourism and hospitality jobs is the lack of decision-making and responsibility given to junior employees. There has been much written about the importance of empowerment in ensuring a healthy and productive workplace. In recent years, scholars such as Donavan (1994), Lashley (1995) and Chow *et al.* (2006) have written about the benefits to hospitality organizations of empowering employees. Hancer and George (2003) have described empowerment as the self-generated exercising of judgment by staff as well as staff being given authority to make everyday decisions. One of the main proponents of using empowerment to generate positive feelings in employees is Lashley (1995, 1999, 2000, 2001). Lashley (2000: 791) claims that to make empowerment happen, employees should be more involved in the management process. He claims that this form of empowerment should include 'some development of personal efficacy and engagement in service performance, but which involves limited decision making apart from that required of their role in service performance'. Jones and Davies (1991) further claim that the idea of empowering employees is to encourage them to be responsible for their own performance and its development. Ripley and Ripley (1993) believe that empowerment will also encourage staff to best utilize their skills and strive to increase their skill set. It has been claimed that by empowering employees, organizations will find that the level of client satisfaction will increase (Johns 1993), and that this increase in customer satisfaction will lead to additional sales and improved profits (Plunkett and Fournier 1991).

One of the main characteristics of the Generation Y employee is that they want responsibility and to be challenged. If the tourism and hospitality industry can begin to offer a greater level of empowerment and autonomy to its workforce, it will help to challenge and drive the younger Generation Y worker. This in turn will increase the employee's satisfaction with their job and encourage them to pursue a career with the organization.

Recognition of formal qualifications

Industry must place a much greater emphasis on professional and academic qualifications, which must be formally recognized and accredited. The industry must also develop remuneration structures appropriate for these qualifications. If it is more heavily involved in curriculum design it will more readily see the benefits and relevance of these programs, therefore being more inclined to recognize these degrees and reward employees appropriately.

Long-term workforce planning

In a highly competitive environment, with new competitors opening every day, companies tend to focus on the day-to-day running of their operations and not think strategically about the long-term impacts today's decisions will have on the workforce of the future. The creation of an efficient and productive workforce requires more than an adequate number of workers. People wanting to work in the industry must be able to find rewarding employment that meets their personal and family responsibilities. If the industry recognizes the importance of long-term workforce planning, it can begin to address the some of the specific issues of skill shortages and workforce development.

Understanding the Generation Y worker to ensure positive experiences

There is a greater need for organizations to focus on current tourism and hospitality students working in their companies. This study has found that this does not currently occur, with all companies interviewed claiming they do not treat students any differently than other employees. It has been stated that the new generation of worker (Generation Y) has many characteristics that are different to previous generations. It is critical that companies understand these characteristics in order to ensure they can offer the Generation Y worker the attributes they are seeking in a career.

Generation Y workers want to be treated differently and individually, and it has been stated in this chapter that for both employers and students to receive maximum benefit from student employment, students should be treated differently to other casual staff. There are a number of reasons why this is the case, including to increase the skills of the student by providing them with cross-training; to provide the organization with more experienced and qualified staff upon graduation; and if students are appreciated and treated differently they are also more likely to continue to work for the employer and stay in the industry upon graduation.

Students are different to regular staff in that they are constantly increasing their skills by undertaking their university courses. These skills should be identified and utilized by employers, not only to benefit the student, but to also benefit the organization by effectively applying the skills the student has acquired. The industry needs to start designing individualized training programs, based on each student's requirements, which students can complete while undertaking their study. This will benefit both parties. First, the student will benefit from being offered a comprehensive and meaningful training program, highlighting many of the roles and duties on offer within the industry. Secondly, industry will benefit upon the students' graduation by having highly trained, highly educated and motivated employees, enthusiastic about developing a career with the company. It has been argued that offering these types of programs will also increase the retention of these students once they graduate, with one of the organizations interviewed, who currently offers a student training program, claiming that many of the students undertaking their training program remain with the company upon graduation.

By offering students challenging and demanding tasks, rather than basic, low-skilled, entry-level tasks, students will feel a sense of responsibility and achievement. By rewarding students when they successfully complete tasks it will also result in students feeling valued and appreciated. It has been argued that responsibility and feeling valued by the company are key characteristics of the Generation Y employee. If companies can offer students either a specific student-oriented training program, or if this is not feasible provide them with meaningful tasks, students are more likely to have a positive experience working in the industry, making it more likely that they will remain in the industry after graduation.

Conclusion

Over the next decade, the growth of positions in the tourism and hospitality industry around the world has been widely reported. In Australia, Minister for Tourism Martin Ferguson AM MP states that labor shortages continue to plague the industry in Australia (2011: 1). 'Nationally we have an estimated 35,800 vacancies in tourism industry jobs and an additional 56,000 people will be needed to fill vacancies by 2015 including 26,000 skilled positions' (Ferguson and Rau 2011). As stated above, the World Travel and Tourism Council (cited in de Jong 2008) predicts that Asia Pacific travel and tourism will require more than 15 million directly related new jobs by 2020 just to service travel demand. If we take the standpoint that students should be encouraged to stay within their trained industry, these findings suggest that industry and educators must work together to solve employment shortfalls by recruiting and retaining skilled and qualified graduates. These graduates will have a combination of core business and management skills, as well as specialist property skills and knowledge. The holistic approach that modern tourism and hospitality degrees undertake enables graduates to identify and articulate the functions and dynamics of the industry. Graduates will also have skills in designing and facilitating strategic thinking and visioning, by using complex theories. They also possess a deeper understanding of sustainability of the environment and understand the role of corporate social responsibility and accountability in today's highly sensitive environment. As well as university training, these graduates usually have some form of training and experience working in the industry while they completed their studies. This combination of the theoretical knowledge as well as the on-the-job experience and training make graduates an extremely valuable resource for the tourism and hospitality industry.

Some may argue that it does not matter if graduates enter fields other than those with which they have studied and been trained. The turnover culture in the tourism and hospitality industry facilitates this argument, because it is seen as the norm (Kraft 1985) to frequently change positions and companies. Tourism and hospitality degree programs can also inadvertently add to this problem, as generally they develop a range of transferable skills, making tourism and hospitality graduates attractive to employers in other industries.

This chapter argues that the attitude that it does not matter if graduates leave or fail to enter the industry is flawed, as the cost of losing these graduates is extremely high. The cost of this turnover has been widely discussed and has financial, as well as psychological, implications for tourism and hospitality organizations. These financial costs include the cost of recruiting, selecting and training a new employee as well as other associated costs (uniforms, induction etc.); the lost productivity while the new staff are trained; and the loss of money spent training and developing the departing staff member. The psychological implications encase staff morale and commitment to the company. Also, if we take Australia as an example, there are only an estimated 2,500 tourism and hospitality graduates each year; therefore the industry must make it a priority to attract as many of these as possible.

This highlights the need for the industry to adopt tactics and strategies aimed at ensuring that potential employees, i.e. tourism and hospitality students, are not leaving the industry or even failing to enter the industry upon graduation. It is clear that there are a number of areas, particularly pay, promotion opportunities and the relationship between respondents and their managers, that the industry must work on to ensure students are receiving positive experiences while they work during their degree. Unless the industry can offer higher wages, facilitate work–life balance by offering flexible work hours, and improve relationships between employees and managers, the industry will continue to lose these highly skilled and highly trained employees, putting at risk the future growth of the tourism industry worldwide.

References

ABS (2006) *Australian Labour Market Statistics*, ABS, online. Available at www.ausstats. abs.gov.au/ausstats/subscriber.nsf/0/C13A89556EEE7941CA25747A00116F59/$ File/61050_jul%202006.pdf (accessed 27 October 2006).

Ayres, H. (2006) 'Career Development in Tourism and Leisure: An Exploratory Study of the Influence of Mobility and Mentoring', *Journal of Hospitality and Tourism Management*, 13(2): 113–123.

Barron, P., Maxwell, G., Broadbridge, A. and Ogden, S. (2007) 'Careers in Hospitality Management: Generation Y's Experiences and Perceptions', *Journal of Hospitality and Tourism Management*, 14(2): 119–128.

Baum, T. (2006) *Human Resource Management for Tourism, Hospitality and Leisure: An International Perspective*, London: Thomson Learning.

Brien, A. (2004) 'Do I Want a Job in Hospitality? Only Till I get a Real Job!', in K.A. Smith and C. Schott (eds.), *Proceedings of the New Zealand Tourism and Hospitality Research Conference*, Wellington, New Zealand, pp. 35–42.

Chow, I.H., Lob, W., Sha, Z. and Hong, J. (2006) 'The Impact of Developmental Experience, Empowerment, and Organizational Support on Catering Service Staff Performance', *International Journal of Hospitality Management*, 25(3): 478–495.

de Jong, P. (2008) 'Four "Mega Forces" are Re-shaping Demand for Travel Services. Discussion notes of the Destination Marketing Association International: 94th Annual Convention', Pacific Asia Travel Association, online. Available at www.pata.org/ patasite/fileadmin/docs/speeches_presentations/2008/080728-30_DMIA_de_Jong.pdf (accessed 15 August 2008).

Deery, M. and Shaw, R. (1999) 'An Investigation of the Relationship Between Employee Turnover and Organisational Culture', *Journal of Hospitality and Tourism Research*, 23(4): 387–400.

Department of Employment and Workplace Relations (2002) *Nature and Causes of Skills Shortages: Reflections from the Commonwealth National Industry Skills Initiative Working Groups*, Department of Education, Science and Training, online. Available at www.skillsinitiative.gov.au/documents/nature_causesskillshortages.pdf (accessed 24 April 2006).

Dermady, M.B. and Holloway, R.W. (1998) 'Recruitment and Retention of Managers: Developing a Management Career Package', *Cornell Hotel and Restaurant Administration Quarterly*, 39(6): 20–25.

Doherty, L., Guerrier, Y., Jamieson, S., Lashley, C. and Lockwood, A. (2001) *Getting Ahead: Graduate Careers in Hospitality Management*, London:CHME/HEFCE.

Domonte, T. and Vaden, A.G. (1987) 'Career Decisions in Hospitality Management', *Hospitality Education and Research Journal*, 11(2): 51–63.

Donavan, M. (1994) 'The Empowerment Plan', *Journal for Quality and Participation*, 17(4): 12–14.

Emenheiser, D.A., Clay, J.M. and Palakurthi, R. (1998) 'Profiles of Successful Restaurant Managers for Recruitment and Selection in the US', *International Journal of Contemporary Hospitality Management*, 10(2): 54–62.

Ferguson, M. and Rau, J. (2011) 'Report Confirms Tourism Job Shortages', Department of Resources, Energy and Tourism, October 13 2011, online. Available minister.ret.gov.au/ MediaCentre/MediaReleases/Pages/TourismJobShortages.aspx (accessed 20 November 2011).

Ferris, G.R., Berkson, H.M. and Harris, M.M. (2002) 'The Recruitment Interview Process: Persuasion and Organization Promotion in Competitive Labour Markets', *Human Resource Management Review*, 12: 359–375.

Fraser, R.A. (2003) 'Why don't Hospitality Students Keep the Faith? A Research Report on Hospitality Students' Committment to Careers in the Industry', in S. Kuslavan (ed.), *Managing Employee Attitudes and Behaviors in the Tourism and Hospitality*, New York: Nova Publishers, pp. 99–134.

Freeland, B. (2000) *Demands of Training: Australian Tourism and Hospitality*, Adelaide: National Centre for Vocational Education Research.

Frogner, M.L. (2002) 'Skills Shortages', *Labour Market Trends*, 110(1): 17–27.

Hancer, M. and George, R.V. (2003) 'Psychological Empowerment of Non-supervisory Employees Working in Full-service Restaurants', *International Journal of Hospitality Management*, 22(1): 3–16.

Heraty, N. and Morley, M. (1998) 'In Search of Good Fit: Policy and Practice in Recruitment and Selection in Ireland', *The Journal of Management Development*, 17(9): 662–685.

Hinkin, T.R. and Tracey, J.B. (2000) 'The Cost of Turnover', *Cornell Hotel and Restaurant Administration Quarterly*, 43(1): 14–21.

International Society of Hospitality Consultants (2006) *Top Ten Issues in the Hospitality Industry for 2007*, online. Available at www.hospitalitynet.org/news/4029554.html (accessed 25 July 2008).

Jenkins, A.K. (2001) 'Making a Career of it? Hospitality Students' Future Perspectives: An Anglo-Dutch Study', *International Journal of Contemporary Hospitality Management*, 13(1): 13–20.

Johns, N. (1993) 'Quality Management in the Hospitality Industry: Part 3. Recent Developments', *International Journal of Contemporary Hospitality Management*, 5(1): 10–15.

Jones, P. and Davies, A. (1991) 'Empowerment: A Study of General Managers of Four Star Hotel Properties in the UK', *International Journal of Hospitality Management*, 10(3): 211–217.

Kraft, R.J. (1985) 'Towards a Theory of Experiential Learning', in R. Kraft and M. Sakofs (eds.), *The Theory of Experiential Learning*, 2nd edn, Boulder, CO: Association for Experiential Education, pp. 7–38.

Kyriacou, C. and Coulthard, M. (2000) 'Undergraduates' Views of Teaching as a Career Choice', *Journal of Education for Teaching*, 26(2): 117–126.

Lashley, C. (1995) 'Towards an Understanding of Employee Empowerment in Hospitality Services', *International Journal of Contemporary Hospitality Management*, 7(1): 27–32.

—— (1999) 'Employee Empowerment in Services: A Framework for Analysis', *Personnel Review*, 28(3): 169–191.

—— (2000) 'Empowerment through Involvement: A Case Study of TGI Fridays Restaurants', *Personnel Review*, 29(6): 791–815.

—— (2001) *Empowerment: HR Strategies for Service Excellence*, Oxford: Butterworth-Heinemann.

Lloyd, S. (2005) 'Young, Smart and Hard to Find', *Business Review Weekly*, 29 September: 25.

Lucas, R. and Johnson, K. (2003) 'Managing Students as a Flexible Labour Resource in Hospitality and Tourism in Central and Eastern Europe and the UK', in S. Kuslavan (ed.) *Managing Employee Attitudes and Behaviors in the Tourism and Hospitality*, New York: Nova Publishers, pp. 153–170.

Morton, D.L. (2002) 'Targeting Generation Y', *Public Relations Quarterly*, 47(2): 46–48.

Mulcahy, J.D. (1999) 'Vocational Work Experience in the Hospitality Industry: Characteristics and Strategies', *Education and Training*, 41(4): 164–174.

National Tourism Investment Strategy Consultative Group (2006) 'Workforce and Training', in Department of Industry; Tourism and Resources (ed.) *National Tourism Investment Strategy: Investing for our Future*, Canberra: National Tourism Investment Strategy Consultative Group, pp. 63–70.

O'Leary, S. and Deegan, J. (2005) 'Career Progression of Irish Tourism and Hospitality Management Graduates', *International Journal of Contemporary Hospitality Management*, 17(5): 421–432.

Oliver, D. (2006) 'An Expectation of Continued Success: The Work Attitudes of Generation Y', *Labour and Industry*, 17(1): 61–84.

Plunkett, L.C. and Fournier, R. (1991) *Participative Management: Implementing Empowerment*, New York: Wiley.

Richardson, S.A. (2009a) 'Student Experiences Working in the Hospitality and Tourism Industry: Issues and Concerns', *Asian Journal of Tourism and Hospitality Research*, 3(1): 62–74.

—— (2009b) 'Undergraduates' Perceptions of Tourism and Hospitality as a Career Choice', *International Journal of Hospitality Management*, 28(3): 382–388.

—— (2010a) 'Attitudes of Malaysian Tourism and Hospitality Students Towards a Career in the Industry', paper presented at the Fourth Tourism Outlook and Third ITSA Conference, Cross-cultural Tourism in and Beyond Asia, Selangor, Malaysia, December 1–3.

—— (2010b) 'Generation Y's Perceptions and Attitudes Towards a Career in Tourism and Hospitality', *Journal of Human Resources in Hospitality and Tourism*, 9(2): 179–199.

—— (2010c) 'Understanding Generation Y's Attitudes Towards a Career in the Industry', in P. Benckendorff, G. Moscardo and D. Pendergast (eds.) *Tourism and Generation Y*, Cambridge, MA: CABI Publishing, pp. 131–142.

Riley, M., Ladkin, A. and Szivas, E. (2002) *Tourism Employment: Analysis and Planning*, Aspects of Tourism 6, Sydney: Channel View Publications.

Ripley, R.E. and Ripley, M.J. (1993) 'Empowering Management in Innovative Organizations in the 1990s', *Empowerment in Organizations*, 1(1): 29–40.

Service Skills Victoria (2005) *Service Skills Victoria's Response to Victoria's Tourism and Events Industry Discussion Paper*, Melbourne: Service Skills Victoria.

Tourism Council of Tasmania (2004) *Tourism and Hospitality Training Demand Profile Project*, Hobart: Tourism Council of Tasmania.

Tourism Division (2002) *Research Report Number 4: Tourism Workforce and Training*, Department of Industry, Tourism and Resources (DITR), April 12 2006, online. Available at www.industry.gov.au/assets/documents/itrinternet/4.ResearchReport No4TourismWorkforceandTraining20050202121253.pdf (accessed 20 July 2009).

Trendle, B. (2005) *Perspectives on Skills Shortages*, Brisbane: Labour Market Research Unit.

11 Sustainability

An issue for the tourism industry in the new millennium?

Werner Gronau

Introduction

Almost two decades have passed since the Rio Conference, where the concept of sustainability was adopted by the United Nations as the underlying idea for facing global environmental challenges. At the same time, the UNWTO was promoting and continues to promote the tourism industry as one of the major driving forces for the development of less developed countries. In connecting these two approaches the logical consequence seems to be the creation of a global sustainable tourism industry as a catalyst for a better future throughout the world. The present contribution aims at a critical analysis of the existing opportunities, challenges and possible barriers for such a vision, by taking a look at the historic developments, the actual situation and possible trends in the future.

The concept of sustainability

The original concept of the Rio Declaration on Environment and Development in 1992 outlines three major dimensions of sustainability: economic, social and environmental. These three pillars of sustainability, however, cause certain conflicts as noted by Jischa (1998: 118):

> Without a doubt, environmental thinking often conflicts with economic considerations [. . .] It is becoming clearer that the social question will also take a central role in political considerations [. . .] The obvious conflicts among the three pillars of sustainability must constantly be reconsidered by society.

When discussing sustainable economic development, aspects such as a sufficient standard of living for all social groups, economic profitability and qualitative instead of quantitative growth are of equal importance.

In the environmental sector, the consumption of resources should not exceed their ability to be recovered and the use of non-renewable resources should be reduced to a minimum. In addition, pollution and the storage of waste should also be kept to a minimum. Furthermore, the diversity and esthetic quality of nature and landscape have to be respected. The final factor, social sustainability, which might gain increasing prominence in the future, can best be described by the preservation of cultural identity, the continuous development of local societies, a share in political power for all social groups and the fair allocation of resources. All the aforementioned aspects are considered to have a bearing on the tourism sector and, vice versa, are influenced by tourism due to its constantly growing role. Therefore, the concept of sustainability implies an alternative form of tourism industry must be developed. The overall social agreement for the sustainability concept, representing the guiding idea for the future, sets new framework conditions for the tourism industry in general: society even expects a certain contribution to overall sustainability by the tourism industry. Consequently, the concept of sustainability should be regarded as a challenge to develop innovative forms of tourism in order to contribute to the concerted efforts towards sustainability.

The concept of sustainable tourism

Since the mid-1990s, sustainable tourism has become a buzzword in development studies in general and tourism research in particular. In spite of the vast literature on the topic, a proper theoretical framework of 'sustainable tourism' has not yet been developed. For example, according to Komilis (1994: 65) most investigations on the topic 'had advanced little beyond the stage of formulating and discussing various principles and assumptions'. Indicating a methodology gap, Wheeller (1991: 93) observes: 'while the case studies which explore the ways of applying sustainable principles to practice, often through small eco- or alternative tourism projects, provide at best a micro solution to what is essentially a macro problem'.

Besides the lack of a theoretical framework, the general assumption predicting that there can be a sustainable form of tourism is often questioned. Objections are, for instance, raised on the various contradictions between the holistic concept of sustainability and the more product-centered perspective of the global tourism industry. Illuminating the holistic perspective, Lane (1994: 106) views sustainable tourism as a balanced triangular relation between 'host areas and their habitats and people, holiday makers and the tourism industry', where no stakeholder upsets the equilibrium. Taking this argument into account, a proper balance of the different stakeholder interests is crucial for a sustainable tourism industry. This view is supported by Sharpley (2000: 9), who states that 'the potential for sustainable tourism development exists if no single factor or stakeholder predominates'. Taking the over-dependence of many destinations, such as Cyprus, on the tourism industry and the dramatically growing market domination of a few global tour operators into consideration, the balance between local benefits and the tourism operator's welfare seems to be simply wishful thinking. Furthermore, a clear contradiction between sustainable principles and tourism development can be identified in the spatial inequality of development. It can be argued that the aim of the improvement of quality of life for all people (Jamrozy 2007) is in contrast to the usual strong spatial concentration of the tourism industry. In many cases, the tourism industry even exacerbates the unequal allocation of resources. In classical 'sun and beach' destinations, such as Cyprus, an increase of spatial disparities can be observed between the coastal tourism regions and the rural areas of the hinterland. Last but not least, there is an ongoing friction between overall societal goals with regards to sustainability and the actual attitude and actions of the individual tourist towards this approach. Whereas Carter and Moore (1993) point to an increasing environmental consciousness of tourists being attracted by sustainable tourism products, fully convincing evidence of a major shift in consumer attitude towards the willingness to pay for more sustainable tourism products is still missing. Concluding the discussion, Sharpley (2000: 14) comes to the eye opening and frustrating conclusion that 'true sustainable tourism development is unachievable'.

Sustainability and the tourism industry: a contradiction?

Based on the last section the following question arises: is there any overlap in the structure of the global tourism industry and the concept of sustainability? As elaborated above, the 1990s were dominated by a theoretical discussion on the opportunity to implement the concept of sustainability in the tourism industry. However, scholars have been rather divided on this issue, but there seems to be a certain agreement on the contradiction between the character of the concept and the tourism reality. In detail, there are three dimensions clearly illustrating the clash between the compatibility of small scale, decentralized, bottom-up concepts with the current tourism industry (Sharpley 2000):

- *Local management/control.* There is no doubt that the dominance of major tour operators poses significant problems for tourism authorities, with a destination management approach towards the reduction of capacities that may be overruled by the strategies of the operators. The heavy dependence of the tourism industry on tour operators seems to be a clear indicator for the centralized top-down approach of the tourism industry being strongly at odds with the bottom-up approach of sustainability.
- *The tourism product.* Sustainable tourism, according to typical policies, is quite often understood as quality tourism. However, quality tourism demands a quality product and, subsequently, a sufficient volume of 'quality tourists' to meet projected arrivals and spending targets. In consequence, a blind faith in an upmarket tourism product is promoted in order to rectify the impacts of mass tourism. Unfortunately, mass tourism is the everyday reality. Mass tourism creates the turnover and, due to its overwhelming market share, the majority of the overall revenue. Alternative forms of tourism are still negligible niche products, at least at the major established mass tourism destinations.
- *Tourism's developmental role.* Perhaps most importantly, tourism in its present form (i.e. principally coastal, summer-sun tourism) has been and remains the engine that drives the tourism industry. Economic growth, high

levels of employment, increasing wealth and the expansion of other sectors of the economy have all resulted from the development of tourism as a volume industry, while tourism has also proven to be an effective agent of modernization and development. To an extent this has been facilitated by the inherent desire and ability of people to take advantage of the opportunities offered by tourism, yet it is the scale of tourism development that has been a principal factor in its successful contribution to development. Quality tourism, in contrast, may lead to higher per capita tourist spending and reduced environmental impacts. But restricting the growth in arrivals will, inevitably, impact upon employment levels, growth in other sectors of the economy and, ultimately, continued development.

While considering the given contradiction, plenty of best-practice examples have been presented at the same time in order to support the compatibility of sustainability and the tourism industry. Concepts of pro-poor tourism or community-based tourism are presented demonstrating benefits for the local community through the tourism industry. Examples from the Amazon and Africa illustrate the opportunities arising from the participative approach to developing tourism products which contribute to a more sustainable community. Li (2006) found that while there was minimal community involvement when implementing a tourism project in the Jiuzhaigou Biosphere Reserve, a World Heritage Site, the entire community received economic benefits and also benefited from the tourism industry through an improvement of the natural environment. Such examples seem to contradict Sharpley's (2000) previously mentioned view, that there is a fundamental incompatability between sustainability and the tourism industry.

In reality it is not a contradiction at all, due to the fact that the perspective is a completely different one. While Sharpley (2000) argues that the tourism industry in its present form does not have the opportunity to become sustainable, scholars such as Li (2006) stress the opportunity of implementing sustainable tourism products. Therefore there has to be a clear separation between the existing mass tourism-oriented, tour operator-based, long-established tourism destinations and upcoming ones that are concentrating on sustainable tourism products. Of course, not all new destinations are going down the road towards sustainable tourism products, but there seems to be a clear trend towards sustainability, especially in less developed countries. It may be argued that costs related to the implementation of large-scale mass tourism are not available in many of these countries, but at the same time there is expertise to develop alternative tourism products brought to these locales, for example by NGOs or international bodies such as the UNWTO.

In brief, the overall dilemma on the compatibility of the tourism industry and sustainability may be reduced to the two following hypotheses:

- The tourism industry in its present form is characterized by an oligopolistic tendency, a centralized top-down organization and a revenue fixation that is not compatible with the overall aim of sustainability.

- The implementation of sustainable tourism products in small niches is possible by avoiding the involvement of the mass market-dominating tour operators, hence tourism can be sustainable.

Summing up these two hypotheses, the key towards sustainable tourism seems to lie in the structure of the overall tourism industry rather than in the contradiction between tourism and sustainability.

'Sustainabilization' of the tourism industry

Based upon the aim of creating a certain kind of sustainable tourism, while accepting the concept that tourism lacks sustainability due to its strong dependency on large-scale tourism business such as large hotel chains or very powerful tour operators, the way forward seems to be evident. The tourism industry has to become more sustainable in order to provide the opportunity for tourism itself to really become sustainable. This approach has to include tourism companies in all present forms and functions. Therefore, the aim for the upcoming decade is evident because the tourism industry, to a large extent, has to integrate sustainability issues into its everyday business. Hence the following sections will elaborate the two major aspects involved in this goal: corporate social responsibility (CSR) and sustainable supply chain management in tourism.

Corporate social responsibility in tourism

The latest trends in management favor the CSR approach as a kind of voluntary action by companies towards the overall welfare of society. Consistent with McWilliams and Siegel (2001), CSR can be defined as situations where the firm goes beyond compliance and engages in 'actions that appear to further some social good, beyond the interests of the firm and that which is required by law'. However, this is just one interpretation of CSR. Numerous definitions have been proposed and often no clear definition is given, making theoretical development and measurement difficult. Also, the differences in the legal framework comparing the situation in the United States and Europe lead to a different understanding. While European legislation forces much stricter requirements, for example, in terms of human resources management upon companies, the need for implementing CSR concepts in Europe has been debated heavily among stakeholders. Nevertheless, CSR can be valuable in Europe as well, while it only refers to going beyond the given legal framework in terms of companies' responsibility for the wellbeing of society overall.

The implementation of a CSR approach, therefore, can be understood as a re-positioning of the overall management strategy of a company. Instead of concentrating only on the maximization of economic benefits in terms of revenue, the company commits itself to its social and environmental responsibilities, in essence, dedicating itself to the aim of sustainability. Therefore, the implementation level of CSR approaches in the tourism industry may be a driving force in the overall move toward a sustainable tourism industry. As one of the most dominant players within the tourism industry, the role of tour operators becoming more sustainable may be interesting. Several European tour operator associations have proposed industry-wide actions to gradually internalize sustainability, with the potential to be used, in the best of cases, as a competitive advantage tool, or in the worst of cases as a means of risk management and regulation avoidance. These initiatives follow the ground-breaking work of the United Nations Environment Programme, the 'Tour Operators Initiative for Sustainable Tourism Development' (TOI). Unfortunately, the dynamic of the initiative has decreased in recent years and the overall involvement of international operators in CSR is still moderately low.

When it comes to real commitment instead of voluntary actions, the implementation of the German TourCERT-Label for CSR in tourism by 'KATE' (Kontaktstelle für Umwelt und Entwicklung), a German non-profit organization engaged in the field of sustainable tourism development, is to be a good example for the retention of important players in the business. The label is given after an external certification process by an independent certification council. Core indicators are:

- CO_2 emissions per guest per day.
- Business ecology: CO_2 emissions generated in the company per employee.
- Percentage of the price paid by the customer that goes to the destination.
- Quality of customer information.
- Index of customer satisfaction.
- Business culture: index of staff satisfaction.
- Business success: cash flow in relation to total turnover.
- Sustainability index partner agencies.
- Sustainability index accommodation.
- Sustainability index tourist guides.

These 10 core indicators are the integral part of the applied CSR reporting standard, which aims at answering crucial questions such as:

- How many jobs are created in the destination?
- What are the job conditions?
- What does tourism contribute to improving the level of education and employment?
- What is the company contribution when supporting economically under-developed regions?
- How does tourism preserve natural ecosystems instead of damaging them?
- Does tourism contribute to reducing poverty and does it respect the human and labor rights of people in the destinations?

All these questions lead to a very detailed quantitative approach, including 80 detailed indicators measuring the level of sustainability in the company to be certified. Since its introduction in 2008, 38 German tour operators have gone through the accreditation process, although none of them are the major players in the sector. TUI or Thomas Cook refer to their voluntary commitment but unfortunately still refuse to take part in an external certification process. Despite of the refusal to take part in such accreditation processes, the tour operator industry takes some action to integrate sustainability into their five main business dimensions: product design and management, supply chain management, internal management, communication with customers and cooperation with destinations. While all five are clearly interlinked, TOI decided early on to pay special attention to the supply chain, since this is where most of the impacts take place (Font and Cochrane 2005a, b).

Sustainable supply chain management in tourism

Supply chain management (SCM) can be defined as:

> A philosophy of management that involves the management and integration of a set of selected key business processes from end user through original suppliers, that provides products, services, and information that add value for customers and other stakeholders through the collaborative efforts of supply chain members.
>
> (Ho *et al.* 2002: 4422)

Sustainable supply chain management (SSCM) adds sustainability to SCM processes, so that these also consider the environmental, social and economic impacts of business activities. In tour operations, this relates to the development of operator purchasing policies and practices that contribute positively to supplier sustainability and at the same time improve the quality of the products and services offered. This is not straightforward, since tour operators' supply chains are diverse and fragmented, including accommodation, transport, excursions/activities, food, craft and other ancillary services. At times, manufacturing and, to a lesser extent, the service sector, have internalized the impacts of the supplier into the production process. This initially focused on environmental impacts that led to lean manufacturing and sometimes to social impacts that enable companies to claim environmentally friendly, organic, or Fairtrade products (Drumwright 1994; Kassinis and Soteriou 2003; Quazi 2001; Wilkinson *et al.* 2001; Williamson and Lynch-Wood 2001). After all, a company is only as sustainable as its suppliers. Much of SSCM literature focuses on the manufacturing industry with little attention paid to the service sector, including the tourism industry.

Nevertheless, several studies have appeared on these supply chains including those of Buhalis and Law (2001), Page (2003), Sinclair and Stabler (1997) and UNWTO (1994). In 2006 Yilmaz and Bititci (2006) developed a tourism value chain model to manage the tourism product as a beginning-to-end seamless entity, which created new groundwork for studies in the sector. However, this is not an issue that tour operators or academics have investigated in much detail. This is due to the multitude of small suppliers under different national legislation, the challenges in measuring sustainability in the service sector and the lack of tangible evidence that addressing this issue would lead to greater willingness by customers to purchase or spend on a product. At the same time, the overall framework of the tourism industry does not really seem to favor an integrated SSCM. As pointed out by Zhang *et al.* (2008), the characteristics of tourism – it is coordination-intensive, perishable, information-intensive, has product complexity, demand uncertainty and complex dynamics – interferes a great deal with SCM issues. Realizing these aspects, the question arises to what extent sustainability plays a role within the decision-making process of setting up SCM of tour operators. Based upon the study conducted by Leeds Metropolitan it can be said:

> The main challenge is to apply existing SSCM practices more widely in tourism. Quality is a key aspect of supplier selection by tour operators, but even though many sustainability issues have significant effects on the quality of holidays experienced by tour operators' clients the tourism sector only rarely includes sustainability issues as part of the quality equation.
>
> (Font and Cochrane 2005a)

The study clearly differentiates the market segment the tour operator deals with:

> Sustainability issues are most evident as a quality issue amongst specialist operators, while mass operators are at the very early stages of incorporating sustainability as a product quality issue, focusing mainly on environmental areas. Increased communication on the relationship of sustainability and quality in order to increase market awareness and demand is the key to driving SSCM forward.
>
> (Font and Cochrane 2005b)

It is evident that there is still a large implementation gap when it comes to SSCM in tourism, but it seems to be filtering into the industry slowly, supported by an increase of academic studies and a growing awareness on the demand side.

Sustainability through new demand

The tourism industry is both supply-led and demand-driven. The provision of sustainable tourist facilities and services may arise as a response to growing demands among consumers or may be an aim to stimulate tourist demand. Whatever the initial impetus, sustainable development in the long term necessitates a balance of supply and demand in terms of range, quality, quantity and price. An evolution on one side of the demand/supply equation will usually be accompanied by changes in the other, whether this represents growth, stagnation, decline, or some qualitative transformation. Therefore, a major driving force for sustainable tourism has to consumer behavior. The demand for a more sustainable tourism industry will surely change the face of the overall industry. Unfortunately, the demand side seems to be rather focused on cheap holidays rather than asking for more sustainable forms of tourism. Indeed, 'Tourism development is a dynamic process of matching tourism resources to the demands and preferences of actual or potential tourists' (Liu 1994: 21). Nevertheless, in recent years there are fields evolving demonstrating a certain interest in more sustainable tourism on the consumer side. CO_2 compensation of flights may be one example of the growing awareness of tourists and at the same time of the public's growing commitment towards sustainability issues. CO_2 compensation of flights follows the overall idea of reducing the ecological impacts of flying through the purchase of CO_2 certificates. In the case of 'atmosfair', a major player in the context of German CO_2 compensation, a doubling of voluntarily compensated flights has been recorded each year since 2005, which shows the significant change in perception and behaviour on the part of consumers in Germany.

The principle of atmosfair follows the common approach of CO_2 compensation in general. The amount of CO_2 for a specific flight is calculated and customers pay a certain amount, which is then invested in CO_2 reduction projects all over the world. This results in adequate reduction of CO_2 comparable to that created by the flight. The success of atmosfair became possible due to the integration of atmosfair services at all major online booking platforms in Germany. Since the end of 2007 flights can also be compensated on the leading online booking platforms for the German market, Opodo and Expedia. These companies included the opportunity to voluntarily compensate the purchased flight within the booking process in their online booking tools by just ticking the relevant option. Also, the German-based holiday airline TUI-fly integrated this tool in their online booking system. As a result, since the end of 2007 CO_2 offsetting for flights is offered with all major German online booking platforms. In addition to the strong presence of atmosfair within online booking tools providing the opportunity for voluntary compensation, the amount of tour operators including CO_2 offsetting in their holiday packages has also clearly increased. TUI-Nordic and three small operators out of Forum Anders Reisen (Alternative Travel Forum) (this includes, for example, the German Alps Club) contribute the same amount paid by the customers to atmosfair, again from the operator side, mainly for promotion and marketing reasons.

Generally speaking, the demand determinants push a tourist into a travel decision while the supply factors pull the tourist towards a particular destination. Therefore, the ubiquity of flight compensation tools will surely further increase their utilization. The size and preferences of global tourist demand are determined by variables in generating countries. As a result, the change of attitude towards sustainability issues in the source markets of tourism industry will strongly influence the performance in target destinations. The spatial distribution of tourist flows will at the same time be influenced by the competitiveness of various tourist destinations. In consequence, neither the tourism industry nor the tourism destinations will be able to reshape the face of tourism industry as long as the demand side (in form of each individual tourist) does not realize their responsibility for a more sustainable future. Demand for sustainable products can be witnessed in several fields. Nevertheless, a critical volume for integrating sustainability dimensions to a great extent in mass-tourism products has not yet been achieved.

Conclusion

The question regarding whether sustainability is still an issue for the tourism industry in the new millennium should be reflected upon. It can be argued that the goals set almost 20 years ago have not been reached by far. Nevertheless, a deeply rooted debate on the issue has led to a clutch of activities from various stakeholders and awareness has been created with regard to the formation of a sustainable tourism industry. Management concepts such as CSR or SSCM have been elaborated in order to change the supply side of tourism industry. Although these concepts still lack large-scale implementation, they are a promising sign for the growing awareness among tourism stakeholders. While a slight change at the demand side is apparent, there also seem to be efforts on the supply side that are increasingly evolving. Nevertheless, the crucial question on the compatibility of sustainability and the tourism sector remains questionable when considering the development of mass tourism in recent years. The transformation of the supply and the demand side at the same time in order to achieve some kind of sustainable tourism industry still seems to be a chimera.

References

Buhalis, D. and Laws, E. (2001) *Tourism Distribution Channels: Practices, Issues, and Transformations*, London: Continuum International Publishing Group.

Carter, B. and Moore, S. (1993) 'Ecotourism in the 21st Century', *Tourism Management*, 14(2): 123–130.

Drumwright, M. (1994) 'Socially Responsible Organizational Buying: Environmental Concern as a Non-economic Buying Criterion', *Journal of Marketing*, 58(3): 1–19.

Font, X. and Cochrane, J. (2005a) *Integrating Sustainability into Business: A Management Guide for Tour Operations*, Paris: Tour Operators Initiative for Sustainable Tourism Development, online. Available at www.toinitiative.org/fileadmin/docs/publications/Sustainability_in_Business_-_Management.pdf (accessed 10 September 2011).

—— (2005b) *Integrating Sustainability into Business: An Implementation Guide for Responsible Tourism Coordinators*, Paris: Tour Operators Initiative for Sustainable Tourism Development, online. Available at www.toinitiative.org/fileadmin/docs/publications/Sustainability_in_Business_-_Implementation.pdf (accessed 10 September 2011).

Ho, D.C., Au, K.F. and Newton, E. (2002) 'Empirical Research on Supply Chain Management: A Critical Review and Recommendations', *International Journal of Production Research*, 40(17): 4415–4430.

Jamrozy, U. (2007) 'Marketing of Tourism: A Paradigm Shift Toward Sustainability', *International Journal of Culture, Tourism and Hospitality Research*, 1(2): 117–130.

Jischa, M. (1998) 'Sustainable Development: Environmental, Economic and Social Aspect', *Global Journal of Enineering Education*, 2(2): 115–124.

Kassinis, G.I. and Soteriou, A.C. (2003) 'Greening the Service Profit Chain: The Impact of Environmental Management Practices', *Production and Operations Management*, 12(3): 386–403.

Komilis, P. (1994) 'Tourism and Sustainable Regional Development', in A.V. Seaton (ed.) *Tourism: The State of the Art*, Chichester: John Wiley, pp. 65–73.

Lane, B. (1994) 'Sustainable Rural Tourism Strategies: A Tool for Development and Conservation', *Journal of Sustainable Tourism*, 2(2): 102–111.

Li, W. (2006) 'Community Decision Making Participation in Development', *Annals of Tourism Research*, 33(1): 132–143.

Liu, Z.H. (1994) 'Tourism Development – a Systems Analysis', in A.V. Seaton (ed.) *Tourism: The State of the Art*, Chichester: John Wiley, pp. 20–30.

McWilliams, A. and Siegel, D. (2001) 'Corporate Social Responsibility: A Theory of the Firm Perspective', *Academy of Management Review*, 26(1): 117–127.

Page, S.J. (2003) *Tourism Management: Managing for Change*, Oxford: Butterworth-Heinemann.

Quazi, H.A. (2001) 'Sustainable Development: Integrated Environmental Issues into Strategic Planning', *Industrial Management and Data Systems*, 101(2): 64–70.

Sharpley, R. (2000) 'Tourism and Sustainable Development: Exploring the Theoretical Divide', *Journal of Sustainable Tourism*, 8(1): 1–19.

Sinclair, M.T. and Stabler, M. (1997) *The Economics of Tourism*, London: Routledge.

UNWTO (1994) *Global Distribution Systems in the Tourism Industry*, Madrid: World Tourism Organization.

Wheeler, B. (1991) 'Tourism's Troubled Times: Responsible Tourism is Not the Answer', *Tourism Management*, 12(2): 91–96.

Wilkinson, A., Hill, M. and Gollan, P. (2001) 'The Sustainability Debate', *International Journal of Operations and Production Management*, 21(12): 1492–1502.

Williamson, D. and Lynch-Wood, G. (2001) 'A New Paradigm for SME Environmental Practice', *The TQM Magazine*, 13(6): 424–432.

Yilmaz, Y. and Bititci, U.S. (2006) 'Performance Measurement in Tourism: A Value Chain Model', *International Journal of Contemporary Hospitality Management*, 18(4): 341–349.

Zhang, X., Song, H. and Huang, G. (2008) 'Tourism Supply Chain Management: A New Research Agenda', *Tourism Management*, 30(3): 345–358.

12 Tomorrow's tourist and the case study of New Zealand

Ian Yeoman

Introduction

Tourism to New Zealand

Today, every country in the world has a tourism proposition, whether it is New Zealand ('100% Pure New Zealand'), India ('Incredible India'), or Afghanistan ('The Last Unconquered Mountains of the World'). New Zealand's share of international arrivals is 0.3 percent, one of the smallest in the world, but tourism is the country's largest earner of foreign currency and competes with agriculture to be the country's largest industry. According to the country's Tourism Satellite Account (Statistics New Zealand 2009), the economic value of tourism is NZ$ 21.7bn, with international markets contributing NZ$ 9.3bn representing 16.4 percent of total exports of goods and services. International tourists to New Zealand visit the country for the landscapes, mountains, Maori culture and outdoor activities. Today, New Zealand is one the world's most successful tourism destinations, and many tourists aspire to visit it. The country tourism brand '100% Pure New Zealand' (Yeoman and McMahon-Beattie 2011) is the world's most successful brand and in 2009 it celebrated its tenth anniversary (more than a lifetime in destination branding circles). Many countries look to New Zealand as a country that has got tourism policy and marketing just right. Tourism New Zealand is often benchmarked as an exemplar of success.

It was Prime Minister William Fox who in 1874 foresaw the tourism potential of his country whilst escaping from a busy parliamentary session to investigate the beauty of the Pink and White Terraces in Hot Lakes District of New Zealand's North Island. He envisioned tourist companies blighting one of the wonders of the world with ostentatious hotels and tea rooms, the Terraces cluttered with beer bottle tops, orange peel and walnut shells. While he enjoyed his seclusion and mused on the nature of tourism, Fox realized the wealth that could bargained from the construction of a sanatorium in the region and the crowds who could be lured there. Torn between the potential earnings and the risks of exploiting nature, he returned home and urged the government to take on the roles of developer and protector of the landscapes (McClure 2004). Like Fox, the present New Zealand government wanted to develop the country's tourism product further, but at the same time not exploit it in an environment of changing worlds and continued uncertainty, whether this is rising oil prices, aging populations or climate change.

The New Zealand Ministry of Tourism, in partnership with the Foundation of Science, Research and Technology decided to take a long-term perspective which was beyond an economic short to medium term of forecasts found in the country's strategies for 2015 (Ministry of Tourism 2008). The Ministry of Tourism and the Foundation for Science, Research, and Technology sought a team of researchers that could look into the future and construct a series of scenarios about that future. This chapter is part of an ongoing research series that looks at the future of tourism in New Zealand to 2050 (http://www.tourism2050.com) and looks specifically at the key drivers that will shape tourists' behaviors, actions and attitudes.

An economic correlation

It is generally accepted that tourism demand depends above all on the economic conditions in major generating markets. When economies grow, levels of disposable income will usually also rise. A relatively large part of discretionary income will typically be spent on tourism, in particular in the case of emerging economies. A tightening of the economic situation, on the other hand, will often result in a decrease or trading down of tourism spending. In general, the growth of international tourism arrivals significantly outpaces growth of economic output as measured in gross domestic product (GDP). When GDP growth falls below 2 percent, tourism growth tends to be even lower. When GDP is at 3.5 percent tourism grows on average 1.3 times faster than GDP (UNWTO 2010), hence the proposition that when GDP growth is good tourist behavior can be labeled a fluid identity; when it is less than good it is proposed it is a simple identity.

New Zealand's future tourist: which identity?

Today's tourist has demanded better experiences, faster service, multiple choice, social responsibility and greater satisfaction. Against this background, as the world has moved to an experience economy in which there is endless choice through competition and accessibility because of the low-cost carrier, what has emerged is the concept of fluid identity. This trend is about the concept of the self which is fluid and malleable in which the self cannot be defined by boundaries, in which choice and the desire for self and new experiences drives tourist consumption. One indicator of this fluidity of identity is the fact that consumers, on average, change their hairstyle every 18 months, according to the Future Foundation (2007). From a tourist's perspective it is about collecting countries, trying new things and the desire for constant change. It means the tourist is both comfortable with a hedonistic short break in Queenstown or six months backpacking across New Zealand. This fluid identity makes it difficult for New Zealand to segment tourists by behavior or attitude. However, as wealth decreases, that identity simplifies, a new thriftiness and desire for simplicity emerges (Flatters and Wilmott 2009). This desire is driven by inflationary pressures and falling levels of disposable incomes, embodied by the squeezing the middle-class consumer. As the economies of wealth slow down, for whatever reason, new patterns of tourism consumption emerge, whether it is the desire for domestic rather than international travel or what some call the *stayvacation*. A fluid identity means tourists can afford enriching new experiences and indulge themselves at premium five-star resorts. They can afford to pay extra for socially conscious consumption, whereas a simple identity means these trends have slowed, halted, or reserved. As resources become scarcer, the mindset of a whole generation of tourists changes.

Between now and 2050 the world will go through a cycle of economic prosperity and decline which is the nature of the economic order. When wealth is great, a fluid identity is the naked scenario; however when a recession emerges, belts are tightened and tourists like other consumers search for a simple identity. This chapter examine the values, behaviors and thinking of the future tourist, whether it is a fluid or simple identity. Each proposition is discussed within the context of the present and what this means for the future.

Fluid identity

'I am taking a holiday weekend break in Vegas and an ecotourism vacation in South Africa this year,' said the tourist. Why? Tourists cannot be labeled according to their attitudes and beliefs – what they say and what they do are two totally different things. This is why segmenting tomorrow's tourist is becoming much more difficult. If the future is rising incomes and wealth accumulation and there is a continuing trend in terms of a richness in new forms of connection and association, this will permit a pursuit of personal identity which is fluid, an identity which is less restricted by background or geography but more by achievement. In the fluid environment, communications channels and technologies are fast-moving and instant, which produces a culture of choice enhancement.

Tourists have the means for endless choice and creative disorder. They have the power to express opinions and they do so, whether it is through TripAdvisor or YouTube. In fact, they form their opinion not on trusted sources from authority but peer review, hence the importance of consumer-generated content and the advocacy of local authentic information as provided, for example, by the citizens of Philadelphia at http://www.uwishunu.com. They are excellent at using networking tools to get a better deal or complain about poor service. A fluid identity allows tourists to be frivolous, promiscuous and just plain awkward. It means tourists want to sample a range of new experiences, hence the rise of the long tail (Anderson 2009) and emergence of bespoke tourism products, for example specialist cruise markets at http://www.insightcruises.com. The drivers that shape the phenomena of a fluid identity that are discussed here include:

- Rising middle classes and wealth distribution
- Fluidity of values
- Demanding consumers, endless choice and a complicated life
- A world without boundaries

- I will try to be more ethical, but . . .
- Immediacy
- The feminization of a have it all society
- Anxious society
- Collective individualism
- Contested hedonism
- Contested liberalism
- Fluidity of luxury
- New life courses
- Something new.

Rising middle classes and wealth distribution

The rising economy in China could lift hundreds of millions of households out of poverty. Over the next 20 years an increasing number of rural Chinese might migrate to the cities to seek higher-paying jobs. These working consumers, once the country's poorest, will steadily climb the income ladder, creating a massive new middle class. Rapid economic growth will continue to transform the impoverished but largely egalitarian society of China's past into one with distinct income classes. This evolution is already creating a widening gap between rich and poor, and tackling the resulting social and economic tension has become a focus of government policy. Projections indicate, however, that China will avoid the 'barbell economy' that plagues much of the developing world and which results in large numbers of poor, a small group of the very wealthy, and only a few in the middle. Even as the absolute difference between the richest and poorest continues to widen, incomes will increase across all urban segments.

FOR THE FUTURE

It is wealth that drives tourism expenditure. Wealth in real terms from the wealthiest OECD countries (Germany and so on) will decrease and be replaced by countries like India and China. China's urban middle class is a strong market for the future, which will spend a great deal of money on out-of-home expenditure and will likely want to travel the world and have the ability to pay for it.

Fluidity of values

In a period where identities are fluid and driven by rapidly changing cultures, connections and technologies, Thomas Rochon's (2000) book *Culture Moves* addresses this complex process and develops a theory to explain both how values originate and how they spread. In particular, he analyzes the crucial role that small communities of critical thinkers play in developing new ideas and inspiring their dissemination through larger social movements. This idea of shifting values drives consumer volatility and diversity, the changing nature of identity and why it is becoming extremely difficult to segment markets. At the same time, this driver explains the increasingly nature of individualism and everyone having more of 'selves' to play with. As this individuality is fluid, brought by context, background and position in life, consumers are comfortable with fluidity and not being labelled A, B or C. The consumer is living a range of fluid identities and performing different roles, a life that is complicated and full of choices. This is a life that isn't simple but shifting, and the concepts that once upon a time we trusted, i.e. church and teachers, are now something else. From a tourist's perspective, it means tourists are comfortable with a variety of experiences, whether it is an ecotourism experience in South Africa or a hedonism short break in Las Vegas. Fluidity of values drives the desire for new experiences and the experience economy (Willmott and Nelson 2005) and is fueled by wealth.

FOR THE FUTURE

This trend will continue to grow, especially amongst middle class consumers in developing countries who experience consumerism and develop new tastes and desires. This driver connects to the changing nature of luxury as a concept of fluidity.

Demanding consumers, endless choice and a complicated life

With the rise of the better-informed and savvy consumer, a cynicism and mistrust of many consumer-oriented companies has emerged. The belief that companies will exploit consumers and that advertisers will deceive consumers wherever possible is widely held. With the media frequently exhorting consumers to be even more demanding, this attitude is becoming culturally ingrained. Rising affluence and education across the world have been instrumental in breeding a society of highly active and engaged consumers with a whole new set of expectations of the companies that sell to them. Demanding consumers are in a vacuum of a complicated life driven by the pressure of a paradox of choice in life that seems to appear too busy and stressful. This is the cliché of modern life, which is well documented in the literature (Wilmott and Nelson 2005). Some writers argue that capitalism and the promotion of materialism inevitability leads to a hurly-burly jostling for position as people compete to differentiate themselves by buying more and more goods. In this argument, it is effectively all the fault of the consumer. Consumers are encouraged to buy more and really don't need to. Others blame technology or erosion of communities. However, the world is simply getting more hectic and life is complicated. The world is richer, has more choice and has more freedom; therefore the consumer has more decisions to make. The discretion of the choice in the modern era requires decisions and multiple options. This doesn't drown the consumer in choice but leaves them with a feeling of being overwhelmed. As consumers gain wealth, life seems to become more complicated with numerous choices, and hence consumers become more demanding.

FOR THE FUTURE

'Demanding' and 'complicated' are a fact of life and this trend will continue to be part of the future. To a certain extent, tourism is part of the solution because it is an escape from our daily lives. The more life becomes complicated, the more tourism benefits. Tourism is also part of the problem because every country now positions itself as a holiday destination, whether it is North Korea to Malta – they are all doing tourism. The key to success is how to manage the consumer's paradox of choice, whether it is anchoring certain types of tourism or a strong brand to make society more human.

A world without boundaries

In the book *The World is Flat*, Thomas Friedman (2007) recounts a journey to Bangalore when he realized globalization has changed core economic concepts. In his opinion, this flattening is a product of a convergence of the personal computer with the fiberoptic micro cable and with the rise of workflow software. As a consequence, information flow between countries is fast and cheap. Studies by Pew (Yeoman 2008), note that the family bond is stronger today compared to 30 years ago because of the ease of communications and social media websites. Penn and Zalesne (2007) observe that only 5 million Americans work from home but 10 million Americans are extreme commuters (taking more than 1 hour to get to work). In Europe, good public transport in urban centers and the importance of the low-cost airline have made greater distance more possible. It is quite common for workers to work in a city Monday to Friday but home is 300 miles away in another: the weekly commute is accepted as mainstream. Ethnic structures are changing; cities like Los Angeles, London and Melbourne are becoming melting pots of different and blended cultures to create richness and diversity. For example, what we mean by 'Britishness' or 'Kiwi' is fluid and changing. As a result, boundaries are being broken and blended and new ones formed as a result of demography, technology and transportation.

FOR THE FUTURE

This trend will only accelerate as technology becomes faster, cheaper and reduces the distance between places. As immigration increases, cultures blend and change. However, identity and who we are become more important as we search for meaning and a sense of belonging.

I will try and be ethical, but . . .

Much has been said about the consumer and climate change, but do they really care? While many trends have encouraged the growth of ethical consumption in recent years, there are some trends which have a negative or at least limiting influence. Ethical tourism is fashionable and is encouraged by the current dynamics of demographic change. However, it sits uneasily with many aspects of modern lifestyles. Greater wealth has made people more willing and more able to express their moral beliefs in how they holiday, but at the same time it has made consumers more demanding – they have high expectations and are unabashed in seeking out the best deal. A growing economy has facilitated greater choice, but it has also come with a demand for lower prices and greater convenience.

For example, Western society has a low-price culture. Yeoman and McMahon-Beattie (2006a) highlight that today's consumer is four times more price sensitive than a decade ago. It seems consumers have got used to flying with budget carriers and sleeping in low-cost branded motels. These goods are basic commodities which suffer deflationary pressures. From an ethical consumption perspective, although surveys regularly report consumers' willingness to pay extra taxes or a premium to stay in green hotels, the magnitude quoted by Yeoman and McMahon-Beattie (2006a), found that only 7 percent of people would pay a premium of 20 percent or more for an ethical product – whereas 31 percent said they would not pay any extra for ethical goods. Ethical experiences still need to compete on price with their *unethical* competitors. The ethical cachet, like a desired brand name, can encourage a consumer to spend more, but even with keen ethical tourists this is balanced by cost constraints. The keenest minority of wealthy ethical tourists are sometimes willing to pay large premiums – but for the wider public steeped in low-price culture, small premiums are still the order of the day. As Kermit the Frog once said, 'it's not easy being green' (Henson 2005). That is the dilemma of today's consumer and tourist.

FOR THE FUTURE

In many cases, ethical consumption is not the easy or glamorous option. Some-times consumers' ethics can clash with the have it all lifestyles, especially in the wealthy groups most influenced by the debate. For instance, lately there has been a great deal of negative press around the environmental responsibility of air travel. However, modern consumers, especially the wealthy, positively expect to be able to take at least one foreign holiday a year. As these two trends clash, the ethical consumer must judge whether they should take only short-haul holidays or, indeed, whether foreign travel is at all compatible with their ethics.

Immediacy

We live in an era where time has become one of the most highly valued commodities in our society. 'Having time', 'making time', 'saving time', and 'buying time' are everyday phrases. They are not just buzzwords or idle descriptions but ideas and (sometimes) aspirations, which have come to define our generations and affect everyday lives as individuals and consumers. Having time for family, friends, or a quiet moment alone has become a luxury for many people, and increasingly many consumers are willing to pay more for goods and services if it means they can save themselves some time. Today, our expectations about sourcing information have been reduced from minutes to nanoseconds as technology has abandoned dial up and embraced broadband. At the same time, the use of mobile technologies in our daily lives means tourists can access anything, anytime, anywhere. There is almost nowhere on the planet where this isn't true. Social media platforms like Twitter allow us to follow our friends or Facebook keeps families connected throughout the world. Google is now part of everyday conversation. Global positioning systems (GPS) allows us to know where everything is and never get lost. Everything is just a click away, as they say.

At the same time consumers have become increasingly used to having to manage time and coping with the often-felt compulsion to be 'wired at all times' – to colleagues, families and friends. Research published in the UPS Business Monitor (Yeoman and McMahon-Beattie 2011) found that senior business executives agreed that 'too many e-mails' was by far the most frustrating techno-issue facing them in their workplace. The same study also found that 90 percent of those same senior executives always respond to their e-mails. Apparently, some 75 percent of the executives interviewed in the UPS survey even stay in touch with their office by phone while on holiday.

FOR THE FUTURE

Augmented reality in which virtual reality is placed in front of a physical object and delivered on a mobile phone platform is changing hotel reservation and information-provision models. Today, in cities like Tokyo and Seoul, 30 percent of hotel reservations are made on the day of arrival via a mobile phone, a concept that allows information-seeking and an immediate reservation (Yeoman 2012). Today, the New York City Visitor and Convention Bureau is using state of the art Google maps and tables in their visitor center (Yeoman 2012). Further into the future, the University of Washington's twinkle (Chen 2009) project might bring similar technologies to contact lenses, giving the impression of Terminator technologies and Arnold Schwarzenegger (Yeoman 2012).

The feminization of a have it all society

Betty Friedan's (1963) ground-breaking book, *The Feminine Mystique*, the idea that women have been enticed into the workforce and are seeking out paid employment as a way to get out from under their second-class status, is now being replicated in developing nations like China and India. Here, the passing of women from father to husband has been disbanded with education, careers, dating and new lifestyles. In the USA, four decades ago nearly two-thirds of all college graduates were men (64 percent). Today's makeup of college campuses looks drastically different, as a majority of graduates are now women. In 2007, 53.5 percent of all graduates were women while just 46.5 percent were men. More women than men have some college education but not a degree as well. As a result of the sharp increase in education, women today are also earning far more income than they were in 1970. Women's earnings grew 44 percent from 1970 to 2007; men's income only grew by 6 percent. This has narrowed the income gap between men and women, but has far from closed it. Median earnings of full-year female workers in 2007 were 71 percent of earnings of comparable men, compared with 52 percent in 1970.

This trend is picked up by Silverstein and Fiske (2005a, b), who argue that in the USA, it has been women who have transformed luxury products and tourism. Yeoman and McMahon-Beattie (2005) note that:

> The typical reader of the Lonely Planet is *18–34, educated to degree level, has strong opinions about social justice and world peace and regards travel as a culturally valuable stage on life's way. Eighty per cent of Lonely Planeters' are single and 72 per cent are female*, therefore leading to the conclusion that the growth in world travel has a feminine perspective.

At the same time, the most important values in society are about family (Yeoman 2008) rather than material possessions, but the pressure to have both a family and a career are enormous given the drive for year on year wealth improvement. The drive to improve one's self is a basic human trend that is set to continue.

FOR THE FUTURE

This trend will continue to increase but with different emphasis; to some it is about a work–life balance or how to manage in a world of technological change given the rise of social media. Families today are asking how they can earn enough to maintain the standard of living they want while having enough time to spend with their children. Families often struggle to find time for the things that make life worth living – family, friends, leisure, just enjoying life. From a tourism perspective, holidays become the meeting place from a 'have it all society' or they are part of the 'bling' and materialism of tourism. To some, tourism is about collecting places. It is part of the development of cultural capital and social cachet about how we talk about places we have visited at dinner parties or the social good of tourism, i.e. volunteerism.

Anxious society

Despite being richer, healthier and safer than ever before, today's consumers seem to worry more than ever – whether about food, crime and diseases and so-called risks of one kind or another. The result is that goods and services are subject to panic effects, whereby a product deemed 'unsafe', or simply tainted by association, suffers a sudden collapse in demand. The tourism market is affected by this, whether it be foot and mouth disease (UK), SARS (Canada) or terrorism (Egypt), where precautionary behavior by tourists has gone far in excess of any rational calculus of risk and probability. Sociologist Frank Furedi (2002) calls this the culture of fear. For example, he notes that in response to a Gallup questionnaire about whether people need to take special care about what they eat for health reasons, the proportion agreeing doubled between 1947 and 1996. Despite improvements in health and diet, more people are worried about what they eat. It seems as though in the lack of any serious dangers in day-to-day life, consumers generate new fears and concerns to supplant the old ones.

Parallel to a culture of fear is a myth of decline (Berstein 2004). A modern socioeconomic analysis in many OECD countries clearly divides itself into two distinct tribes. On the one hand, there are those who interrogate the relevant data and broadly conclude that, over the last generation, many consumers have done rather well in the world, citing as examples rising disposable incomes, price stability, greater levels of educational attainment and relative social harmony. On the other, there is a well-supported camp which insists that we are less content than we used to be; that families/communities are not as strong and as tight as before; that the neurosis of competitive individualism makes us incapable of consuming wisely; that the boom in antidepressant consumption and therapies of all kinds shows how much we have lost our way as a society (Yeoman 2012).

FOR THE FUTURE

An anxious society and excessive worrying means the state will regulate even more in the future. To a certain extent this phenomenon of excessive worrying is actually taking the fun out of pleasure. A society that worries to excess results in a sclerosis in commercial activity as a result of regulations and the extent to which red tape and rising insurance premiums impact on choice – resulting in tourism businesses being unable to operate viably. Yeoman (2008) argues that an anxious society will always be here and one of the ways to deal with the situation is building trust with your consumers. That is why destination brands have to be based upon truth and trust, which has a mental connection with tourists.

Trust, volatility and identity

It must be universally accepted by now that few consumers are going to proactively love a special personal inventory of big brands. And fewer still are, in the motive presence of better/cheaper/different offers, going to be devoted to them forever throughout their consuming lifetimes. But one has to wonder whether this whole borrowed idiolect of human intimacy and 'relationships', built on some notion of sustained exclusivity, really packs analytical heat any more. We make no over-cute verbal leap here but how many individuals may, across their lifetimes, enjoy a combination of only one partner, only one family, only one home? There is generally an age of experimentation before settlement and then inertia and then, quite possibly, re-experimentation.

However, the success of '100% Pure New Zealand' as a destination brand is unique in the tourism industry. Not only did the brand celebrate its tenth birthday in 2009, it is also one of the most iconic brands in the world (Yeoman and McMahon-Beattie 2011). Really successful brands can pursue what we might call an *elasticity of loyalty*. Here, consumers are prepared to embrace new ideas and products from them – even if they were to move into sectors where they previously had neither presence nor credibility. This is brand nirvana, a special space occupied only by the few and (tellingly for more old-fashioned marketing analysis) not necessarily by the oldest. We also notice too, that some modern offers make barely any discourse with the theme of loyalty at all. Ryanair's (http://www.ryanair.com) market is held in place by ultra-cheap flights, easy booking and multiple destinations. Beyond these features, the brand (in the sense we mean here), does not pretend to be lovable. It is indeed almost totally de-glamorized. It virtually says to customers: 'if you can get a better deal, take it' (Yeoman and McMahon-Beattie 2011).

In a society based upon a fluid identity, Willmott and Nelson (2005) argue this fluidity is grounded in a rootless society, as the church, elders in the family, or class distinction has being abandoned as a sign of guidance. For many people this is a liberating experience in which they can guide their own destiny. With fewer set courses, life becomes more complicated.

FOR THE FUTURE

The world of tourism is becoming more commoditized, with many destinations offering similar types of experiences. Even Norway promotes itself to the British market as 'not as far as New Zealand' (Yeoman and McMahon-Beattie 2011). If this trend continues, everywhere might look like New Zealand. What is important for the future, whatever the brand is, is a promise that has to be matched on the supply side. In advanced capitalist societies, consumption has been intrinsic to self-expression and tourism is a prime example of this. As affluence grows, so also does our cultural and social knowledge and people's expectations (and the way in which this informs consumption) become more important considerations. The cultural capital is how tourists talk about the places they have visited, the food they have eaten, the museums they have visited and the people they have met. Trust is generated in the conversation hence also creating cultural capital and social cachet. As most destinations' marketing organizations are a function of government most consumers are less trusting of government, hence the scrabble across the world for social responsibility and ethical behavior. Brands must appear simple and transparent to the consumer, with no contradictions. In a networked society where no one can hide, where information is freely available, the same is true about brands.

Collective individualism

Broadly speaking, individuals have become more powerful in relation to institutions over the last generation. Witness the devolution of increased buying power to consumers since the 1970s and 1980s, a function of macroeconomic growth, higher skills and enhanced employability as well as reasonably efficient systems of income distribution. Or the explosion of choice characterizing the evolution of so much human experience in recent years – the result of everything from the evaporation of monolithic public utilities to competition in the high street to the ease with which one can change spouse, to the widespread tolerance of lifestyles once regarded as unusual or unacceptable. Individualism is symbolized by the growing trend of expression of identity through tattoos in society or from a business perspective Tesco, the largest retailer in the UK, knows that if you are buying premium ice cream you will also buy fresh pasta (Humby 2008), such is the power of the prediction based upon their customer loyalty scheme (http://www.tesco.com/clubcard).

Yet it is also the case that even the most individualistic modern consumer sees an advantage in joining forces with others, finding the best sources of intelligence, pursuing economies of scale and sharing experiences – leveraging the input, knowledge and network of groups and communities and entering into a kind of 'sharing' engagement more generally. Individuals are expressing their identity with others with whom they have associated themselves through groups. Oliver (1999) discusses the phenomenon of tattoos as a process of identification with groups, sports teams, or culture. It is as if we all want to be individuals with a sense of belonging. The tattoo has become the timeless symbol of identification, to the point that Air New Zealand leveraged a marketing campaign using temporal tattoos (Yeoman and McMahon-Beattie 2011).

FOR THE FUTURE

Individualism is a key driving force for the future of tourism, because individualism is an expression of identity and escapism. Tourism allows people to be who they want to be, but also provides space for collectivism. Collective individualism is expressed in the 100% Pure New Zealand brand. New Zealand tourism is saying who they are and who they want to identify with. With the growth of social media, individualism is growing at an exceptional pace allowing tourists to share ideas via blogs, or is the future something akin to *Avatar* in which we all can be something else?

Contested hedonism

The term 'hedonism' is used in several contexts. In moral philosophy it denotes the view that a good life should be a pleasurable life. In psychology it stands for the theory that pleasure-seeking is a main motivator of human behavior. There is a longstanding discussion about the merits of this hedonism. Some praise it as natural and healthy, but others equate hedonism with overindulgence and moral decay. The mixed feelings about hedonism are reflected in the connotations surrounding the word. On one hand, hedonism is associated with good taste and the art of living well, on the other hand with addiction, superficiality, irresponsible behavior and short-sighted egoism (Veenhoven 2003). As such, the world's most successful city tourism destination is Las Vegas, which has always promoted itself as an adult Disneyland with a hedonistic outlook. Vegas is about undiluted fun and pleasure. Yeoman and McMahon-Beattie (2011) notes that a great deal of product positioning and product promotion has been rooted in the concept of 'sanctioned indulgence', and holidays are no exception. But this concept is not quite what it was. As a concept, both personal and political, indulgence is having to respond to new pressures, redefining itself for a more health-conscious but still pleasure-seeking age. Health hedonism is a term which brings together the following factors:

- The ever more insistent invitation from health professional to the consumer citizen to scrutinize and review all habits in their own interests including sunbathing, drinking and sex.
- The new forms of social and cultural status which can flow from being seen to be in charge of one's own personal development, fitness, appearance and aging process.
- The awareness that there are multiple forms of pleasure and that what is objectively good for you should impart just as much fun and quality.

FOR THE FUTURE

Veenhoven (2003) raises an interesting question about hedonism: does it add to happiness? How long does that happiness last? If hedonistic behavior is as unhealthy as some doctors say it is, it could shorten an otherwise happy life. So the key to the future is making sure that hedonism is healthy. Very few markets now make the promise of undiluted, you know it's not good for you but go on anyway excess – holidays are moving this way. Many markets in fact just have to deal with the critical cultural/commercial contradiction of the times. The consumer wants quality to the point of luxury, but might not want to look like a slob or appear as someone who is wantonly insensitive to their own health. On the other hand because consumers have a fluid identity that concept of hedonism is contested. Future tourists are happy with a range of hedonistic concepts, whether it is healthy or not.

Contested liberalism

It goes without saying that the way in which contemporary society defines value and identifies virtue is shaped in shifts in wealth and education. In general terms, as society becomes richer and more educated, it becomes more liberal. There is the expectation that an increasingly liberal society will deal with issues such as gay rights, abortion, immigration and sex. However, in a society which has seemed to have banned discrimination against women, many of these issues still have a degree of discomfort. Sex is an issue to be discussed in the home rather than in public. In China, the country's first sex theme park was demolished (BBC 2009) because the authorities felt uncomfortable with the idea. However, at the same time, attitudes towards Internet dating have changed, with the success of websites such as http://www.findsomeone.co.nz. In the UK, every major town has an Ann Summers shop (http://www.annsummers.com/) in the high street selling everything from rampant rabbits (vibrators) and fluffy handcuffs, to erotic lingerie. American liberal and European attitudes towards lingerie have seen the successful growth of brands such as Victoria's Secret. Across the world we have seen same-sex marriages become legal in predominantly Catholic countries such as Italy and Spain. Homosexuality is no longer banned in many countries but carries a death penalty in others. Immigration is a thorny issue: in times of economic prosperity businesses cry out for immigrate labor, but during recessions we see organized pockets of severe disquiet in many places and the rise of nationalist politics. Abortion is an issue that divides nations, especially in the USA.

So, is the consumer liberal? According to the social forecaster William Higham (2009), today's teens are hugely different to Generation X or the Baby Boomers. Like Saffy from *Absolutely Fabulous*, many are reacting against the hedonism and youthful 'cool' of their parents and older siblings, exhibiting more 'adult' traits than their elders. They are increasingly drawn to moral certainties and the assurance of tradition. They seem to be conservative rather than liberal.

FOR THE FUTURE

The notion of multiculturalism, so central to the specific form of liberalism we have known over the last generation, is being seriously contested by a growing worry that many parts of the world are referring to as tribalism and not enough common purpose. Sex will always be an issue that divides opinion. Places with liberal attitudes towards sex and drugs such as Amsterdam are curtailing the emphasis on such virtues (but not abandoning them). Liberalism is in conflict with many religions around the world, whether it is the Roman Catholic Church or Islam. At another level, a heightened sense of personal freedom might increase the growth in world tourism, where identity is built on liberal attitudes reinforced through education and knowledge. The exposure of tourists to a multicultured society allows greater expression of individuality, whether this is sexual behavior or unconventional lifestyles.

Fluidity of luxury

The concept of luxury is incredibly fluid and changes dramatically across time and culture. In the past it was associated with champagne, caviar, designer clothes and sports cars. Nowadays with increased affluence, luxury is a blurred genre which is no longer the preserve of the elite. More and more consumers have traded up as the old values of tradition and nobility have become less important. People are enjoying much more material comfort in comparison to previous generations, resulting in a trend of a cultural shift for personal fulfillment and aspiration through experience. Therefore, it could be argued that luxury is increasingly about experience and authenticity rather than monetary value. This is not to say that luxury is about status, but luxury is more than monetary value. Indeed, they run side by side. This focus on aspiration and experience means increasing emphasis on personal transformation through for example, wellbeing and travel. It means that consumers want to improve their life. This is what Yeoman and McMahon-Beattie (2005) identify as the feminization of luxury, where luxury has moved on from its male trophies and status symbols towards experience and indulgence.

This is perhaps attributed to women's increasing buying power in society which is driving luxury markets such as wellbeing, clothes and tourism. Therefore, luxury is becoming a lot more difficult to define, because the language has changed. Luxury today is not a necessity or necessarily expensive. It can be mass market, not traditional, but personal, authentic and experiential. However, the old-world luxury of consumption and elitism still prevails.

FOR THE FUTURE

As consumers' incomes across the world rise, their aspirations grow. While air travel has become a commodity, many experiences and products have seen the benefit of consumers trading up. The rising middle classes of the world are now experiencing luxury, the like of which their forefathers would have never imagined. No longer is it uncommon to take several holidays a year, to have a second home or dine in an award-winning restaurant. However, different consumers view luxury different ways: developing economies view luxury as materialism whereas developed countries view luxury as aspiration. By 2050, countries like China may no longer be developing countries but developed, so their perception of luxury might be similar to today's developed countries if levels of wealth continue to grow.

New life courses

When many futurists argue about an uncertain world, whether it is oil prices, technology, the economic performance of China or climate change, the only certain prediction is birth and death. According to the United Nations in 2050 there may be 9.1 billion people in the world compared to 2.5 billion in 1950. In 2008, the global population might be 6.8 billion with 5.6 billion living in less-developed regions. Demography changes life courses, consumer attitudes and beliefs. Research by Yeoman and Butterfield (2010) on the singles market and travel in the UK identified that by 2030, single females who live alone could represent 19 percent of households and holidays for this market may act as a meeting place for singles. For companies such as http://www.exploreworldwide.com the core market is the single traveler, while http://www.elenasmodels.com provides holidays for men looking for Russian wives. The main purchasers of *Lonely Planet* guides are single, middle-class females, and are portrayed in the films about Bridget Jones, a 30-something single woman living in London trying to make sense of life and love.

Longevity and smaller core families have led to the family structure becoming more vertical rather than statically horizontal in form. Because there are more, longer-living grandparents and fewer children, grandparents are enjoying more time with their grandchildren. Consider the following: in 1900, the life expectancy of a woman in the United States was 47 years, today it is 80. Today, grandparents can expect to enjoy several more years with their grandchildren than could grandparents of the 1960s. One of the emerging markets of today is the grand traveler, where grandparents holiday with grandchildren.

Demography may be the single most important factor that might change tourism behavior. For example, in order to maintain a healthy lifestyle in old age, consumers are searching for a means to extend healthy retirement years. This means, for example, that we have seen an increase in healthier foods and better access to a variety of physical activities as a way of combating growing anxiety problems and expanding waistlines. Another example of change is the future of the German market. The Germans are the biggest outbound travelers of the world. In a more long-term perspective, aging populations could become problematic for Germany and propensity to travel and actual travel patterns will fall due to less wealth per capita, health issues and stagnated house prices.

Something new

Incomes have grown enormously across the world since the World War Two, new middle classes are emerging in real terms in China and India, whereas forecasts of population growth in USA, Australia and the UK may drive even more wealth creation. In Australia, disposal income has grown threefold since the early 1950s and has led to major material wellbeing. Not only have televisions and mobile phones become the norm but an increasingly large proportion of discretionary income is spent on holidays, health and leisure activities. As people's basic materials needs are increasingly satisfied, they turn their marginal incomes on post-material wants such as personal services that generate self-fulfillment, self-esteem and a better quality of life.

As economies mature, an ever greater proportion of consumer spending is going in search of services rather than physical goods. Only about one-third of all household spending is now devoted to what economists call 'tangibles' (Yeoman 2008), a reflection that consumers increasingly prefer to spend money on things that give them temporary enjoyment, rather than on things they can keep. Of course, one of the effects of exposure to a broader range of activities than was available in the past is that certain activities are no longer regarded as 'special'. For example, most people do not feel that going out for a meal is something out of the ordinary. This is not to say that they don't enjoy going out for a meal or that a meal can't be a special occasion, but simply that eating out is now regarded as a more everyday activity than in the past. There is a profound yearning for new experiences – which has resulted in a 'checklist mentality' when it comes to trying new things. Consumers increasingly try out something once so they've had the experience but won't necessarily do it again – a one-off experience that doesn't have to enter their regular portfolio of activities. With increased wealth comes a desire for change and something new, research by the Future Foundation (http://www.futurefoundation.net) highlights that the average UK consumer changes their hairstyle every 18 months, when buying a new car seeks a new model and make, is constantly meeting new friends and therefore seeking novelty and change (Yeoman 2012).

FOR THE FUTURE

We are seeing a big increase in hobbies, leisure activities that are carried out on a regular basis compared to the rest of the population. This could mean the experience of becoming engrossed in a sport and playing at club level, or the experience of becoming an art, wine, or food connoisseur. In short, new experiences are defined by becoming passionate about a specific activity. As long as disposable income continues to increase, these hobbies and pastimes are being turned into holiday activities, whether it is knitting or tramping. Chris Anderson (2009) has coined the term *The Long Tail*, in which the future of the world is based upon everything micro, including tourism. Now many destinations focus on promoting niche market to short break tourists.

A simple identity

According to Yeoman (2012), during an economic slowdown, tourists tend to travel less, stay nearer home (increase in domestic tourism) and seek simplicity such as http://www.exploreworldwide.com value-based holidays focusing on basic facilities, meeting locals, lots of free time and cheapness, in exotic locations throughout the world. The drivers identified here are the opposite of an affluent society and a fluid identity, but there is some overlap especially as it is our interpretation that future tourists from China and India will be like today's tourists from the UK and Germany, who have a mature outlook to consumption; rather it is inconspicuous consumption than conspicuous. The section explores the drivers that when grouped together are called 'simplicity':

- Resources are the new luxury.
- Decline of deference.
- Advancement of discretionary thrift.
- Sense of security.
- Speeding up mercurial consumption.
- Dominance of simplicity.
- A background of authenticity.

Resources are the new luxury

Half of humanity lives in cities and by 2050 most regions of the world will be predominantly urban. Every day, 193,107 new city dwellers are added to the world's urban population, which translates to slightly more than two people every two seconds. This means that the world's urban population will swell to almost 5 billion in 2030 and 6.4 billion by 2050. Cities have long been the center of tourist activity, from the early times of civilization through to their highly developed state in the global economy. However, what is the future for the city of Los Angeles? According to study by Scott *et al.* (2004), California and the cities of San Diego and Los Angeles could be classified as an optimal climate for tourism and all year round visitation. But what does the future hold given warmer climates,

rising sea levels, water shortages, Peak Oil and the continuing trend of urbanization? Scott *et al.*'s (2004) study examined climate change scenarios for tourism in
US cities through 2030 to 2080 and found that Los Angeles tourism would be
marginally better off in the winter months but overall would move from 'excellent' to 'marginal/unfavorable' as the climate would become unbearable for
tourists.

FOR THE FUTURE

In 2350, New Zealand is a place with a dystopian society and the consumption of
resources is managed and maintained in equilibrium by the simple expedient of
demanding the death of everyone upon reaching the age of 30, thus avoiding the
issue of overpopulation. Auckland, the nation's domed capital city, is a hedonistic
adventure ground with casinos, lap dancing establishments and luxury hotels.
Ecotourism holidays to the Abel Tasman National Park and Milford Sound are
now a visit to the holodeck. Food and wine tourism is recreated using molecules
from the memory bank of the city's Replicator. Auckland has constructed a range
of indoor sporting venues that create an authentic experience whether it is a round
of golf or surfing. Auckland is certainly a super city.

Imagine a world in which climate change really did change the world. A world
where water shortages, rising temperatures, urbanization, Peak Oil and demography could combine into a type of *Logan's Run* scenario (Yeoman 2012). Does
this scenario mean that tourism in New Zealand becomes more exclusive because
we have natural resources and places like California are just too hot?

Decline of deference

In an economic slowdown, the role of authority changes as governments intervene
to stabilize markets, bring assurance and confidence to markets, create jobs and
increase public expenditures. As such, many countries have increased destination
spending on marketing, particularly in domestic markets to entice tourists to stay
at home, hence the term *stayvacation* as international markets fall in many countries. The tourism industry in particular turns to government to offer support and
strategic leadership when the private sector is failing. Therefore, trust in authority
increases and destination brands that offer value, honesty and can deliver on brand
promise become more important (Yeoman 2012).

FOR THE FUTURE

The decline of deference will resume its trajectory as tourists become even savvier
as information-gatherers and decisions-makers bypassing traditional government
sources. However, in an environment of too much choice and too much information, government sources of information are seen as reliable and honest and help
the tourist make informed decisions.

Breaks on green consumerism

Green consumerism is deeply rooted in consumer mindset and consumers are increasingly embracing green products and services. Yeoman and McMahon-Beattie (2006b) highlight that consumers will increasingly pay a premium for a green product such as Fair Trade. But increasingly consumers that have embraced ecoism will abandon such desires when recessions arrive. Consumers are cutting back on pricy green credentials (known as badging), and ramping up cheap and value-based experiences. Paying to be green has slowed whereas the simplicity of being green is on the rise i.e., hiking, being with nature etc.

FOR THE FUTURE

However, green consumerism is expected to be a long-term trend as many government policies and legislation become embedded in such a philosophy. Today, schoolchildren discuss a wasteful planet, being green and recycling, which therefore indicates a future of green consumerism as a basic requirement.

Advancement of discretionary thrift

Thrift as a trend is not new: during the boom year prior to global financial crisis (GFC), consumers got used to trading down. Retailers in the USA like Walmart, Costco and Kohls had reduced costs and margins in order that consumers were able to enjoy everyday low prices (Silverstein and Fiske 2005b). Consumers have come to expect falling prices and intense competitive activity, especially in the tourism sector. Today, the air transport sector is dominated by low-cost carriers and a low-cost price culture dominates and sharpens resistance to price increases.

As the GFC has heightened, many consumers have had no choice but to become thrifty and increasingly affluent consumers are economizing as well. Research by Flatters and Wilmott (2009) identifies mounting dissatisfaction with excessive consumption. Many desire a more wholesome and less wasteful life. They are recycling more, buying used goods and imbuing their children with traditional values – behaviors that dovetail with the demand for simplicity. Economic downturn makes being thrifty the norm; it is not about becoming dull and austere. It was US President Barack Obama who observed at the 2009 G20, that a 'voracious consumer market' is unlikely to reemerge.

Such trends prevail and make providers turn to innovation, for example the Pod Hotel in Manhattan (http://www.thepodhotel.com), where accommodation usually costs US$300 a night, the Pod offer single beds from US$89 a night including bunk beds. The UK firm Eurocamp, which offers an upscale back to nature experience, is expanding as an economical alternative to high-end vacations.

IN THE FUTURE

The use of technology and social media assists tourists in the search for bargains, whether it is the use of augmented technologies in smart phones or contact lenses which view availability and prices as we view them in the street or recommendations from a network of friends on social media sites. Thrift and simplicity also combine to drive the trend of visiting friends and relatives, as incomes fall getting back to basics and developing human relationships is very important, and the most important aspects of tourists' lives are friends and relatives (Yeoman 2012).

Focus on the boardroom and assault of pleasure

In times of economic squeeze, media focuses on the boardroom, excessiveness and corporate governance. Misbehavior that boards might get away with in the good times arouse the ire of consumers and regulators when the economy goes south, as the lynch mob respond to executive bonuses at AIG or New Zealand Telecom. Excessive pay amongst executives has prompted blogs, media hounding and death threats to some high-profile executives. The trend of 'focus on the boardroom' has been building for years, given the present crisis in car manufacturing and world banking. As a result, government intervention against companies with unethical or ineffective governance will increase.

In the life sciences industry, the perceived excessiveness of free jollies and hospitality given to doctors has resulted in the regulation of excessiveness. In March 2009 (Yeoman 2012) the state of Massachusetts finalized its Pharmaceutical and Medical Device Manufacturer Code of Conduct, which regulates interactions between drug and device companies and health care practitioners, placing restrictions on meetings venues, gifts, meals and entertainment. It also requires companies to disclose any gifts or payments to health care practitioners worth US$50 or more. This practice is replicated across the world whether it is the European Federations of Pharmaceutical Industries and Associations (EFPIA) code of practice or similar codes in Australia, New Zealand, Japan or Canada.

The following quote highlights how governments can respond to such a phenomenon:

> What do Reno, Orlando and Las Vegas have in common? To some pockets of the federal government, they just seem like too much fun. Instead, employees at some big agencies, like the U.S. Department of Agriculture, are being encouraged to host meetings in more buttoned-down places such as St. Louis, Milwaukee or Denver. When a conference planner for MGM Mirage's New York-New York Hotel and Casino in Las Vegas tried to book a conference with the Federal Bureau of Investigation, she received a polite refusal. The Department of Justice 'decided conference[s] are not to be held in cities that are vacation destinations/spa/resort/gambling,' according to a May email from an FBI employee obtained by the U.S. Travel Association and viewed by The Wall Street Journal. 'Las Vegas and Orlando are the first 2 on the chopping block.' According to an Agriculture Department employee familiar with the guidelines, the agency issued internal travel guidelines in the spring that encourage employees to hold meetings in cities that display three key attributes: a travel hub; low in cost; and 'a non-resort location.' The employee

said cities on the list with those three attributes included Chicago; Denver; Portland; Oregon; St. Louis; Washington, D.C.; Milwaukee; Phoenix and Fort Collins, Colorado. Resort locations aren't banned, 'but you have to provide robust justification' to supervisors for approval to hold an event there, the employee said.

(Audi 2009)

FOR THE FUTURE

Focus on the boardroom will endeavor to increase with more accountability. As wealth in the world increases combined with a desire for traceability and safety, a regulation culture becomes the norm. In a society where ethics becomes more important, corporations and governments are held accountable. As a consequence, the fun and excessiveness could be taken out of tourism. Maybe the future of tourism is in boring places rather than fun spots like Queenstown.

Sense of security

This backdrop of anxiety forces the consumer to decide between two courses of action. Fear leads to risk minimization so that perceived dangers will be avoided. However, over time, a sense of complacency develops and people think that 'whatever happens, will happen' so a wider choice opens up again. From a macro political point of view, anxiety leads to a dual crisis of security and trust as organizations change their vision of the world. In Shell's Global Scenarios (2007), this trend plays out that individuals and companies have to prove who they are. The state plays a major role in providing security to the nation and overseeing the process whereby trust in the market is preserved through the duration of market abuses or dysfunctions. This involves a stronger coercive and discretionary power for the state and independent regulatory agencies. Regulators themselves are not trusted and must demonstrate that they take the interests of investors, consumers and other stakeholders into proper consideration. It is against this background that the post-9/11 world has emerged, of which tourism in the United States is a symptom.

Yeoman (2008) highlights that consumers think they live in a riskier world than they did in the past. Many of our everyday decisions appear surrounded by external risks; eating, traveling, talking on the mobile or even breathing seem to encompass a huge array of hazards aimed at challenging our wealthy and secure lives. However, by most measures, the world is actually a much safer place compared to previous periods in history, and we are leading healthier and longer lives. Overall, despite being healthier, richer and safer, consumers perceive themselves to be living in a more 'risky society'. Dr Pita Sharples recently commented on racism in New Zealand, quoting from Edwina Pio's (2010) book *Longing and Belonging* in which Asian immigrants found it difficult to be accepted in New Zealand, therefore raising the question 'how does this make tourists feel?'

From a tourism perspective, the tourist has to feel safe and secure. If the trend is anxious and feels unsafe, tourists won't come. Destinations that can position themselves around a perception of security will succeed. However, this is not about overregulation which stifles innovation. '100% Pure New Zealand' has resonance with safety because of distance and isolation. This is New Zealand's strength.

Speeding up mercurial consumption

Consumers in pre-recession times were agile and fickle. They could instantly find a brand to meet their needs. They would spend NZ$8 on a Starbucks coffee but nowadays have migrated to cheaper alternatives that are just as good. The instantaneous spread of word of mouth through online social media has only accelerated this trend. Mobile phones can read barcodes in supermarkets and combined with price comparison software, this allows the consumer to make decisions of whether to purchase or not.

From a tourism perspective, tourists have become canny at searching for bargains. Economists call this mercurial consumption, whether it is using price comparison software, or grabbing last minute offers from websites such as http://www.grabaseat.co.nz which offers last minute air travel deals to New Zealand consumers, or http://www.5pm.co.uk which offers diners the chance of discounted meals after 5p.m. that evening. Technology and social media network-enabled purchasing strategies further accelerate this trend of mercurial consumption. Technology applications such as http://www.farecast.com advise airline travelers of the optimal time to book a seat.

The trend of mercurial consumption can only increase as parts of the tourism experience become more commoditized and tourists can easily find alternatives and use technology to find out about everything. In an environment where destination products and experiences become similar and offer no product difference, customers will choose based upon the best deal that is made available to them.

Dominance of simplicity

Downturns are stressful and accelerate consumers' desire for simplicity. Even prior to the recession consumers were feeling overwhelmed with profusion of choices and 24/7 connectivity and were starting to simplify. A US publisher realized this in 2000 and capitalized on it by launching Real Simple (http://www.realsimple.com). Simplicity is about uncomplicated products, transparency and trust. Do you trust your granny? Would you like her to knit you a pair of socks? There isn't anything more simple at http://www.netgranny.ch in which a relationship is formed with a 'granny' who knits you a pair of socks for a premium price.

Innocent, makers of natural fresh fruit drinks, are the brand leader in the smoothie market in the UK. Since its birth in 1999, Innocent has fast increased its market share. In 2006 the company sold 1 million smoothies a day, it has 63 percent of the market and turnover is projected at UK £75 million. The smoothies are designed as a product that is healthy and tastes good. Innocent is in tune with the healthy living aspirations of so many consumers and it has succeeded in making fruit fun and being healthy easy. What is it that makes Innocent so different? What is it about this brand that consumers cannot resist? (Yeoman 2012).

Part of the success undoubtedly rests on their communication strategies. Maintaining a consistent voice throughout all the aspects of the brand from the language to the packaging, Innocent has managed to position itself as a friendly, honest, open, ethical, fun and personal brand. The ingredient list on the side of an Innocent drink, might say 'a few small pebbles hidden amongst the crushed strawberries and mashed bananas'. Only a bit further down the list you find: 'we lied about the pebbles'. A link to Innocent's online gym is titled 'I'm fat. Let me in.' The company recently published a book called *Stay Healthy. Be Lazy* (Innocent 2004). Consistent with its overall voice, the book sets an honest straightforward tone. 'Are you lazy? Great, that makes two of us.' Also, the laid-back and earthy approach to business fits with the prevailing suspicion towards the ethics of global conglomerates. Innocent is committed to running its business in a sustainable way. These values underpin every decision the company makes from sourcing its fruit to choosing green electricity to run their offices – and it donates 10 percent of profits to charity each year.

The website http://www.skittles.com is an example of a product site with virtually no corporate content; all of the content is generated by the users. The website fundamentally connects a range of social media user-generated sites, whether it is Twitter or Facebook. Hence the website resonates with a high degree of trust amongst users because of the simple nature of the application.

FOR THE FUTURE

Many consumers are feeling overwhelmed by the profusion of choices and 24/7 connectivity, so they tend to simplify and get back to basics. From a tourism perspective, '100% Pure New Zealand' is a simple brand that represents purity, unspoilt landscapes and an authentic experience.

A background of authenticity

Research by the Trajectory Group (Flatters and Wilmott 2009), highlights a trend in that it seems that affluent consumers have revealed mounting dissatisfaction with excessive consumption. Many desire a wholesome and a less wasteful life. As such, there is a desire to get back to nature, something that is tranquil, basic, rooted, human and simple (Yeoman 2008). As a consequence, the desire for more authentic and simple luxury experiences accelerates. An example of simple luxury are tree house hotels which offer a unique experience in a natural setting: this is a new experience which is not seen as conspicuous consumption, but overtly inconspicuous. The Costa Rica Jungle Hotel is based in a rain forest around Arenal Volcano, surrounded by wildlife and birds (http://www.treehouseshotelcostarica.com). Another example is haycations, where holidaymakers pay to stay and work on farms. Holidaymakers are turning to haycations to experience a world far removed from their daily life. At Stoney Creek Farm (http://www.stoneycreekfarm.org), tourists are charged up to US$300 a night to work on the farm. This is an experience where tourists pick their own food, then cook it that evening in a location with no cellphone reach. During times of recession tourists are searching for back to basics experiences that are simple, with a sense of community and authenticity. About 50 percent of the tourists to Stoney Creek Farm are locals from the same county. This is a typical example of inconspicuous consumption and a desire for a simple identity.

FOR THE FUTURE

As consumer desires mature and as time is squeezed, they become more educated. Authenticity is at the heart of simplicity. This is an everlasting trend based upon an increased preference for non-conspicuous consumption and a move away from mass consumerism. Yeoman (2008) even discusses authenticity as the new luxury for certain markets.

So, what does this all mean?

The profile of the future tourist depends upon wealth. As wealth and identity grow, the proposition of fluid identity becomes more prominent. At the same time, if the future of wealth is less, then the proposition of simplicity is proposed. What does this all mean for New Zealand? If the future is a tourist with a fluid identity, it is extremely important for New Zealand to offer a variety of experiences and products in which diversity is the key driver. This identity means the tourist is sampling experiences, looking for novelty, wants to be entertained, is influenced by peer recommendation and likes to experiment. Therefore, New Zealand cannot be one thing but rather a collection of high-quality experiences. Here, the tourist is frivolous, materialistic, liberal and awkward. The tourist typical of Generation Y (Yeoman and Butterfield 2010) is not bounded by conformity, has seen the world and does not tolerate poor service. This tourist will have abandoned sustainability as it has no depth and meaning but rather is treated with tokenism, sometimes forgotten but other times cherished. Typically, the tourist will not be from traditional markets such as the UK and Australia but rather China and India. This tourist will have opinions about New Zealand tourism shaped by friends and social media and will be active in forums and blogs about a variety of topics. As the typical Chinese tourists doesn't have brothers or sisters the importance of friends and connections will shape and influence destination choice and activity. Singleton group travel will be very important for places where tourists can share experiences and find connectivity such as social spaces in backpackers' hostels.

The future tourist in general will be older than previous cohorts and more likely female given the impact of demography change in many countries. It is expected that tourists living longer will seek out new places that previous generations haven't been to. Space tourism will become the ultimate experience and with New Zealand's lack of population density and great capacity for air space, combined with a wonderful landscape, space tourism will have a future in New Zealand as a day trip experience into the stratosphere. Longevity and wellbeing will be important in a future in which natural and authentic experiences play an important part in the product mix of New Zealand.

In this proposition, one of the problems for New Zealand is how does it position itself and how will tourists talk about New Zealand? On one hand, it will be increasingly difficult to label and segment tourists, rendering segmentation models useless due to constant change; therefore does destination marketing have a future? Increasingly tourists are becoming sceptical about advertising and marketing. What does this mean for Tourism New Zealand?

To a certain extent, fluid identity is about wealth and a have it all society, these tourists can afford holidays several times a year and a multitude of short breaks. This is a tourist that can afford to be concerned about the environment so doesn't mind paying a little bit extra. In a have it all society, the desire is for sociality, economic gain, family involvement, leisure and self-improvement which are less delineated by stages of life or gender, all of these desires are reflected in holiday activity. The expectation amongst the tourist with a fluid identity is they want a richer and fulfilling life, but at the same time there are pressures and expectations. Although rising wealth means more opportunity it also means a fear of loss, in which society is portrayed as in decline. Here the tourist will turn to therapies and antidepressants, is anxious about the future and thinks society has lost its way. The tourist who had been envied for their wealth and opportunities will now display shallowness and a crisis of confidence.

A heightened sense of personal freedom has undoubtedly increased the growth of tourism to New Zealand, where identity is built on liberal attitudes reinforced through education and knowledge. The exposure of tourists to a multicultured society allows greater expression of individuality, whether this is sexual behavior or unconventional lifestyles; however this degree of liberalism differs around the world. Fundamentally, as economies grow they become more liberal in outlook and seek to push out their identity. As such, they will try new things and visit new places, destinations in the faraway places that seemed inaccessible to previous generations. The concept of luxury tourism is very fluid in this proposition, although materialism is important, time and aspiration play their part as well. In the experience economy the concept of culture evolves to something akin to a no-brow culture where high and low brow cultures have merged. Culture is important for the future, so a continued festivalization of society will continue where comedy fringe and ballet work together.

The GFC plummeted the value of the high net worth population by US$32.8 trillion or 19.5 percent according to the World Wealth Report (2009) published by Capgemini and Merrill Lynch. So the rich as less rich than they were before the

GFC. Flatters and Wilmott (2009) argue that in most developed economies pre-GFC, the pre-recession consumer behaviour was the product of 15 years of uninterrupted prosperity. The GFC changed that, propelling tourist trends into slowdown, halting or even reserving the trajectory of growth in world tourism. So, is this a sample of the future, an era of the pension crisis, scarcity of oil, inflation and falling levels of disposal income in which tourism expenditure falls year on year? If so, what will the future tourist look like? Rather than having a fluid identity, it will more likely tend toward simplicity. During an economic slowdown, tourists tend to travel less, stay nearer home (increase in domestic tourism) and seek simplicity (such as http://www.exploreworldwide.com). Tourists will seek value-based holidays focusing on basic facilities, meeting locals, lots of free time and cheap exotic locations throughout the world. This trend is accelerated in a scenario of falling incomes as a simple and functional product that will suffice. The emergence of new technologies such as augmented reality changes how tourist book accommodation. Today, 30 percent of hotel bookings in the cities of Seoul and Tokyo are on the day arrival via the mobile phone (Yeoman 2012). The use of this technology assists tourists in the search for bargains. Thrift and simplicity also combine to drive the trend of visiting friends and relatives: as incomes fall getting back to basics and developing human relationships is very important, and the most important aspects of tourists' lives are friends and relatives. With the proposition of a simple identity, tourists have mounting dissatisfaction with excessiveness, as a consequence destinations like Queenstown with its bungy jumping and five star resorts will suffer. But organizations like the Youth Hostel Association and the Department of Conservation hut network will thrive given the desire to get back to nature and basic experiences. In a simple identity, ethical consumption declines as paying a premium falls by the wayside. From a tourism perspective, many of the ethical tourism projects will fail because consumers simply can't afford them any more. Price is the number one consideration within this proposition. As a consequence, New Zealand's distance and cost become barriers of choice for many tourists. As travel becomes more expensive attitudes to travel change as other forms of leisure expenditure become more dominant. This trend is dominant in Japanese society where gaming has changed the Generation Y's attitude towards travel (Yeoman and Butterfield 2010). To some tourists authority will be important; therefore it is important for New Zealand to maintain a strong brand image that is honest, clear and based upon the values of simplicity.

Conclusion

Tourism is an unpredictable industry, shaped by events, the world economy and the sociopolitical environment. Tourists are fickle and when times are good they will spend large amounts of disposable income on tourism. To a certain extent, tourists retrench and focus on lower order basic needs when times are hard, so tourism declines. Given the GFC and the forthcoming demographic and pensions time bomb we could see a year on year decline in tourism expenditure with 2050 being the flip point. When tourists do have money, they possess a fluid identity of constant change in a fast-moving world, in which they are easily bored, seek novelty, desire thrill, something new, aspiration and enrichment. Tourism has always been about fun, relaxation, entertainment, enrichment and enjoyment. But will it be simple or fluid? Only time will tell. The point of this chapter is make readers think about the future, challenging many of the common ideas and assumptions that are held. No one can predict who exactly the future tourist will be.

References

Anderson, C. (2009) *The Long Tail*, Auckland: Random House Publications.

Audi, T. (2009) 'Government Meetings: Stay Away from Sin City', *USA Today*, 22 July, online. Available at online.wsj.com/article/SB124822843228670879.html (accessed 12 February 2010).

BBC (2009) 'China Sex Theme Park Demolished', BBC, 18 May, online. Available at news.bbc.co.uk/2/hi/asia-pacific/8054893.stm (accessed 9 February 2010).

Berstein, G. (2004) *The Myth of Decline*, London: Pimlico.

Capgemini and Merrill Lynch (2009) *World Wealth Report*, online. Available at www. capgemini.com/resources/thought_leadership/2009_world_wealth_report/ (accessed 20 September 2009).

Chen, B. (2009) 'Digital Contacts Will Keep an Eye on Your Vital Signs', online. Available at www.wired.com/gadgetlab/2009/09/ar-contact-lens/#ixzz0s8B4SmU6 (accessed 12 June 2010).

Flatters, P. and Wilmott, M. (2009) 'Understanding the Post Recession Consumer', *Harvard Business Review*, 87(7/8): 106–112.

Friedan, B. (1963) *The Feminine Mystique*, London: Penguin.

Friedman, T. (2007) *The World is Flat: A Brief History of the Twenty-first Century*, New York: MacMillan.

Furedi, F. (2002) *The Culture of Fear*, New York: Continuum Press.

Future Foundation (2007) *nVision Central Scenario*, London: Future Foundation.

Henson, J. (2005) *It's Not Easy Being Green: And Other Things to Consider*, London: Hyperion Books.

Higham, W. (2009) *The Next Big Thing: Spotting and Forecasting Consumer Trends for Profit*, London: Kogan Page.

Humby, C. (2008) *Scoring Points: How Tesco Continues to Win Customer Loyalty*, London: Kogan Page.

Innocent (2004) *Stay Healthy. Be Lazy: An Easy Detox by Innocent*, London: Boxtree.

McClure, M. (2004) *The Wonder Country: Making New Zealand Tourism*, Auckland: University of Auckland Press.

Ministry of Tourism (2008) *New Zealand Tourism Strategy 2015*, online. Available at www. tourism.govt.nz/New-Zealand-Tourism-Strategy-2015/ (accessed 12 June 2008).

Oliver, R. (1999) 'Whence Consumer Loyalty', *Journal of Marketing*, 63(1): 33–44.

Penn, M. and Zalesne, E.K. (2007) *Microtrends*, New York: Penguin.

Pio, E. (2010) *Longing and Belonging*, Wellington: Dumore Books.

Rochon, T. (2000) *Culture Moves*, Oxford: Oxford University Press.

Scott, D., McBoyle, G. and Schwartzentruber, M. (2004) 'Climate Change and the Distribution of Resources for Tourism in North America', *Climate Research*, 27(2): 105–117.

Shell (2007) *Global Scenarios for 2025*, online. Available at www.shell.com/home/content/aboutshell/our_strategy/shell_global_scenarios/previous_scenarios/previous_scenarios_30102006.html (accessed 12 June 2008).

Silverstein, M. and Fiske, N. (2005a) *Trading Up: The New American Luxury*, New York: Portfolio.

—— (2005b) *Trading Up: Why Consumers want New Luxury Goods and how Companies Create Them*, New York: Portfolio.

Statistics New Zealand (2009) *Tourism Satellite Account*, online. Available at www.tourismresearch.govt.nz/Documents/Tourism-Satellite-Account/2009/tourism-satellite-account-2009-web.pdf (accessed 20 June 2009).

UNWTO (2010) *Economics of Tourism*, online. Available at www.unwto.org/facts/eng/economy.htm (accessed 17 July 2010).

Veenhoven, R. (2003) 'Hedonism and Happiness', *Journal of Happiness Studies*, 4(4): 437–457.

Willmott, M. and Nelson, W. (2005) *Complicated Lives: The Malaise of Modernity*, Chichester: Wiley.

Yeoman, I. (2008) *Tomorrow's Tourist*, Oxford: Elsevier.

—— (2012) *2050: Tomorrow's Tourism*, Bristol: Channelview.

Yeoman, I. and Butterfield, S. (2010) 'Demography and Tourism: An Overview', in I. Yeoman, C. Hsu, K. Smith and S. Watson (eds.) *Tourism and Demography*. Oxford: Goodfellows, pp. 1–22.

Yeoman, I. and McMahon-Beattie, U. (2005) 'Luxury Markets and Premium Pricing', *Journal of Revenue and Pricing Management*, 4(4): 319–328.

—— (2006a) 'Everyday Low Prices', *Journal of Revenue and Pricing Management*, 6(1): 2–8.

—— (2006b) 'Tomorrow's Tourist and the Information Society', *Journal of Vacation Marketing*, 12(3): 269–291.

—— (2011) 'The Future Challenge', in Morgan, N. Pritchard, A. and Pride, R (eds.) *Destination Branding: Managing Place Reputation*, Oxford: Elsevier, pp. 169–182.

Part IV
Concluding thoughts

13 Future tourism

Where to now?

James Leigh and Craig Webster

Introduction

In a sense, you have been reading a history book, actually a book on future history as we considered what the future of tourism may be as it confronts a whole new world with unique challenges and threats along with some facilitators. Tourism experts have crystal ball-gazed to assess precedents and current trends, and even future trends to take a futuristic view of tourism in the context of contemporary and looming world conditions in this dramatically challenging third millennium.

Setting the scene for unfolding events

One confounding problem with the book is that the future has not yet occurred, and thus many of the projections that have been made may prove to be untrue or not entirely correct. Unplanned or unexpected events may also make the future very different from the one that the authors projected it would be. For example, the emergence/discovery of an energy source to adequately replace petroleum would make a world of difference in the future, making the probable depletion of petroleum unimportant or less important for the future economy, although the transition may be tricky and tough. Certainly a power source that has not yet been invented or perfected that could power jet travel in the future would ensure that transoceanic travel would continue, even if petroleum runs out. However, it would be a mistake to anticipate that some unexpected or unplanned events in the future may save humanity and the tourism industry from issues that are capable of being planned for now.

Another issue with the book is that it is written at a time of 'economic crisis' or 'financial crisis'. The fact that the global economies are currently in a crisis must play a role in influencing how the authors have responded to thinking about the future. Those who have a more optimistic view will see the crisis as a temporary hurdle that will be overcome by political will or simply by muddling through. Those with a more pessimistic view will see the crisis as part of more long-term problems with serious implications for tourism and humanity. Only time will really be able to inform us which perspective turned out to be the most accurate.

Many of the authors anticipate we are entering a new world epoch, an axial era, with unprecedented opportunities and challenges as we grapple with demographic trends of overpopulation in some places and declining aging population in others, war and peace issues, violence and terrorism, declining cheap energy supplies, pollution, extreme erratic weather and natural disasters, food and water shortages, threats of worldwide pandemic disease, economic crises, social change and civil unrest, tectonic shifts in the world balance of power and the rise and fall of superpowers with the ensuing geopolitical challenges and conflicts. Alternatively some authors think there is a chance for continued economic development to fuel the prosperity and wealth needed to support choices across the whole range of touristic experiences within sumptuous amenities-based mass international tourism.

As we have already seen, some experts expect that tourism has formidable hurdles to surmount. However, the movers and shakers in the tourism sector have not been known for a penchant to consider how future dramatic challenges (or opportunities) may drastically affect – hinder or facilitate – the industry. We can hope it is within the human intellectual capacity to surmount any problems and make the best of opportunities, with innovation in technology and the ability to organize and plan, and even change our attitudes and values along with improved understanding and skills.

What have we learned so far?

The chapters in this book have highlighted some dramatic challenges for tourism in the looming future of this century. Let us take a backward glance at the book, and from this vantage point, consider how tourism in the future may finally be forged out of these trends and events.

We first looked at Peak Oil in Chapter 2 to get a glimpse of the catastrophic effects these could have on society if played out fully with declining commodities and rising prices. We considered that there may also be a great opportunity for society and tourism to change, so that tourism would not be addicted to a sumptuous amenities base, requiring massive doses of energy. Tourism would transform to be more local, frugal and simple, for a less wealthy and less mobile peoples. Scarce energy and commodities supplies would lead to more conservative energy use in a parochial and agricultural community-based sustainable society. We need to prepare for the coming imminent shocks so that their impact will not be so dramatically shocking.

From there a grand view was taken of future tourism in the context of looming trends in political economy in Chapter 3. In that chapter we considered the likely trajectory of the tourism industry. We explored the looming general world economic, social and political conditions. This included looking into issues of human population growth, resource depletion and food supplies. We also considered the political regimes of tourism management and the importance of tourism for economic development. Finally, we viewed two very different futures that may be approaching – one an extension of the post-World War Two affluence and its related growth of tourism and successful liberal economies, and the other, a far less optimistic scenario with more meager means.

We subsequently examined the vital issue of international security and the likely impact on future tourism in Chapter 4. We placed tourism within its larger political and economic context and discussed contemporary trends in such issues as war, terrorism and political instability and their potential effects on tourism worldwide. We then turned to socially produced insecurities and their impact on the world consumer classes which make up global tourists both at home and abroad. We suggested that many future global tourists will travel in a manner to continually seek out safety and protection – actually a mirror of the way they live their lives at home.

In Chapter 5, we considered the under-researched and unglamorous phenomenon of 'social tourism', that is supported holidays for the poorer who otherwise could not enjoy leisure tourism. We examined the supply of supported holiday opportunities, with reference to agents, including national governments and the private sector. We also provided an outline of international agreements and declarations. A novel perspective on social tourism was taken by considering the social equity dimension inherent in the concept of sustainable development. We viewed the relevant EU developments including the Barcelona Declaration and the implications for an assessment of any future 'right to tourism'. While implementing a European right to tourism may be desirable, the challenges may be formidable, due to declining welfare budgets. However, this may open up a vacuum for the commercial tourism sector to more fully participate if the touristic fiscal environment remains strong enough.

Then, Chapter 6 discussed key trends and expectations about future tourism, including economic, sociocultural and demographic, technological, environmental and political dimensions. However, we were critical that many tourism forecasts are based on false assumptions by simply following historic trends and extrapolating them into the future. This linearity does not always exist, and in reality there is great uncertainty around timescales and the magnitude of changes. To better differentiate between the drivers of change that are likely to overthrow a system and change it fundamentally, the concept of shifters and shapers was introduced. The impact of Peak Oil on global transportation was discussed as one example of a shifter, as increasing oil scarcity and rising costs of transportation may force global tourism towards redefinition.

We then viewed the future relationship between tourism and quality of life, in Chapter 7. The new millennium has witnessed major changes in tourism and so tourism service providers are posed with a range of challenges in an ever-competitive world. It has now become more important than ever for service providers to enhance awareness of quality of life and its relationship with tourism. New domains in the area are dealing with different aspects of the quality of life and tourism, addressing the health, sociological and psychological impacts as well as the factors affecting the quality of life in relation to both economic and community wellbeing, and health and safety, to mention only a few.

Then we moved to take a social constructivist position on the future of tourism and look to identify the factors that are shaping contemporary tourism and tourism studies to consider possible futures, in Chapter 8. Emphasis was placed on issues of institutions and power and key factors that are influencing the future of tourism. We argued that these factors get limited coverage in tourism discourses, with the likely result that tourism will be less sustainable than ever before in the foreseeable challenging future.

We saw in Chapter 9 that information technology and its developments are major drivers to change tourism both from within the industry as well as from the outside, from that of the consumer experience perspective. While it was recognized that technological change is hard to predict, this chapter looked at current efforts, for example, in the areas of interface design, artificial intelligence, robotics, search engines and social media, to sketch out potential impacts on tourism. It was also suggested that this will critically reflect on the haves and have-nots in such an emerging world. The chapter also discussed the potential drawbacks of technology dependence in tourism and even deliberate decisions by tourists and tourism businesses to avoid technology.

Subsequently, in Chapter 10, we saw that major challenges facing the tourism and hospitality industry worldwide are labor and skills shortages. We highlighted that attracting and retaining qualified workers is an urgent concern globally. It was suggested that demography, failure to adequately address worker dissatisfaction and a reputation for long hours and low pay, all contribute to challenge tourism. In this context we examined how students, studying tourism and hospitality in Australia, the United States and Malaysia, perceive a career in the industry. It was found that these students do not believe the industry offers them the attributes they want in a future career.

Chapter 11 reviewed the current implementation level of sustainability in the tourism industry. After a brief introduction on the roots of sustainability and its interrelation with tourism, actual trends such as corporate social responsibility and sustainable supply chain management were introduced and screened for the possible impacts on tourism. Examples of corporate social responsibility labels and CO_2 compensation in tourism rounded off the overview of where the sustainable tourism debate is standing at the turn of the millennium.

Then, in Chapter 12, we saw that today's tourist demands better experiences, faster service, choice, social responsibility and greater satisfaction. Against this background, as the world has moved to an experience economy with endless choice through competition and accessibility with low cost, the concept of fluid identity has emerged. This identity is fickle and malleable, with a desire for choice and new experiences, and these drive tourist consumption today. However, as wealth decreases identity becomes simpler, with thriftiness and a desire for simplicity driven by inflationary pressures and falling levels of disposable incomes, squeezing the middle-class consumer. As the economies of wealth slow down, new patterns of tourism consumption emerge, whether it is the desire for domestic rather than international travel, or a stayvacation. Finally, based on the highlighted present and likely unfolding trends, we considered implications for New Zealand's future tourism.

Developing a comprehensive view

We can now begin to tie up all the loose ends into a comprehensive integrated view of what we suspect future tourism may be like. We have considered that future tourism could take two possible routes. One would be within growth in sustained prosperity and wealth, even expanding around the globe to fuel the maintenance of choice in ever-growing sumptuous amenities-based mass international tourism. The other view is that the future of tourism will have to exist within declining wealth in problematic social and political arenas. However, viewing the future in an optimistic versus pessimistic dichotomy, although useful as an analytical tool, is oversimplification of the future realities that may appear. It may be better to express this in a continuous manner, with a more pessimistic vision of the future and optimistic vision of the future on two very different ends of a spectrum. To simplify, we propose looking at the possible future in a trichotomy as shown in Table 13.1, in which we envision a more optimistic and pessimistic future mitigated by a more middle of the road approach.

We see in Table 13.1 that there are three different views of the future, each of them having very different implications for tourism. In the most pessimistic outcome, humanity will not have dealt with its major challenges and succeeded; indeed, much of humanity will perish. In the more optimistic visions of the future, we see that humanity has overcome the major problems it faced and has created an economy that can sustain growth and create more affluence.

A final peek at future tourism

This book, however, has tended to consider the potentially more challenging future scenario for tourism. Future tourism in this route would be in a world in economic decline, with the possibility of energy, food and other commodities in short supply, therefore making tourism very expensive. Future tourism, under such a scenario, would likely be very expensive and therefore more local. And in an extreme case, society would be forced to completely transform to local communities with an agricultural base in self-sufficiency. Tourism then would have to change greatly, with the likely revival of hospitality integrated into 'proximity tourism' which would be, in the most distant form, an intercity or interprovincial experience. Proximity tourism would become typical.

Mixed with these futures for tourism is the menace of pandemic disease outbreaks, encroaching social instability and civil unrest, terrorism and security threats which could be further exacerbated by economic decline and urgent political issues and problems. It appears these problems will be around, and even worsen.

In a world with sustained economic development, the commercial sector could begin to be involved in social tourism, to subsidize tourism for the elderly and otherwise disadvantaged citizens. However, in a world with encroaching austerity and declining prosperity and budgets, the involvement of the commercial tourism

Table 13.1 Competing futures

	Most optimistic	In-between	Most pessimistic
General state of global economy	• Continued expansion of global economy and increased affluence enjoyed by populations worldwide	• Continuation of recessions and expansions of economic development in successive peaks and troughs	• Long-term depression and general decrease in living standards globally, especially in the more developed countries, and possibly a collapse of global and national societal systems
Energy	• Petroleum in abundant supply to support the global population's energy needs at high levels of energy consumption • Alternative energy sources continue to be developed and take up the slack, whenever petroleum supplies seem to be inadequate	• Petroleum generally enough to support the global population's energy needs at high levels of energy consumption • Alternative energy sources continue to be developed and take up some of the slack, when petroleum supplies are insufficient	• Petroleum depletion and no adequate replacement for petroleum as an energy source, and a dearth of energy in general • Alternative energy is gravely insufficient to significantly compensate for drastically declining petroleum supplies
Globalization	• Globalization continues to encompass the globe • Civilization clash and terrorism minimized so peace and prosperity continue	• Globalization continues to encompass the globe generally, and civilization clash and terrorism loom larger due to declining wealth	• Protectionism and the high cost of transport put an end to globalization to be replaced by trade and commodity wars, civilization clash and pervasive terrorism
Food security	• Technology and climate control enable increases in food production to keep up with global needs • Soil depletion and desertification from modern chemical farming remain a challenge to food supply	• Continued disparity in food shortages and overproduction • Erratic climate, soil depletion and desertification from pollution and modern chemical farming exacerbate food shortages	• Widespread hunger and famine leading to civil and geopolitical conflict, exacerbating civilization clash and terrorism • Erratic climate, soil depletion and desertification from pollution and modern chemical farming further exacerbate shortfalls in food supply

(Continued on next page)

	Most optimistic	*In-between*	*Most pessimistic*
Human population	• Increases in affluence enable population increases although diffusing consumerism leads to population decline	• Stabilization of population globally, but disparate across regions with pockets of growth and decline	• Decreasing population because declining petroleum hinders the capability of humanity to increase food production, leading to widespread famine, severely impacting on all levels, economically, civilly, politically, geopolitically
Erratic climate change	• Not an issue, since it is not anthropogenic or can adequately be managed via geoengineering and global environmental policies and taxes	• Can be largely managed via geoengineering and global environmental policies and taxes	• Increase in pollution and erratic environmental temperature swings cause major environmental challenges and catastrophes like hurricanes, flooding and droughts
Tourism	• Increasing and diffusing universal economic development continues to increase middle classes' consumption of mass international tourism services • Rapid tourism development in currently less-developed countries • Aging populations fuel tourism service demands • Space travel and increasing demand for sumptuous amenities-based mass international tourism	• Continuation of mass tourism for middle classes in more developed countries • Some less developed countries will have an emerging middle class able to enjoy more tourism services • Continued ups and downs of the economy challenge tourism services and sales to maintain steady continuous growth	• End of mass tourism and mass international jet travel • Severe reduction in the percentage of the population with the means to enjoy tourism services • Rise of frugal proximity tourism with simple hospitality and human-based activities

sector in social tourism, through whatever form of subsidy or supplement may be innovatively developed, would appear to be problematic.

Quality of life is an issue and tourism is considered a constituent leisure activity. Improving our life's quality may require more and higher 'quality' tourism. Life-quality needs are influenced by identity, however, and if simple identity replaces a fluid identity, in more austere times life quality would be simpler, and tourism likewise would be met with more simple, frugal and local needs. Popular transport would not be by plane, but more likely by bus and train, and possibly ship. It may be that hospitality and quality interpersonal experiences will become more sought after. In this way we see that identity and perceived needs are a function of the socioeconomic milieu's realistic offerings, all as a manifestation of humans adjusting to their newfound environment.

Issues of sustainability will test the competencies of leaders and their staff in tourism, and we need to train and educate tourism's workers in vital issues and competencies to equip them for the looming era's challenges, whether it be a time of plenty or of more meager means. These leaders and staff would also need to address working conditions in the industry, which might be difficult to improve if approaching circumstances are overly challenging. In any transitioning phases, leaders and workers will also need to be resilient and adaptable to accommodate new circumstances along with tourism's changing possibilities and challenges.

Technological development has made it possible for tourism to become mass and intercontinental beginning in the 1960s. With growing prosperity it seems logical to expect that technology in general and information technology would continue to be used more extensively in tourism. However, if the worldwide economic crises deepen, this could have the effect of flattening the demand for tourism's general use of expensive technology, and so technology avoidance could loom larger. Alternatively, in tougher times increased technology could be used in specific areas of tourism, for example new technologies for cheap alternative energy production.

Demographic shift may also greatly impact future tourism. Declining population trends are becoming a reality in many countries. This means populations will be older with a higher proportion of pensioners who are feebler and less wealthy. These venerable citizens will likely avoid extremes of weather and culture, and so seek out more frugal and serene tourism. They would also prefer vacationing in destinations with good back-up medical services just in case of a health crisis. Generally then for these tourists it would seem a temperate climate, in economically developed destinations with care and security, would be sought out. It may also be that aging populations in the developed world, with worldwide economic decline and lower personal discretionary budgets and spending, along with longer working hours, less vacation time and rising retirement ages, will have a negative effect on tourism.

A general trend of violence and terrorism may be looming large as factors for consideration in tourism. Specifically hostile acts are being targeted at tourists and this is diffusing, beyond the typical danger zones, to the extent that it can unexpectedly and suddenly pop up anywhere at any time. Obviously this will impact tourism in a negative way, and it may be that protection measures will have to be taken for secure tourism to be maintained.

In recent years the frequency and intensity of catastrophes and extreme natural catastrophes and weather conditions, like earthquakes and tsunamis, hurricanes, droughts and floods have increased to truly unprecedented dramatic record levels – overwhelming humanity's ability to cope. Of course in such circumstances, the chaos of lawlessness and crime also often abounds. This has repercussions for the economy and the environment and its infrastructures, making large areas totally incapable, at least temporarily, of supporting tourism or even being hostile to it.

We may ask what in a nutshell, will future tourism be like? It seems there are two possibilities, one being more likely than the other. As we have seen, one possibility is a world of dramatic challenges which would demand a great metamorphosis of the tourism industry to confront myriad factors that largely challenge the viability of tourism as we know it today. Tourism in this dramatically challenging world would be in uncharted waters to battle unprecedented levels and frequency of across the spectrum events and trends of natural and human-made problems.

Fundamentally, it may be that tourism needs to consider how it can meet society's needs, in a sustainable cost-effective way, with fewer, poorer and older tourists, in an increasingly problematic world of decreasing supply and more expensive resources, and also in a world with escalating economic, political and social turmoil.

Alternatively, if the world is to continue to have ongoing economic development and prosperity, across even larger swathes of humanity from newly developed poorer regions, there will still be the challenge of growing mass international tourism's physical and cultural pollution, which destroys the environment at both levels. Also increasing levels of mass international tourism will surely conflict with conservation of energy and resources, and there will still be the persistent issues of scarcer commodities, older and poorer tourists, natural catastrophes, pandemic disease outbreaks, security and terrorism, geopolitical conflicts and so on.

Notwithstanding, tourism is a human activity, and by its very nature will be changed by the unfolding events and trends. The problem is how promptly and effectively tourism will change to survive and even thrive in the increasingly dramatic world.

Whatever route the world takes in its future history, of increasing or declining wealth and plenty, of enhanced or inhibited human wellbeing, the challenges are still formidable and will test the resolve and resilience of tourism and its stakeholders, and even the leaders and citizens, in future tourism's greater society.

Index

Page numbers in **bold** refer to figures and tables